# The Complete Guide
# To
# Thematic Units:
## *Creating*
## *The*
## *Integrated Curriculum*

# The Complete Guide
# To
# Thematic Units:
# *Creating*
# *The*
# *Integrated Curriculum*

Anita Meyer Meinbach

Liz Rothlein

Anthony D. Fredericks

Christopher-Gordon Publishers, Inc.

Norwood, MA

# Credits

Every effort has been made to contact copyright holders for permission to reproduce borrowed material where necessary. We apologize for any oversights and would be happy to rectify them in future printings.

**Chapter 2:**

Excerpts from *Miss Rumphius* by Barbara Cooney (New York: Puffin Books, © 1982) used with permission of the publishers.

Figure 2.3, from "K-W-L: A teaching model that develops active reading of expository text," by Donna Ogle, reprinted with permission of Donna Ogle and the International Reading Association.

**Chapter 3:**

The Developmental Inventory, from Ruddell, M.R. (1993). *Teaching content reading and writing*, is reproduced permission from M. R. Ruddell, 1993.

*Thematic Unit: Folktales Around the World:*

Pages from *Frantic Frogs and Other Frankly Fractured Folktales for Readers' Theatre* (© 1993) are used with the permission of the publisher, Teacher Ideas Press and the author.

Christopher-Gordon Publishers, Inc.
480 Washington Street
Norwood, MA 02062

Printed in the United States of America
10  9  8  7  6  5  4  3  2        99  98  97  96  95

ISBN:0-926000-0-0

# Dedication

*To Liz Rothlein and Tony Fredericks —*

*my coauthors, my mentors, and most importantly, my friends.*

*—A.M.M.*

*There are rare, beautiful human beings on this earth who radiate such giving, caring, and love*

*that all who come in contact with them are forever blessed.*

*One such person is my daughter Terri.*

*—L.R.*

*This one's for all the kids — whose imagination, creativity, and joie de vivre*

*make teaching the most exciting profession on earth!*

*—A.D.F.*

# Introduction

What an exciting time to be a teacher! The infusion of children's literature throughout the elementary curriculum, the whole language movement, and the invitational classrooms being established in schools all over the country make this a vibrant and fascinating time to be in education. With more than fifty years of combined teaching experience between the three of us, we have seen the ebb and flow of several educational "movements." Some have lasted longer than they should have and others, quite thankfully, have passed on to that great schoolyard in the sky.

What we find so dynamic and stimulating about the "reforms" taking place today is that they are not new! The concepts behind whole language were first proposed by John Dewey and his colleagues in the 1920s. The foundation for literature-based reading programs were advocated and delineated by Louise Rosenblatt in the 1930s. What is happening in today's classrooms is a renewal of the ideas and strategies that have "been around" for many years. The research is not new; it is how it is being used that is so electric!

We believe that learning through children's literature, in authentic invitational classrooms, can be intensely exciting and magnificently stimulating. As classroom teachers and reading specialists we have had the pleasure of working with hundreds of youngsters — helping them experience the joys of a book sumptuously savored or a story richly shared. We have had the honor of working with fellow teachers throughout the country as they seek to convey the magic of literature to their students in new and dynamic ways. And we have experienced the thrill of working with pre-service teachers — sharing with them the excitement and enthusiasm of a literature-rich reading program and a student-centered learning environment. Indeed, it is an exciting time to be a teacher!

As authors, we have also had the honor of sharing our zeal about teaching and our zest for learning with fellow educators around the country. We hope that, within the pages of this book, you will not only observe the magical experiences possible in literature-rich learning environments, but also embrace a belief of ours that the best teachers are those who are willing to learn alongside their students — exploring new territories and examining new vistas. Indeed, we are strong advocates of the idea that the best teachers are those who have as much to learn as they do to teach. In fact, we approached the writing of this book as a new and exciting learning experience — seeking new ways to use children's literature, exploring new dimensions of literature-rich classrooms, and examining new ideas about the learning process and the role of teachers. We believe that that process has helped us to grow as writers and has surely helped us to grow as teachers. We hope that our discoveries along the way may be guideposts for your professional growth and certainly increase your students' growth as lifelong readers and learners.

We have worked hard to fill the pages of this book with a plethora of ideas and a host of practical strategies for your classroom and your students. We sincerely hope that you will find our recommendations and suggestions appropriate in building exciting frameworks for your entire curriculum. We believe that thematic teaching and thematic units offer a wealth of learning opportunities for learners of all ages — opportunities without limits and without restrictions. As you and your students set your sails for new lands and new destinations, we hope that this book will serve as a guide for those journeys and as a companion for the literature-rich discoveries that will be made along the way. May your classroom be filled with all the excitement that thematic units can bring; and may your students be filled with all the wonder and imagination books can offer.

What an exciting time to be a teacher!

Anita M. Meinbach
Liz Rothlein
Anthony D. Fredericks

# Contents

# PART I:

Thematic Units: Structure and Design

# CHAPTER 1

# Developing and Using Thematic Units

A light breeze swept in off the Pacific Ocean. Sunlight echoed off the cliff faces and bounced throughout the small cove. Shadows cast by the rocks and outcroppings were splayed across the warm sand like surrealistic photographs. The day was warm and the air held the faint smell of a beach at low tide. It would have been a quiet, peaceful expanse except for the chatter and commotion of twenty-six of Chris Terriman's fourth graders clambering over the rocks and scampering over the sands of that small expanse of real estate.

"Hey, Mrs. Terriman, look at all the neat creatures in this pool!"

"Hey, Mrs. Terriman, look at the way these rocks have been worn by the waves!"

"Hey, Mrs. Terriman, look at the weird-looking plants that are growing down from the rocks on the cliffs!"

"Hey, Mrs. Terriman, look at the different types of seaweed growing near these rocks!"

There was an intense excitement in the air as Chris's students scampered over rocks, collected samples of flora and fauna, and recorded observations and notes in their journals. Chris smiled, knowing that this field trip was but one part of a larger thematic unit she had developed for her class. In fact, this was more than just a field trip — it was an opportunity for Chris's students to make connections between some of the literacy events in the classroom and their world outside the classroom.

Chris had grown up in Newport Beach, California, and had always had a love affair with the ocean. As a child, she had become an accomplished sailor and body surfer. During high school, she and her friends would play endless hours of beach volleyball during the summer months. But, what she enjoyed most was exploring some of the small beaches and coves that dotted the Southern California coastline. One of her favorite sites was "Little Corona" — a small rocky cove, flanked by cliffs and frequented by body surfers and skin divers. It was here that she was able to examine the life of tide pools and cliff faces. It was here that she was able to enjoy the quiet solitude of the cove or watch the endless progression of waves wash up upon the shore. It was here that she was able to record the geological symmetry of the landscape through a collection of color photographs. And it was here that Chris brought her students to experience the miracles and majesty of an ever-changing ecological wonderland.

On that particular November morning, Chris's students were scattered in a hundred different directions. A small group of three boys was moving between several tide pools, recording the number of sea urchins and sea anemones they found. Two girls were examining strands of seaweed that had washed up on the beach. Another group of students was collecting small samples of rocks to examine back in the classroom. Three students were drawing illustrations of the cove for presentation in a class scrapbook. Two different groups of students were collecting various samples of sand and soil for later analysis. Two boys were recording the social habits of a small flock of sea gulls bouncing on the water just outside the surf line.

Later that day, when the class returned to school, students began working on a host of extending activities. One group of students began preparations for a short video series on the ecology of the area, using videotapes recorded during the morning visit. Robert and Marcello were off to the library to locate addresses of various geological groups to whom they could send a list of questions about the rocks discovered on the beach. Carole and Elsie began looking through several books to collect information about the life of sea anemones and some of the other fauna discovered in the tide pools. Another group of students was developing a special brochure on how the ecology of the cove was endangered by the trash and debris left by sunbathers. Inez and Paul were putting together a "visitor's guide" to the cove, as it might be seen by an approaching flock of sea gulls.

Enthusiasm was rampant throughout the classroom. Students were excited by the opportunities to share information, discuss possibilities for presenting data discovered during the field trip with other classes, and make decisions on how their "book knowledge" could be used in productive ways. Some students chose to pursue independent activities, while others worked quietly in small groups. Cooperative learning was evident throughout the room as students assembled ideas and shared possibilities in an atmosphere of mutual respect and support. Competition was scarcely evident, as students helped each other with ideas, resources, and extensions of activities. It was clearly apparent that this was a true "community of learners" -one in which students were all working toward common goals, making decisions and following through on those decisions, and taking responsibility for how they learned as much as for what they learned.

Chris's students were not engaged in haphazard activities, but rather in a well-planned and thoroughly engaging process of thematic learning. The morning field trip was but one event in the thematic unit on "Oceanography" designed by fourth grade teachers at Chris's school. This unit combined an assortment of children's literature and whole language activities into a sequential series of lessons designed to assist students in appreciating the oceans of the world as well as the oceanic events that occurred less than ten miles from their school. Chris had introduced the unit with a collection of books about the oceans — including those dealing with life forms, explorations of the oceans, trade routes, the effects of the oceans on climate, and significant oceanic discoveries. Included in the unit were books such as *Our World: Seas and Oceans* by David Lambert (New York: Silver Burdett and Ginn, 1987); *Animal's at the Water's Edge* by Charles P. Milne (Minneapolis, MN: Raintree, 1988); *Oceans* by Seymour Simon (New York: Morrow, 1990); *The Rock Pool* by David Bellamy (New York: Clarkson Potter, 1988); *How to Hide an Octopus* by Ruth Heller (New York: Grosset, 1985); *A Day in the Life of a Marine Biologist* by William Jasperson (Boston: Little, Brown, 1982); *Night Dive* by Ann McGovern (New York: Macmillan, 1984); and *The Seashore* by James Pope (New York: Franklin Watts, 1985). These books (only several of the dozens selected and collected by the school librarian and other fourth grade teachers) were the impetus for the unit. The literature selections (for the unit) became the vehicle for a host of holistic activities. Some activities had been planned by teachers; however, a large majority were suggested by students as an outgrowth of the books read and shared in class. Some of these extending activities included:

   a.   the creation of a undersea poster covering one wall of the classroom;

   b.   the "invention" of a homemade desalinization device;

   c.   a "semantic octopus" which recorded new words and terms learned throughout the unit;

   d.   life-size illustrations of blue whales and other large ocean creatures on the school playground;

   e.   a scrapbook of amazing facts and figures;

   f.   a video series devoted to the changing ecology of various sections of the Southern California coastline;

   g.   a display of letters written to various scientific groups and universities;

   h.   surveys of family members and relatives on environmental concerns related to oceans;

   i.   a photographic collection (with annotations) of tide pool life;

j.  a skit on the life and death of various ocean creatures; and

k.  a set of brochures on currents and tides and their effect on land masses.

Chris is one of a growing legion of teachers who have discovered the enormous value and impact thematic teaching can and does have on the lives of her students. In many ways, thematic teaching allows Chris to "energize" her curriculum and demonstrate the natural connections that exist between reading, language arts, science, social studies, math, and the creative arts. Chris's students are also provided with opportunities to take responsibility for their learning — making choices, making decisions, and making judgments on the material and processes used throughout a designated unit. In essence, Chris's classroom is one in which children's literature provides both a foundation and a launching pad for her students' self-initiated discoveries. A thematic unit provides breadth and depth to the entire curriculum — offering innumerable opportunities for students to become immersed in the dynamics of their own education. In short, *a thematic unit is the epitome of whole language teaching: students use language productively to answer self-initiated questions and satisfy their own inherent and natural curiosity about the world around them.*

Let's take a look at some of the other advantages of thematic units — for teachers (Table 1-1) as well as for students (Table 1-2).

---

## TABLE 1-1

## Advantages of Thematic Teaching
## (for teachers)

- There is more time available for instructional purposes. Material does not have to be crammed into artificial time periods, but can be extended across the curriculum and across the day.

- The connections which can and do exist between subjects, topics, and themes can be logically and naturally developed. Teachers can demonstrate relationships and assist students in comprehending those relationships.

- Learning can be demonstrated as a continuous activity — one not restricted by textbook designs, time barriers, or even the four walls of the classroom. Teachers can help students extend learning opportunities into many aspects of their personal lives.

- Teachers are able to relinquish "control" of the curriculum and assist students in assuming a sense of "ownership" for their individual learning destinies.

- Teachers are free to help students look at a problem, situation, or topic from a variety of viewpoints, rather than the "right way" frequently demonstrated in a teacher's manual or curriculum guide.

- The development of a "community of learners" is facilitated and enhanced through thematic teaching. There is less emphasis on *competition* and more emphasis on *collaboration and cooperation*.

- Opportunities for the teacher to model appropriate learning behaviors in a supportive and encouraging environment is enhanced.

- Assessment is more holistic, authentic, and meaningful and provides a more accurate picture of students' progress and development.

- Authentic use of all the language arts (reading, writing, listening, and speaking) is encouraged throughout all curricular areas.

- There is more emphasis on *teaching* students; less emphasis on *telling* students.

- Teachers are provided with an abundance of opportunities for integrating children's literature into all aspects of the curriculum and all aspects of the day.

- Teachers can promote problem solving, creative thinking, and critical thinking processes within all aspects of a topic.

- Teachers can promote and support children's individual autonomy and self-direction by offering students control over their learning.

- Teachers are also engaged as *learners* throughout the development and implementation of a thematic unit.

## Table 1-2

## Advantages of Thematic Teaching
## (for students)

- Focuses on the *processes* of learning more so than the *products* of learning.

- Breaks down the "artificial barriers" that often exist between areas of the curriculum and provides an integrative approach to learning.

- Provides a child-centered curriculum — one tailored to their interests, needs, and abilities; one in which they are encouraged to make their own decisions and assume a measure of responsibility for learning.

- Stimulates self-directed discovery and investigation inside and outside of the classroom.

- Assists youngsters in developing relationships between ideas and concepts, thereby enhancing appreciation and comprehension.

- Offers realistic opportunities for children to build upon their own individual background of information in developing new knowledge.

- Respects the individual cultural background, home experiences, and interest levels of children.

- Stimulates the creation of important concepts through first-hand experiences and self-initiated discoveries.

- Students are encouraged (and supported in their efforts) to take risks.

- Students develop more self-direction and independence through a variety of learning activities and opportunities.

- Students understand the "why" of activities and events instead of just the "what."

- Students are encouraged to make approximations of learning, rather than focus on the absolutes of learning.

- Children have sustained time and opportunity to investigate topics thoroughly and to engage in reflective inquiry.

# Teaching Thematically

As indicated above, thematic units offer teachers and students some unique opportunities to examine all the dimensions and ramifications of holistic learning. Thematic units are not, however, a simple hodgepodge of random activities or an "Irish Stew" of cross-curricular projects. We would like to offer a definition of thematic units we have used in a previous book — a definition we have found particularly useful in designing and implementing our own units:

*A thematic approach to learning combines structured, sequential, and well-organized strategies, activities, children's literature, and materials used to expand a particular concept. A thematic unit is multidisciplinary and multidimensional; it knows no boundaries. It is responsive to the interests, abilities, and needs of children and is respectful of their developing aptitudes and attitudes. In essence, a thematic approach to learning offers students a realistic arena in which they can pursue learning using a host of contexts and a panorama of literature.*

(Fredericks, Meinbach, & Rothlein; 1993)

In short, we like to think of thematic units as an instructional device to **expand** the learning opportunities of students and the teaching opportunities of teachers.

Perhaps you're wondering how thematic teaching works. That is, your question may be How does a thematic unit work within the structure of daily lesson plans and curriculum guides? To assist you we have provided a daily plan from David McManus's thematic unit on "Communities." David is a second grade teacher in Northwestern Oregon and has been developing and using thematic units for four years. He has discovered that thematic teaching provides him with a multitude of teaching opportunities that not only excite his students, but get him excited as well. As a result, he has developed several units for various areas of his second grade curriculum. Since the district requires all teachers to follow a specific curriculum guide in each subject area, there are selected objectives David must include in his lessons. However, he has found that these can be easily incorporated within the parameters of a thematic unit and, in fact, provide some of the framework for developing a unit.

The daily plan which follows illustrates how David has captured the spirit and excitement of thematic teaching for an entire day. Please note how subjects have been integrated, how students are able to take responsibility for their own learning, how David can act as a facilitator for learning, and how literature is a stimulant for the events that can and do happen in David's classroom.

---

### THEMATIC TEACHING: A SAMPLE PLAN

**Theme: Communities**

*8:30 - 9:00 Opening*
   As students are entering the classroom they put away their lunch boxes and continue work on any activities still unfinished from the previous day. They may work independently or in small groups according to the nature of the activities. Activities may include journal writing, video-taping, poster creation, silent reading, library research, skit practice, or a cooperative learning venture.

*9:00 - 9:45 Required/Optional Activities*
   **Group 1** — Students begin to build a dual diorama (one half depicts an urban environment, the other half depicts a rural environment). Using plastic figures, clay, pipe cleaners, and a shoe box, the scenes are created using ideas from several selected pieces of literature.
   **Group 2** — Students are composing a letter to a class in another state telling them about some

---

of the information they have collected and facts they are learning (the pen pals have been established by the two respective teachers [who are former college classmates]). The pen pals communicate regularly about some of their activities and field trips.

**Group 3** — Students visit several classrooms throughout the school, collecting data about home towns. Teachers, students, and administrative staff are interviewed about the places they have lived throughout the United States. After students complete their data collection, a large map will be constructed to illustrate their results.

**Group 4** — After viewing a filmstrip on some of the problems normally associated with urban life (pollution, traffic congestion, crime) students work together to draft a letter to the editor of the local newspaper, suggesting a series of solutions to address problems in their own community.

**Group 5** — Using a large sheet of oaktag, students create a community calendar of events. Listings in the local newspaper are added to school events and posted in a prominent place in the classroom.

**Group 6** — Three students are completing a reading of the book *Country Mouse, Town Mouse* by Lorinda B. Cauley and will begin work on a puppet show that will be shared with another second grade class.

### 9:45 - 10:05 *Sustained Silent Reading*
Students obtain books from the classroom library and scatter throughout the room. Books selected include: *The Village of Round and Square Houses* by Ann Grifalconi (Boston: Little, Brown, 1986); *All About Things People Do* by Melanie and Chris Rice (New York: Doubleday, 1989); *Efan the Great* by Roni Schotter (New York: Lothrop, 1986); *The House on Maple Street* by Marcia Sewell (New York: Morrow, 1987); *We Keep a Store* by Anne Shelby (New York: Orchard, 1990); *Town and Country* by Alice and Martin Provensen (New York: Crown, 1984); and *The Little House* by Virginia Lee Burton (Boston: Houghton Mifflin, 1969). Most students engage in independent reading while three pairs of students read their books to each other.

### 10:05 - 10:25 *Writing Process*
**Journals** — Several students open their journals and take on the role of an urban house. Each student writes about a day in the life of his/her house as seen through the "eyes" of that house. Students are involved in different stages of the writing process, including drafting, revising, and editing.

**Reader's Theater** — A small group of four students continues work on a reader's theater adaptation of *Shaker Lane* by Alice and Martin Provensen (New York: Viking, 1987). Students create scenarios about some of the events from the book. The reader's theater will be presented at a later date.

**Big Book** — Another group of students creates an oversized book which has been cut from cardboard into the shape of a factory. Sheets of paper have been stapled inside the covers. Students prepare essays about some of the events that take place inside a factory. The completed book will be shared with several first grade classrooms.

**Fact Book** — A small group of students heads to the library to collect data for inclusion in a "fact book" — a collection of interesting facts about urban and rural life. The final project will be donated to the school library for permanent display.

### 10:25 - 10:40 *Read-Aloud/Storytelling*
*Miss Rumphius* by Barbara Cooney (New York: Viking, 1982) is read to the entire class [this book discusses the world travels of a lady and what she does when she returns home]. Afterward, discussion centers on comparisons between the life of "Miss Rumphius" and the lives of some of the students' grandparents.

*10:40 - 11:10 Teacher-Directed Activities*

**Opening** — To begin the lesson, students are asked to create a list of all the words used to describe communities. These words are recorded on the chalkboard in a vertical list. Students are told that these words are examples of adjectives.

**Book Study** — The book *In Coal Country* by Judith Hendershot (New York: Knopf, 1987) is introduced to students. During the oral reading students are asked to listen for adjectives used in the story. As words are noted, they are added to the list on the board.

**Group Work** — Students are divided into several heterogeneous groups. Each group is "assigned" four to five specific U.S. communities (urban or rural areas) and asked to generate adjectives (from the list on the board) that could be used to describe each. Each group prepares a narrative about their location, using identified adjectives. Each narrative is read to the whole class and differences and similarities in adjective use are discussed. Stories are posted on the bulletin board.

*11:10 - 11:50 Responding To Literature*

(Students have just completed *Farm Morning* by David McPhail [New York: Harcourt, Brace, 1985]).

**Group 1** — Students select one of the animals mentioned in the book and write about a day in the life of that animal. They draw the shape of the animal on a sheet of construction paper. They cut out the animal and, using it as a pattern, make pages and construction paper covers for student books. Students use these materials to write their story. Students have time to share their stories.

**Group 2** — Students prepare a letter to the county extension agent inviting her to visit the classroom and share information on the care of various farm animals.

**Group 3** — Students are involved in a discussion: Which is more demanding — living on a farm or living in the city? Students establish "mini-teams" and debate the merits of each lifestyle.

*11:50 - 12:10 Recess/Sharing*

*12:10 - 12:40 Lunch*

*12:40 - 1:25 Special Class*

Students go to music, art, computer room, library, or physical education.

*1:25 - 2:10 Math*

**Group 1** — Students survey the adult members of their families and friends and collect data on the variety of occupations in which people have worked. The information is combined into charts and graphs that record jobs, the number of people who have worked in each job, and the number of jobs held by individuals.

**Group 2** — Small teams of students (with their parents) survey the prices of selected food items (one pound of hamburger meat, a 16-ounce box of cereal, a quart of milk, and a jar of peanut butter) in different stores throughout the local community. The data is gathered together in class and displayed on a comparative chart. Discussions about the "cost of living" in various sections of the community is initiated.

**Group 3** — Students bring in recipes for cultural or ethnic foods that are prepared by the families of students in the class. A "Cultural Feast Day" is planned, with an emphasis on the measurements used in the preparation of various dishes.

*2:10 - 2:40 Teacher-Directed Lesson*

**Opening** — Students are asked to brainstorm the various reasons why people live in different

sections of a community (ethnic group, housing costs, distance to work, and so forth).
**Group Work** — Each student selects a reason and gets into a group identified with that reason (for example, all who believe that people live where they do because of housing costs are formed into one group). Each group prepares a written argument for their selected reason and presents their case(s) to the class. Groups research their selected reasons (via interviews, library work, and so forth) and share their findings with the whole class.
**Closure** — A professor of sociology from the local college is invited to speak on the ethnic and cultural composition of the local community. Students will have prepared a list of questions prior to her visit.

*2:40 - 3:00 Daily Closure*
Students review daily activities. A summary statement about the day's activities is generated by the class and recorded on a large wall calendar in the front of the classroom. Each student transcribes the summary statement onto a personal calendar which is taken home and shared with parents at the end of each week.

*3:00 - 3:15 Dismassal*

As you look over David's plan for one day of his "Communities" unit, you will note a variety of learning options for students. As you might suspect, the entire unit encompassed more than a single day — in fact, the unit is planned for three weeks of intensive investigation into all aspects of "Communities." Succeeding days included such topics and activities as:

- populations and communities of animals
- populations and communities of plants
- civic responsibilities of community members (voting, etc.)
- field trips to city hall, a senior citizen center, and the post office
- a letter-writing campaign to the local newspaper
- read-alouds by various community members, including the town mayor
- geological study of the local community
- historical study of the local community
- creation of a diorama to be posted in the local bank
- creation of an almanac of local weather patterns and climatic conditions over the past 100 years
- an investigation of the major industries and agricultural resources of the region
- creation of a community map for new families

What is most striking about David's thematic unit is not that it was based on a required component of the social studies curriculum (which he would have had to teach anyway), but rather that the events, activities, and projects included within the unit evolved from the suggestions and interests of his students. In a real sense, David has created an "invitational" classroom — one in which students take an active role in the design, structure, and formation of any thematic unit. While David may begin the process with the district's curriculum guide in a particular area, a collection of teacher resource books, input from colleagues and friends, or information collected at conferences and from professional journals, it is his students who provide the bulk of the ideas and investigations David builds into his units. In so doing, he is offering his students an opportunity to take an active role in their own learning and an equal opportunity to assume a measure of responsibility for their own scholastic endeavors.

# Planning Thematic Instruction

As you might expect, thematic teaching requires some planning and organization in order to make it successful. Our own experiences, as well as those of teachers with whom we have talked around the country, have indicated that there are five primary areas to consider in designing an effective and successful thematic unit. These include:

A.  Selecting the theme

B.  Organizing the theme

C.  Gathering materials and resources

D.  Designing activities and projects

E.  Implementing the unit

Let's take a look at each of those components in a little more detail. To assist you in designing your own units, we will periodically share with you the processes Jean Ziebel, a fourth grade teacher in West Virginia, used in the development of a thematic unit on "The Environment."

## A.  Selecting the Theme

The topics for thematic units can come from many sources. Here are a few to consider:

*   *Curricular topics*   Themes or topics outlined in a basal textbook or in the district's curriculum guide(s).

*   *Issues*   Local concerns or topics that affect students or their families directly.

*   *Problems*   Concerns or questions which have a more universal application or appeal.

*   *Special events*   A local or national celebration or holiday.

*   *Student interests*   Special topics that capture student interest or reflect their hobbies and/or leisure activities.

*   *Literary interests*   Genres of literature, author studies, or a special collection of related books.

The following chart provides you with a few possibilities to consider for the development of your own thematic units.

| Theme Topics | Primary (Grades 1-3) | Intermediate (Grades 4-6) |
|---|---|---|
| Curricular Areas | Animals<br>The seasons<br>Dinosaurs<br>Weather<br>Plants<br>Staying healthy<br>The changing earth<br>Sun and moon<br>Magnetism<br>Simple machines<br>Light and heat<br>Neighborhoods<br>Communities | Body system<br>Inventors<br>The enviroment<br>Oceanography<br>Life cycles<br>Work and energy<br>Electricity<br>Sound and light<br>Solar system<br>The changing earth<br>Space<br>Mythology<br>Geography |

| Theme Topics | Primary (Grades 1-3) | Intermediate (Grades 4-6) |
|---|---|---|
| Curricular Areas (con't) | Transportation<br>Growing up<br>Family life<br>Holidays<br>Celebrations<br>Sports<br>Native Americans | Discovery<br>Becoming a nation<br>Pioneer life<br>War and peace<br>Multiculturalism<br>Careers<br>Ancient cultures |
| Issues | Homework<br>Family matters<br>Siblings<br>Trash disposal<br>Rules | Pollution<br>Water quality<br>Toxic wastes<br>Air quality<br>Nuclear power |
| Problems | Energy use<br>Crime<br>Natural resources<br>The environment<br>Food | Ozone layer<br>Starvation<br>Population<br>Oil spills<br>Wildlife<br>Solar power |
| Special Events | Birthdays<br>Winter holidays<br>Circus<br>Field trip<br>Olympics<br>Summer vacation | Shuttle launch<br>Elections<br>World Series<br>Super Bowl<br>Unusual weather<br>Legislation |
| Student Interests | Dinosaurs<br>Monsters<br>Sharks<br>Airplanes<br>Friends and neighbors<br>Vacations<br>Space exploration<br>Ocean creatures<br>Scary things | Computers<br>Famous people<br>Ecology<br>Environment<br>Sports heros/heroines<br>Sports<br>Relationships<br>Clothes<br>Vacations |
| Literary Interests | Nursery rhymes<br>Fairy tales<br>Sports stories<br>Adventure<br>Mystery<br>Poetry<br>Fiction<br>Books by a favorite author | Romances<br>Legends<br>Mysteries<br>Autobiographies<br>Sports heros/heroines<br>Horror stories<br>Outer space<br>Books by a favorite author |

The chart above is only a partial listing of potential topics that can be developed into thematic units. The textbooks you use for your classroom, your school district's curriculum guides in various subjects (and the policies related to the use of those guides), and your students' interests and suggestions can all be used as resources for the selection of thematic topics.

### B. Organizing the Theme

Once you have selected a theme topic, your next step is to determine the skills and objectives for the unit, as well as the activities that will be used to foster an understanding and appreciation of those elements.

We have found two strategies to be particularly useful at this stage — one is called "Themewebbing"; the other "Bookwebbing."

Themewebbing provides you with an outline form with which you can interrelate and integrate aspects of the elementary curriculum with a specific thematic topic. In so doing, you can offer students an opportunity to understand the universality of a topic as well as how that topic can be expanded and enlarged within each curricular area.

Indicated below is the outline Jean used as she began developing her thematic unit on "The Environment." She began by placing the title of her thematic unit in the center space on the Unit Planning Form (see Figures 1-1 and 1-2). For each of the curricular areas, she brainstormed some possible activities and projects related to the general theme. She also invited her students to participate in this brainstorming effort — offering them opportunities to suggest whole language activities that might expand their understanding of and participation in the unit. What Jean discovered, as you will, is that whenever students are offered genuine opportunities to contribute to the learning milieu they are more inclined to participate in that environment and, hence, learn from that environment. Thus, the successful planning of a unit involves input from your students as much as it involves input from you.

Figure 1-1

# Unit Planning Form

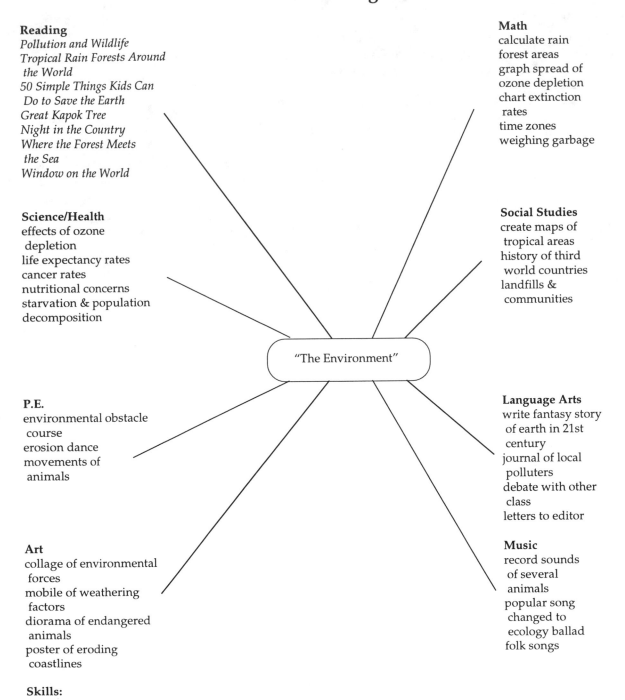

**Reading**
*Pollution and Wildlife*
*Tropical Rain Forests Around*
 *the World*
*50 Simple Things Kids Can*
 *Do to Save the Earth*
*Great Kapok Tree*
*Night in the Country*
*Where the Forest Meets*
 *the Sea*
*Window on the World*

**Math**
calculate rain
 forest areas
graph spread of
 ozone depletion
chart extinction
 rates
time zones
weighing garbage

**Science/Health**
effects of ozone
 depletion
life expectancy rates
cancer rates
nutritional concerns
starvation & population
decomposition

**Social Studies**
create maps of
 tropical areas
history of third
 world countries
landfills &
 communities

"The Environment"

**P.E.**
environmental obstacle
 course
erosion dance
movements of
 animals

**Language Arts**
write fantasy story
 of earth in 21st
 century
journal of local
 polluters
debate with other
 class
letters to editor

**Art**
collage of environmental
 forces
mobile of weathering
 factors
diorama of endangered
 animals
poster of eroding
 coastlines

**Music**
record sounds
 of several
 animals
popular song
 changed to
 ecology ballad
folk songs

**Skills:**

Figure 1-2

# Unit Planning Form

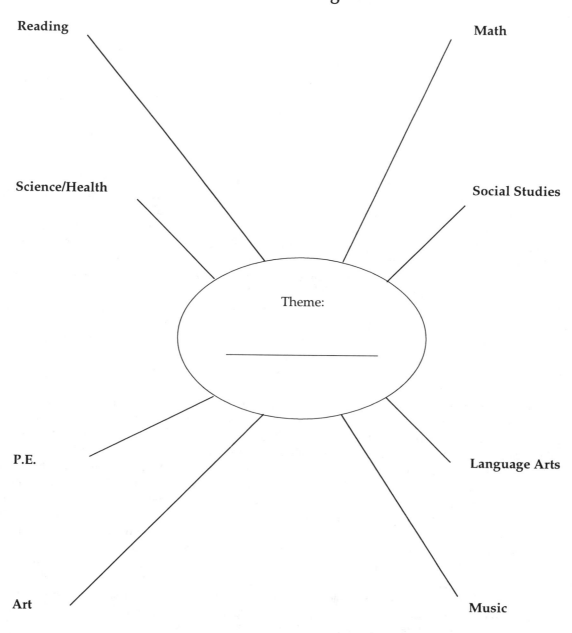

Reading

Math

Science/Health

Social Studies

Theme:

_____

P.E.

Language Arts

Art

Music

**Skills:**

You will note on the "Unit Planning Form" that there is a space to record the skills to be taught during a thematic unit. Thematic teaching does not mean the elimination of skill work for students. Instead, it means that skills are still taught, but in a more meaningful, realistic, and holistic manner. Depending on where you are teaching, you may be required to adhere to a district curriculum guide or a publisher's scope and sequence chart of skills. Using a thematic unit does not negate the teaching of skills, rather it offers a host of teaching possibilities for sharing those skills with your students and assisting students in using their newly learned skills in "real-life" situations and authentic literature. The "Sample Plan" presented earlier in this chapter is an example of how the grammatical skill of adjective use was incorporated into the structure of a thematic unit. We encourage you to consider the utilization of skills as a requisite part of the thematic units you create or the thematic units you use from this book.

Another strategy Jean uses to plan thematic units is called "Bookwebbing." Bookwebbing is similar to Themewebbing, except in this strategy a literature selection is featured as the central focal point for the webbing procedure. That is, curricular extensions are tied to the material in a book — providing students with opportunities to expand the information in a book into all the other areas of the elementary curriculum.

Indicated below is how Jean used the book *The Great Kapok Tree* by Lynn Cherry (New York: Gulliver, 1990) as an initial literature selection for her "Environment" thematic unit. (See Figure 1-3.) It should be noted that "Bookwebbing" can be done with several related books selected for a unit. For example, what follows is a preliminary outline for a *single book* within a larger thematic unit. To continue the development of the thematic unit, Jean would also use "Bookwebbing" with two or three other similarly related books (see Figure 1-5, "Unit Guide," on page 17). For example, she may wish to "bookweb" additional books such as *The Wump World* by Bill Peet (Boston: Houghton Mifflin, 1970); *One Day in the Tropical Rainforest* by Jean Craighead George (New York: Crowell, 1990); and *Going Green: A Kid's Handbook to Saving the Planet* by John Elkington (New York: Puffin, 1990). All four of these respective "bookwebs" could then be combined and assembled into a well-rounded and thorough thematic unit on "The Environment."

In planning activities for a book, you will find it advantageous to consider (1) "Pre-reading Activities" — those activities which "tap into" students' background knowledge and allow them to relate that knowledge to the information in a selected book; (2) "During" or "After" whole language activities that students can pursue within or across selected curricular areas (see Chapter Two); and (3) a selection of open-ended questions used as "discussion starters" between yourself and students or among students. Obviously, these questions are not intended to "test" students on what they have read, but to help students think about the implications and ramifications of a piece of literature as it relates to the general theme. The "Literature Planning Guide" provides you with a duplicable planning sheet which can assist you in this process. (See Figure 1-6.) You may wish to consider this sheet as a supplement to, or a replacement for, the "Book Planning Form." Please feel free to use both or either one according to your own teaching or planning style.

Many teachers have discovered that "Bookwebbing" is an easy and practical way with which to design thematic units. Unit construction begins with a single book — then, two or three additional books are "linked" to the initial literature selection to create the basic structure for a thematic unit. The most advantageous aspect of this strategy is that students can be invited to actively participate in the design of the unit — particularly when they have been exposed to a plethora of children's literature and other thematic units. Their contributions in the form of ideas and related activities help make the planning process meaningful and relevant and the eventual thematic unit a positive addition to any content area. Some teachers have discovered that students can be major developers in the preliminary design of an unit — a factor that contributes to its eventual impact and success.

Figure 1-3

# Book Planning Form

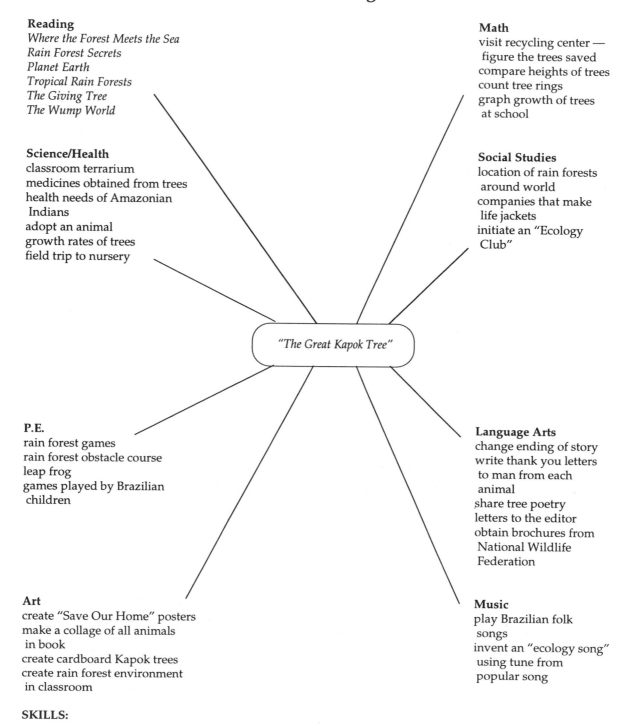

**Reading**
*Where the Forest Meets the Sea*
*Rain Forest Secrets*
*Planet Earth*
*Tropical Rain Forests*
*The Giving Tree*
*The Wump World*

**Science/Health**
classroom terrarium
medicines obtained from trees
health needs of Amazonian
 Indians
adopt an animal
growth rates of trees
field trip to nursery

**P.E.**
rain forest games
rain forest obstacle course
leap frog
games played by Brazilian
 children

**Art**
create "Save Our Home" posters
make a collage of all animals
 in book
create cardboard Kapok trees
create rain forest environment
 in classroom

**SKILLS:**

**Math**
visit recycling center —
 figure the trees saved
compare heights of trees
count tree rings
graph growth of trees
 at school

**Social Studies**
location of rain forests
 around world
companies that make
 life jackets
initiate an "Ecology
 Club"

**Language Arts**
change ending of story
write thank you letters
 to man from each
 animal
share tree poetry
letters to the editor
obtain brochures from
 National Wildlife
 Federation

**Music**
play Brazilian folk
 songs
invent an "ecology song"
 using tune from
 popular song

*"The Great Kapok Tree"*

Figure 1-4

# Book Planning Form

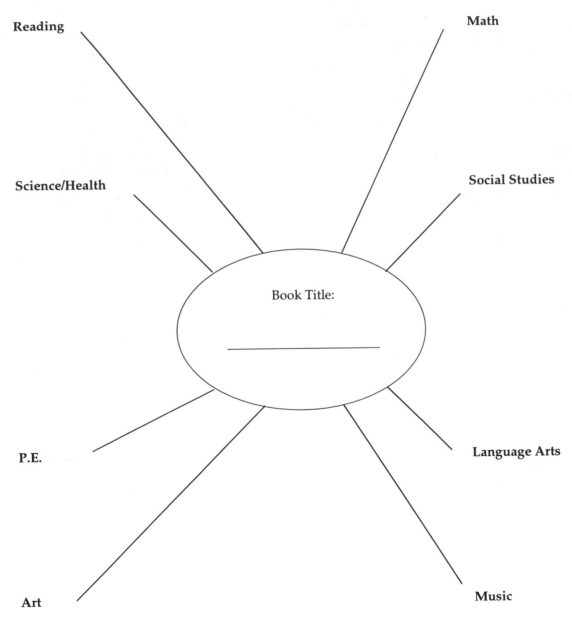

Reading

Math

Science/Health

Social Studies

Book Title:

_____

P.E.

Language Arts

Art

Music

**Skills:**

Figure 1-5

# Unit Guide

Theme: _____

Focus: _____

Objectives: (1) _____
            (2) _____
            (3) _____

Initiating Activity (whole language activity shared with students at the beginning of a unit to heighten interest in the unit):

_____
_____
_____
_____
_____

General Activities (cross-curricular activities to introduce, teach and extend the unit objectives):

| Reading: | Math: | Science/Health: | Social Studies: |
| --- | --- | --- | --- |
| | | | |

Literature Selections:

| Book#1: | Book #2: |
| --- | --- |
| | |
| Book #3: | Book #4: |
| | |

Specific Skills: _____

_____

Culminating Activity (one or more whole language activities used to "round out" a unit and bring closure for students):

_____

_____

_____

_____

_____

Mini-Themes (one or more mini-units related to the larger unit. These can be used in place of, or as a supplement to, the larger unit):

| Mini-Theme #1: | Mini-Theme #2: |
|---|---|
| Mini-Theme #3: | Mini-Theme #4: |

Evaluation/Assessment Strategies:

_____

_____

_____

_____

_____

Figure 1-6

# Literature Planning Guide

Book Title: _____

Author: _____

Pre-Reading Activity: _____

_____

_____

_____

Cross-Curricular Activities (related to book):

| Reading: | Math: | Science/Health: | Social Studies: |
|---|---|---|---|
| | | | |
| P.E.: | Language Arts: | Art: | Music: |
| | | | |

Specific Skills: _____

_____

_____

_____

_____

Open-Ended Questions:

1. _____

2. _____

3. _____

4. _____

5. _____

## C. Gathering Materials and Resources

Thematic units differ from textbook-based units not only in their design, but also in the variety and types of materials used. Suffice it to say that thematic units can encompass a host of materials and resources — thus ensuring an abundance of opportunities for students to experience a "hands-on, minds-on" approach to learning. Obviously, your first consideration will be the types of literature you wish to use within a unit. After that, you and your students can work together suggesting and planning any number of materials and resources for use within a unit. Indeed, when students are provided with active opportunities to suggest resources, they will be more inclined to use those items throughout the duration of a unit.

Here are some possible resources for you to consider in designing your own units:

### Printed Resources

newspapers
pamphlets
notices
travel guides
junk mail
journals
letters
maps
advertisements

brochures
flyers
encyclopedias
dictionaries
magazines
booklets
journals
catalogs

### Visual Resources

videos
filmstrips
computer software
slide programs

films
CD-ROM
movies
overhead transparencies

### Literature Resources

1.  Printed:
    a.  *Eyeopeners* by Beverly Kobrin (New York, NY: Penguin Books, 1988)
    b.  "Outstanding Science Trade Books for Children" (March issue of *Science and Children*).
    c.  "Notable Children's Trade Books in the Field of Social Studies" (April/May issue of *Social Education*).
    d.  "Children's Choices" (October issue of *The Reading Teacher*).
    e.  *Science Through Children's Literature* by Carol Butzow and John Butzow (Englewood, CO: Teacher Ideas Press, 1989).
    f.  *Social Studies Through Children's Literature* by Anthony D. Fredericks (Englewood, CO: Teacher Ideas Press, 1991).
    g.  *The Literature Connection: Using Children's Books in the Classroom* by Liz Rothlein and Anita Meinbach (Glenview, IL: Scott, Foresman and Co., 1991).
    h.  *A to Zoo — Subject Access to Children's Picture Books* by Carolyn W. Lima (Ann Arbor, MI: Bowker, 1985).
    i.  *Booklist Magazine* published by The American Library Association (50 E. Huron St., Chicago, IL 60611).
    j.  *Children's Books in Print* (Ann Arbor, MI: Bowker, annual).
    k.  *Children's Literature in the Reading Program* by Bernice Cullinan (Newark, DE: International Reading Association, 1987).
    l.  *Fiction, Folklore, Fantasy, and Poetry for Children* by S.S. Dreyer (New York: Bowker, 1986).
    m.  *Best Books for Children: Preschool Through the Middle Grades* by J.T. Gillespie and C.B. Gilbert (New York: Bowker, 1985).

n. *A Critical Handbook of Children's Literature* by Rebecca Lukens (Glenview, IL: Scott, Foresman and Co., 1995).

o. *Adventuring with Books: A Booklist for pre-K to Grade 6* by Diane Monson (Urbana, IL: National Council of Teachers of English, 1985).

p. *Through the Eyes of a Child: An Introduction to Children's Literature* by Donna Norton (Columbus, OH: Merrill, 1983).

q. *Children's Literature from A to Z: A Guide for Parents and Teacher* by J.C. Stott (New York: McGraw-Hill, 184).

r. *The Scott, Foresman Anthology of Children's Literature* by Zena Sutherland and Myra Cohn Livingston (Glenview, IL: Scott, Foresman, 1984).

s. *The Read-Aloud Handbook* by Jim Trelease (New York: Penguin, 1982).

t. *The WEB: Wonderfully Exciting Books* (The Ohio State University, 200 Ramseyer Hall, Columbus, OH 43210) (periodical).

2. Librarians
   a. Your school librarian
   b. The public librarian
   c. College librarian

3. Book Clubs
   a. *Scholastic Book Clubs*, 2931 East McCarty St., P.O. Box 7500, Jefferson City, MO 65102.
   b. *Troll Book Clubs*, 320 Route 17, Mahwah, NJ 07498.
   c. *The Trumpet Club*, P.O. Box 604, Holmes, PA 19092.
   d. *Weekly Reader Paperback Clubs*, 4343 Equity Dr., P.O. Box 16628, Columbus, OH 43272.

### *Artifacts*

Depending on the nature and scope of your thematic unit you can use a variety of artifacts within that unit. For example, if you and your students were designing a unit on "Simple Machines," you might bring in artifacts such as a screwdriver, a pair of pliers, a knife, a doorknob, a small pulley, a can opener, and a small piece of wood. A unit on "Insects" might include artifacts such as a pair of tweezers, a magnifying lens, pins, display mounts, and a microscope. Obviously, the types of artifacts appropriate for a unit will depend on the topic of the unit. However, here are some who can assist you in obtaining and selecting necessary artifacts:

parents (see "Parent students Letter" following)

| | |
|---|---|
| school media specialist | computer specialist |
| colleagues | teachers in other districts |
| pen pals | relatives/guest speakers |
| community members | local high school teachers |
| college professors | social agencies |
| public officials | senior citizens |
| shop/store owners | students |

Dear Parents:

One of the sections of the local newspaper many people turn to for information is the weather report. The weather report is also a staple of the evening news on television. Indeed, most of us are very interested in the weather and often plan our outings and social events around the predicted weather for the day or weekend.

Children, too, are very interested in the weather. In fact, we are about to begin a science unit in our classroom entitled "The Weather and You." We would like to invite you to help us in this unit by donating some common household objects and items. Your child has checked the items below which he/she feels you might be able to share with all the students in our class. We hope that you might be able to contribute some or all of these items. Please feel free to contact me if you should have any questions. Thanking you in advance.

Sincerely,

| | |
|---|---|
| _____ soda bottle | _____ plastic wrap |
| _____ plastic cups | _____ measuring cup |
| _____ straws | _____ string |
| _____ cotton balls | _____ spray bottle |
| _____ spoons | _____ toothpicks |
| _____ various thermometers | _____ cardboard strips |
| _____ cellophane | _____ food coloring |
| _____ shoe boxes | _____ paper plates |
| _____ lunch bags | _____ eye dropper |
| _____ wax paper | _____ balloons |
| _____ funnel | _____ rubber bands |

P.S. If you are interested, here are some children's books on "The Weather" you and your child may wish to check out from the school library or local public library:

Craig, Jean. *Questions and Answers About Weather*. New York: Four Winds, 1969.
Ford, Adam. *Weather Watch*. New York: Lothrop, 1982.
Gibbons, Gail. *Weather Forecasting*. New York: Four Winds, 1987.
Simon, Seymour. *Storms*. New York: Morrow, 1989.
Webster, Vera. *Weather Experiments*. Chicago: Children's Press, 1982.

## D. Designing Activities and Projects

As you will note in the preceding sections, whole language activities are the crux of a well-designed and fully functioning thematic unit. We have discovered that the first few thematic units we have written have been the most difficult, simply because we were trying to organize a vast amount of information, ideas, and resources into a systematic and sequential framework. However, we also discovered — as have many other teachers — that once the first few units have been written, the rest become increasingly easier. That's not to say, however, that every unit will be straightforward and easy. It does mean that practice in designing units makes the creation of future units that much more uncomplicated.

Here are some suggestions we have learned "along the way." We hope you find these useful in designing the activities and projects you wish to include in your units. Activities should:

- integrate the language arts — reading, writing, speaking, listening;
- be holistic in nature;
- emphasize a "hands-on, minds-on" approach to learning;
- be cross-curricular in nature;
- result from the ideas and suggestions of students;
- focus on the relationship(s) between a piece of children's literature and the "real world";
- allow students to "tap into" their background knowledge and relate that information to what they are learning;
- be based in a meaningful format that engages students in productive work (as opposed to "busy work");
- be designed to last for differing periods of time (for example, one hour, one day, one week);
- be both instructional and motivational in nature; and
- relate to the general topic of the unit or the specific topic of a piece of literature.

It is important to point out that a thematic unit is **NOT** an arbitrary collection of random activities. It is a well orchestrated assembly of whole language activities designed to help students appreciate and comprehend a specific topic or a general idea. To accomplish these goals requires an attention to the *types* of activities, the *variety* of activities, and the *purpose* of the activities selected. In other words, there must be a specific reason for the use of selected activities within a unit.

## E. Implementing the Unit

Teaching thematically is not necessarily an "all or nothing" proposition. By that we mean that it is not necessary to use a thematic unit for a full day, a full week, or a full month. What it does mean is that you will have several options to consider in terms of how you will want to present a thematic unit to your class, how much you want it to dominate your daily curriculum, and how involved you and your students want to be. Obviously, your level of comfort with thematic teaching and the scope and sequence of your classroom or district curriculum may determine the degree to which you utilize (or do not utilize) a thematic unit. We offer the following options for your classroom. This listing, however, is only a partial collection of ideas. The dictates of your own particular teaching situation, personal experience, and student needs may suggest other possibilities or other alternatives to this register of ideas.

- Teach a thematic unit throughout a school day and for an extended period of several school days (see "Thematic Teaching: A Sample Plan" presented earlier).
- Teach a thematic unit for half a day for several days in succession.
- Use a thematic unit for two or more subject areas (for example, science and math) in combination and the regular curriculum for the other subjects.
- Use a thematic unit as the "curriculum" for a selected subject area (for example, science, social studies) and the regular curriculum for the other subjects.
- Teach a thematic unit for an entire day and follow up with the regular curriculum in succeeding days.

- Use a thematic unit as a follow up to information and data presented in a textbook or curriculum guide.

- Provide students with a thematic unit as independent work upon completion of lessons in the basal textbook.

- Teach cooperatively with a colleague and present a thematic unit to both classes at the same time (this can be done with two classes at the same grade or two different classes — each at a different grade level).

- Use a thematic unit intermittently over the span of several weeks.

How you use the thematic units you and your students design will be determined by any number of factors. It is safe to say that there is no ideal way to incorporate thematic units into your classroom plans. We would like to suggest, however, that you consider a multiplicity of options — not only in the design of units, but also in their use.

The following Lesson Planning Forms, Figures 1-7, 1-8, and 1-9 will help you organize your thematic units in terms of your particular classroom and curricular parameters. Figure 1-7 provides a framework for considering various whole language options and the ways in which each can be used to enhance your thematic unit. The planning form in Figure 1-8 considers classroom dynamics, group planning and content area instruction, while Figure 1-9 offers an open ended plan in which you can designate time frames for activities thus enabling you to plan thematically for extended periods of time — day, week, month.

## Figure 1-7

# Lesson Planning Form — I

Theme: _____

Opening (Time: _____ to _____): _____
_____
_____

Required Activities (Time: _____ to _____): _____
_____
_____

Optional Activities (Time: _____ to _____): _____
_____
_____

Sustained Silent Reading (Time: _____ to _____)

Writing Process (Time: _____ to _____): _____
_____
_____

Read Aloud/Storytelling (Time: _____ to _____): _____
_____
_____

Teacher Directed Activities (Time: _____ to _____): _____
_____
_____

Responding to Literature (Time: _____ to _____): _____
_____
_____

Recess/Sharing (Time: _____ to _____)

Lunch (Time: _____ to _____)

Special Classes (Time: _____ to _____)

Teacher Directed Lesson (Time: _____ to _____): _____
_____
_____

Daily Closure (Time: _____ to _____): _____
_____
_____

Additional Activities:
(Time: _____ to _____): _____
(Time: _____ to _____): _____

## Figure 1-8

## Lesson Planning Form — II

Date: _____ Theme: _____

Introduction: _____
_____
_____
_____

Whole Group: _____
_____
_____

Mini-Lesson(s): _____
_____
_____

Learning Centers:
  Reading: _____
_____
  Writing: _____
_____
Music/Art: _____
Listening: _____
_____

Math: _____
_____
_____
_____

Science: _____
_____
_____

Social Studies: _____
_____
_____

Closing: _____
_____
_____
_____

Figure 1-9

## Lesson Planning Form — III

Monday
_____
_____
_____
_____
_____
_____
_____

Tuesday
_____
_____
_____
_____
_____
_____
_____

Wednesday
_____
_____
_____
_____
_____
_____
_____

Thursday
_____
_____
_____
_____
_____
_____
_____

Friday
_____
_____
_____
_____
_____
_____
_____

# CHAPTER 2

# Strategies for Success

*January 13*

*Dear Journal:*

  *Sometimes my little sister really bugs me! She sometimes sneaks into my room and takes some of my stuff and doesn't return it. My mother says that I have to understand that she is younger than I am and sometimes doesn't understand what she is doing. I don't care…it still bugs me. I don't go into her room and take her stuff. I hope she learns what the word "private" means — it means STAY AWAY FROM MY STUFF.*

                     *— Ramona*

*January 18*

*Dear Journal:*

  *We've been working on our "Africa" unit for the last couple of days. Mrs. Yoshida has been reading to us the book "Mufaro's Beautiful Daughters" about two sisters and some of the fights and stuff they get into. It's a folktale about a king who wants to marry the most beautiful woman in the land. Two sisters want to get to the city, each one before the other. I think there's some kind of lesson in this book about how kindness will win over greed. I really like the illustrations in this book, especially the drawings of the people who have such unusual kinds of clothing. I wonder whether those clothes are worn by lots of people in Africa or just by certain tribes. Maybe Mrs. Yoshida can help me find some more books about African folktales or about the different kinds of clothes that people in Africa wear.*

                      *— Ramona*

*January 20*

*Dear Journal:*

  *Mrs. Yoshida has finished reading "Mufaro's Beautiful Daughters" to the class. We talked about how the sisters in the book were like our own brothers and sisters at home (Mrs. Yoshida showed us the new word "siblings"). Everybody had something to say about their younger brothers and sisters especially. Sonia and I have decided to write our own puppet show on the book and present it to Mr. Carrick's class next week. Sonia's mother does a lot of sewing and can help us with the puppets. My father has a word processor at home and can help us with the writing of the play. We plan to practice it a few times and maybe we will have someone videotape it for us and give it to the school library. We want to show how brothers and sisters can be alike and different even though they come from the same family.*

*— Ramona*

Ramona Javier is a student in Taro Yoshida's third grade classroom in Minneapolis, Minnesota. In the diary entries above she has penned some thoughts and perceptions about a book in Taro's thematic unit — "African People and Their Culture." What Ramona has recorded are some thoughts, feelings, background information, and perceptions concerning the notion of sibling rivalry, the family relationships that transcend geography and culture, and how the lessons learned through quality children's literature can be enlarged and expanded by using realistic and meaningful literacy activities. Indeed, Taro and her third graders have discovered that thematic units open up many doors for discovery and investigation and provide innumerable opportunities for students to take an active role in their own learning as well as the learning of their classmates.

Taro's students come from a wide variety of backgrounds and cultures. Students from Cambodia, The Bahamas, South Africa, Vietnam, and Belgium help make her classroom a "mini-United Nations." Taro, herself of Japanese ancestry, celebrates the diversity in her classroom and takes advantage of the different cultures, lands, and languages to create unique thematic lessons that build upon the natural diversity in her room and expand the cultural awareness of all students regarding their classmates and the diverse population of the Minneapolis area. Taro has found that thematic units provide a host of opportunities to engage students in the dynamics of reading, the dynamics of other cultures, and the dynamics of a truly integrated curriculum — one that celebrates the "power" of children's literature and is founded on the utilization of all the language arts in a concert of holistic activities. What Taro and thousands of other elementary teachers have discovered is that thematic units help students use their developing literacy skills in meaningful contexts and as "tools" for further explorations and investigations.

Taro is one of a growing legion of elementary teachers who subscribe to the notion that reading involves an active and energetic relationship between the reader and the text. That is, the reader-text relationship is reciprocal and involves the characteristics of the reader as well as the nature of the materials. This philosophy of reading, often referred to as a *transactional approach to reading* is based on the seminal work of Louise Rosenblatt (1978) and has particular applications for teachers integrating literature into the curricular framework of any subject area. As you might expect, it serves as a foundation for the construction, implementation, and effectiveness of thematic units. Here are some principles of *reading instruction and reading literature* (adapted from Rosenblatt, 1978) that are particularly useful for classroom teachers:

1.   Reading is a lived-through experience or event. The reader "evokes" the text, bringing into the process a network of past experiences with the world, with language, and with other texts.

2.   The meaning is neither in the reader nor in the text, but in the reciprocal transaction between the two.

3.   There is no single correct reading of a literary text.

4.   In any specific reading activity — given agreed-upon purposes and criteria — some readings or interpretations are more defensible than others.

In brief, this suggests that we all have our own unique backgrounds of experience which we bring to any reading material. As a result, we will all have our own unique and personal interpretation of that material — an interpretation which may or may not be similar to the interpretations of others reading the same text. Thus, reading a piece of literature opens up interpretive possibilities for youngsters and provides opportunities for extending that literature in personal and subjective ways. The point we wish to defend is that children's literature (within the context of a thematic unit) enhances the curriculum and enhances children's thinking, interpretation, and appreciation of that curriculum in meaningful and personally reflective ways.

Encouraging youngsters to become actively and meaningfully engaged with text demands a systematic approach to reading instruction. Traditional practices (for example, Directed Reading Activity) have placed the burden of responsibility on the shoulders of teachers because they directed much of the learning and much of the interpretation of textual material. Current views (for example, transactional views) place a great deal of responsibility on the shoulders of students. Two different models predominate here and are illustrated in Table 2-1 (adapted from Pincus, 1986).

## Table 2-1

### Traditional vs. Transactional Teaching

| **Traditional**<br>Directed Reading Activity | **Transactional**<br>Before, During, After Paradigm |
|---|---|
| Readiness & Motivation<br>* teacher sets purposes for reading<br>* teacher talk predominates<br>* teacher discusses vocabulary and<br>    predetermined concepts<br>* no writing is involved | Before<br>* students make predictions about story<br>* teacher helps activate prior knowledge<br>* students share in multiple grouping formats<br>* students write, talk, listen, and read with<br>    each other |
| Oral/Silent Reading<br>* students read silently<br>* sometimes students read in round<br>    robin situations | During<br>* teacher may read aloud or students may read<br>    silently<br>* students relate what they are reading to prior<br>    experiences<br>* students annotate while they read (i.e.,<br>    questioning, journaling, comparing) |
| Follow-up Activities<br>* students answer comprehension questions<br>    (with pre-determined answers)<br>* teacher selects writing topics<br>* students complete worksheets (with pre-<br>    determined answers)<br>* teacher teaches specific skills | After<br>* students discuss and share what they have<br>    read<br>* students engage in problem-solving activities<br>* students participate in self-initiated activities<br>* students initiate discovery activities |

The transactional approach described in Table 2-1 organizes instruction in three phases:

*Before Reading*:     Strategies designed to link students' background knowledge and experiences to the text.

*During Reading*:     Strategies designed to help students read constructively and interact with text.

*After Reading*:      Strategies designed to deepen and extend students' responses to text.

Table 2-2 illustrates each of these three divisions, along with suggested activities and strategies teachers can promote and students can examine independently. This list, while not finite, suggests possibilities for the literature you use within your reading program and within the context of any thematic unit. Suffice it to say, you would not want to utilize all of these ideas; rather, you may wish to consider possibilities within each of the three major areas as options for the design of any literature-based lessons. In so doing, you will be assisting your students in becoming responsible readers and will be encouraging them to interact with all the dimensions of text.

## Table 2-2

### Before, During, and After
### Activities and Strategies

| Context | Teacher Responsibilities | Student Tasks/Activities |
|---------|--------------------------|--------------------------|
| *Before Reading* | • Encourage students to activate background knowledge<br>• Help students establish purposes for reading<br>• Encourage students to generate questions<br>• Invite students to make predictions about text<br>• Encourage students to construct semantic webs<br>• Stimulate prediction-making<br>• Encourage journal entries<br>• Present skills | • Brainstorm concepts and key ideas<br>• Journal past experiences<br>• Categorize, web, and map<br>• Establish own purpose for reading<br>• Create self-initiated questions<br>• Survey material<br>• View film, filmstrip, slides, video<br>• Make predictions<br>• Draw, build, sketch<br>• Link with previous readings |
| *During Reading* | • Model metacognitive and cognitive processes<br>• Invite students to verify and/or reformulate predictions<br>• Encourage students to integrate new data with prior knowledge<br>• Help students think about what they are reading<br>• Invite students to summarize text<br>• Read aloud | • Locate answers to self-initiated questions<br>• Role playing<br>• Silent reading<br>• Journaling<br>• Partner reading<br>• Read aloud<br>• Ask questions<br>• Add information and concepts to previously constructed webs |

| Context | Teacher Responsibilities | Student Tasks/Activities |
|---|---|---|
| | • Encourage additional questions<br>• Incorporate skills | • Taking notes<br>• Re-reading as necessary<br>• Small group sharing |
| *After Reading* | • Encourage retellings<br>• Encourage students to reflect on what was read<br>• Invite students to evaluate predictions and purposes<br>• Promote closure between pre-reading and post-reading<br>• Develop questions that guide reading<br>• Encourage students to respond to text through a variety of holistic endeavors<br>• Assist students in linking background knowledge with text knowledge<br>• Encourage students to seek additional information<br>• Reflect on skills | • Retellings<br>• Discussions<br>• Debates<br>• Panel discussions<br>• Dramatization<br>• Readers theatre<br>• Simulations<br>• Role playing<br>• Oral presentations<br>• Mapping<br>• Journaling<br>• Pen pals<br>• Reading related materials<br>• Viewing slides, videos, etc.<br>• Interviews<br>• Library research<br>• Storytelling<br>• Response groups<br>• Writing conferences<br>• Puppetry<br>• Book talks<br>• Story mapping<br>• Problem solving |

What is evident from the chart above is that children's literature provides a vehicle through which students can begin to assume some responsibility for their own learning and through which teachers can become facilitators for that process. When literature is organized within the framework of a thematic unit, then youngsters are provided with a multitude of learning possibilities and a plethora of reading discoveries.

# Strategies You Can Use

If you support the importance of weaving children's literature woven throughout the elementary curriculum, you would want to use that literature in ways that stimulate reading development and conceptual understandings in a host of contexts. We would like to share with you some techniques and strategies you may find helpful, not only in terms of specific books and reading selections, but also in terms of the overall impact of a thematic unit within a particular subject area. Periodically, we would like to share with you how selected strategies were used by the three teachers (Chris Terriman, David McManus, and Taro Yoshida) you met earlier in this book. We invite you to use their experiences as models for the implementation of a *transactional approach to reading* in your classroom.

We do not mean to suggest that all of these ideas should be used at one time with a single book; instead, our intent is to offer you a selection from which you may choose and begin to build meaningful and lasting experiences with all sorts of literature — either singularly or within the framework of a thematic unit. As before, this is not intended to be a finite list but, rather, a starting point from which you can create lesson plans that assist your students in becoming competent and energetic readers.

## Before Reading

### Semantic Webbing

One method used as a framework for linking prior knowledge and knowledge encountered in text is semantic webbing. Semantic webbing is a graphic display of students' words, ideas, and images in concert with textual words, ideas, and images. A semantic web helps students comprehend text by activating their background knowledge, organizing new concepts, and discovering the relationships between the two.

1. A word or phrase central to the story is selected and written on the chalkboard.

2. Students are encouraged to think of as many words as they can that relate to the central word. These can be recorded on separate sheets or on the chalkboard.

3. Students are asked to identify categories that encompass one or more of the recorded words.

4. Category titles are written on the board. Students then share words from their individual lists or the master list appropriate for each category. Words are written under each category title.

5. Students should be encouraged to discuss and defend their word placements. Predictions about story content can also be made.

6. After the story has been read, new words or categories can be added to the web. Other words or categories can be modified or changed depending upon the information gleaned from the story.

David McManus uses semantic webbing in his classroom for individual books, thematic units, or topics and ideas he wishes to explore with his students. For the "Communities" unit, David wrote the word **COMMUNITIES** on the chalkboard and invited his students to brainstorm for all the words or concepts they knew about "Communities." After the chalkboard had been covered with words, David invited students to work in small groups to organize the words into several selected categories and to provide a title for each category. Afterward, David asked separate groups to record their categories on the board and to explain their choice of the words they had placed within groupings to the entire class. Discussion then centered on selecting the most representative categories for the forthcoming unit. A "Master Web," developed by the students, was drawn on the chalkboard. The identified category titles were drawn in white chalk, and the items selected for each category were recorded on the radiating "spokes" in yellow chalk (see Figure 2-1). During the course of the unit, as new ideas and concepts were being learned, students added more words and ideas to the "Master Web" in pink chalk. Thus, students were able to see the relationships that can exist between their background knowledge (yellow chalk) and the knowledge they were learning within the thematic unit (pink chalk).

## Figure 2-1

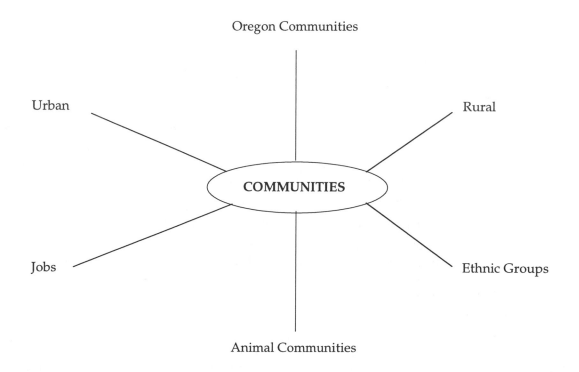

Oregon Communities

Urban

Rural

**COMMUNITIES**

Jobs

Ethnic Groups

Animal Communities

### Student Motivated Active Reading Technique (S.M.A.R.T)

S.M.A.R.T. is a comprehension strategy providing students opportunities to become personally involved in reading—both expository and narrative. Self-initiated questions and concept development underscore the utility of S.M.A.R.T. throughout a wide range of reading situations and abilities.

S.M.A.R.T, which is appropriate for individuals as well as small and large groups, can be organized as follows:

A.  A book, story, or reading selection is chosen for the group to discuss.

B.  The title of the book is recorded on the chalkboard and the group members are encouraged to ask questions about the title of the contents of the selection. All questions are recorded.

C.  The group makes predictions about the content of the selection. Students decide on the questions they feel to be most appropriate for exploration.

D.  Any illustrations found in the book or story are examined and additional questions are proposed. The initial prediction(s) is modified or altered according to information shared based on the illustrations.

E.  The group reads the selection (either orally or silently), looking for answers to the recorded questions. Also, new questions may be generated for discussion as well. As answers are found in the text, the individual or group talks about them and attempts to arrive at mutually satisfying responses.

F.   The procedure continues throughout the reading of the selection: (1)seeking answers to previously generated questions, and (2) continuing to ask additional questions. Upon completion of the book, all recorded questions and answers provided in the selection are discussed. The group decides on all appropriate answers. Questions that were not answered from the text are also shared. Students are encouraged to refer back to the book to answer any lingering questions.

## Prediction Cards

Prediction Cards allow students to tap into their background knowledge about the topic of a book, share that information with classmates, and make predictions about the content of a piece of literature. At the same time, students can manipulate their vocabulary and share ideas related to word study and comprehension of text. Although this strategy works particularly well with non-fiction materials, it can also be used with narrative text.

A.   Before students read a book, select 20-25 words from the book. It is preferable to have words from the front, middle, and back of the book. Include words you know students are familiar with, words essential to comprehension of text, and a few unknown words.

B.   Print each set of words on index cards and distribute each set of cards to a small group of students.

C.   Invite students to assemble the cards into categories of their own choosing. (*NOTE*: Do not tell them a specific number of categories or the number of "word cards" that should be in each grouping.) Encourage students to place words in categories according to their own knowledge of those words or their predictions of how those words might be used in the forthcoming text.

D.   Invite student groups to share their various categories and groupings and provide their rationale for the placement of word cards within specific groups.

E.   Invite students to read the text, looking for the words on the index cards. After reading, encourage students to rearrange cards or manipulate words into new categories or groupings based on the information gleaned from the text. Afterward, invite students to discuss reasons for any rearrangements and compare their placements with those of other groups.

As part of the unit on "African People and Their Culture," Taro Yoshida and her students wanted to investigate some of the flora and fauna of different regions of the African continent. Taro was able to introduce her students to a wide range of literature describing the animal and plant life of Africa. One of the books she used was *Hippo* by Caroline Arnold (New York: Mulberry Books, 1989). [This book describes the life and habits of hippos — those that live in captivity as well as the various species which live throughout Africa.] In preparation for their study of the book, Taro prepared several sets of Prediction Cards. She selected 25 words from the book and typed each word on five separate index cards (thus creating five sets of 25 words each). Taro selected words from throughout the book, including words known by her students as well as additional vocabulary important to their overall comprehension. The words illustrated in Figure 2-2 are those Taro used with her students.

Figure 2-2

| enclosure | banks | mammals | youngster | territory |
|-----------|-------|---------|-----------|-----------|
| pygmy | enormous | underwater | enemies | herd |
| newborn | appetite | submerged | nostril | preserves |
| bristles | kilograms | alfalfa | vegetarian | molars |
| dung | nutrients | incisors | captivity | exhibit |

Taro presented each of five separate groups of students with a set of Prediction Cards and invited them to arrange their cards in categories of their own choosing. Afterwards, each group was invited to share their categories and groupings with the entire class. Discussion centered on some of the differences between the groups and the various types of background information shared within groups.

Later, Taro read the book to her students, inviting them to listen for the words identified on the Prediction Cards. Upon finishing the book, Taro asked her students to rearrange and reassemble the cards according to the information they learned in the book. As before, students worked in groups, sharing and comparing data and facts learned from the book. Students were encouraged to discuss any differences between the arrangement of cards before the reading of the book and new arrangements made after hearing Taro read the book aloud. Students were amazed to discover the ways in which their background information could be combined with the book information to create a host of new categories and groupings.

### K-W-L

K-W-L (Ogle, 1986) is a three-step framework that helps students access appropriate information in expository writing. It takes advantage of a student's background knowledge and helps demonstrate relationships between that knowledge and the information in text.

K-W-L (What I *Know*, What I *Want* to Learn, What I *Learned*) involves students in three major cognitive steps — accessing their background knowledge about a topic, determining what students would like to learn about that subject, and evaluating what was learned about the topic. Figure 2-3 sets up a paradigm through which teachers and students can begin to read expository text. The following steps can be utilized (each number is keyed to Figure 2-3, K-W-L Strategy Sheet):

1.  Invite students to talk about what they already know about the topic of the text. This information should be freely volunteered and written on the chalkboard or in the first section (K — What we know) of the chart (which can be duplicated and given to the class).

2.  Encourage students to categorize the information they have volunteered. This can be done through various grouping strategies, such as semantic webbing. These groupings can be recorded in section 2 on the chart.

3.  Invite students to make predictions about the types of information the text will contain. These predictions should be based on their background knowledge as well as the categories of information elicited in step 2.

4.  Encourage students to generate their own questions about the text. These can be discussed and recorded in the "W — What we want to find out" section of the chart.

5.  Invite students to read the text and record any answers to their questions. Students may wish to do this individually or in small groups.

6.  Upon completion of the text provide students with an opportunity to discuss the information learned and how that data relates to their prior knowledge. Talk about questions posed for which no information was found in the text. Help students discover other sources for satisfying their inquiries.

## Figure 2-3

# K-W-L Strategy Sheet

| 1. K — What we know | 4. W — What we want to find out | 6. L — What we learned and still need to learn |
|---|---|---|
|  |  |  |

2.    *Categories of information we expect to use:*

A.                                    E.

B.                                    F.

C.                                    G.

D.                                    H.

3.    *Predictions on the information included in the text:*

A.

B.

C.

D.

5.    *Answers to self-initiated questions discovered in the text:*

*Source*:    Adapted from Ogle, D. "K-W-L: A Teaching Model That Develops Active Reading of Expository Text," *The Reading Teacher*, February 1986, pp. 564-570. Reprinted with permission of Donna Ogle and The International Reading Association.

## *Anticipation Guide*

Anticipation guides alert students to some of the major concepts in textual material before it is read. As such, students have an opportunity to share ideas and opinions as well as activate their prior knowledge about a topic before they read about that subject. It is also a helpful technique for eliciting students' misconceptions about a subject. Students become actively involved in the dynamics of reading a specified selection because they have an opportunity to talk about the topic before reading about it.

1.  Read the story or selection and attempt to select the major concepts, ideas, or facts in the text. For example, in a selection on "Weather" the following concepts could be identified:

    a.  There are many different types of clouds.

    b.  Different examples of severe weather include tornadoes, hurricanes, and thunderstorms.

    c.  Precipitation occurs in the form of rain, snow, sleet, and hailstones.

    d.  Many types of weather occur along "fronts."

2.  Create five to ten statements (not questions) that reflect common misconceptions about the subject, are ambiguous, or are indicative of students' prior knowledge. Statements can be written on the chalkboard or photocopied and distributed. [Using the concepts for "weather" above, the statements indicated in the example below could be used.]

3.  Give students plenty of opportunities to agree or disagree with each statement. Whole class or small group discussions would be appropriate. After discussions, let each individual student record a positive or negative response to each statement. Initiate discussions focusing on reasons for individual responses.

4.  Direct students to read the text, keeping in mind the statements and their individual or group reactions to those statements.

5.  After reading the selection, engage the class in a discussion on how the textual information may have changed their opinions. Provide students with an opportunity to record their reactions to each statement based upon what they read in the text. It is not important for a consensus to be reached, nor that the students agree with everything the author states. Rather, it is more important for students to engage in an active dialogue that allows them to react to the relationships between prior knowledge and current knowledge.

As part of Chris Terriman's unit on "Oceanography," students had expressed an interest in the weather patterns that form over the oceans of the world and the effect those weather patterns had on various land areas. The effects of a recent hurricane which had swept in off the ocean and destroyed areas of Florida had received front-page coverage in the *Los Angeles Times* and had sparked students' curiosity about how those storms originated over the Atlantic Ocean. Based on her students' interests, Chris introduced her class to the book *Weather Forecasting* by Gail Gibbons (New York: Aladdin Books, 1993). In preparation for their study of the book, Chris composed the following Anticipation Guide:

---

*Directions*: Look at the sentences on this page. The statements are numbered from 1 to 6. Read each sentence; if you think that what it says is right, print *"Yes"* on the line under the word "BEFORE." If you think the sentence is wrong, print *"No"* on the line under the word "BEFORE." Do the same thing for each sentence. Remember how to do this because you will do it again *after* you read the selection.

**Before**   **After**

_____   _____   1.   Hurricanes are the most destructive form of weather.

_____   _____   2.   Precipitation is any type of moisture that falls from clouds.

_____   _____   3.   Thunderstorms occur when a cold front meets and rises over a warm front.

_____   _____   4.   There are five basic types of clouds.

_____   _____   5.   Fog can be defined as a cloud on the ground.

_____   _____   6.   Typhoons occur in the Pacific Ocean.

---

Working as a class, students responded to each of the statements on the Anticipation Guide. Class discussion centered on reasons for their choices and predictions about what they might discover in the forthcoming book. Chris then provided multiple copies of the book to the students and invited them to read and locate confirming data related to each of the identified statements. Afterward, students completed the "AFTER" column of the guide and shared their reasons for placing "Yes" or "No" on each line. Follow-up discussions revealed some differences of opinion, yet the conversation was lively as well as supportive. Students found that they each brought different perspectives to a book, yet they could all benefit from those differences in a mutually stimulating learning environment.

Anticipation Guides are also appropriate for use with fictional material. Note how the book *The Salamander Room* by Anne Mazer (New York: Knopf, 1991) could be developed into an anticipation guide [as part of a thematic unit on "Animals" or "Ecology"].

---

*Directions*: Look at the sentences on this page. The statements are numbered from 1 to 5. Read each sentence; if you think that what it says is right, print *"Yes"* on the line under the word "BEFORE." If you think the sentence is wrong, print *"No"* on the line under the word "BEFORE." Do the same thing for each sentence. Remember how to do this because you will do it again *after* you read the book "The Salamander Room."

**Before**   **After**

_____   _____   1.   Salamanders live under dried leaves.

_____   _____   2.   Most salamanders are orange in color.

_____   _____   3.   Salamanders eat crickets and other insects for food.

_____   _____   4.   The diet of salamanders is similar to the diet of frogs.

_____   _____   5.   Salamanders are an important part of the ecology of the forest.

_____   _____   6.   People should not remove animals from their natural habitat.

---

## Semantic Feature Analysis

This strategy provides opportunities for students to share ideas about word concepts and vocabulary used in a piece of literature. It can assist students in making decisions about how words are related and stimulates discussions about the features of both familiar and unfamiliar vocabulary.

A. Identify a major topic from a forthcoming book. Using the SFA Grid (Figure 2-4) select a category of words that can be described with multiple features. (For example, the topic is "Transportation," words could be *bus, motorcycle, airplane, barge, skateboard,* and so forth; features might be *on land, on water, in the air, motorized, has wheels,* and so forth.)[Figure 2-5 is left blank so that you can duplicate it and use it for your own classroom purposes.]

B. Invite students to brainstorm for words which relate to the general category. These words should be listed down the left hand side of the SFA Grid (for example, bus, motorcycle). Then, encourage students to brainstorm for features of some of those words, These should be listed across the top of the Grid (for example, on land, on water).

C. Invite students to match a word with a feature by placing a "+" (match) or "-" (no match) in the place where a row and a column intersect.

D. Upon completion, invite students to discuss words with common features or features represented by more than one word. Encourage conversation about any agreements or disagreements.

## Figure 2-4

## **SFA Grid**

| Transportation | on land | on water | in the air | on tracks | motorized | has wheels | can carry more than 3 people at a time | | |
|---|---|---|---|---|---|---|---|---|---|
| motorcycle | + | - | - | - | + | + | - | | |
| airplane | - | - | + | - | + | + | + | | |
| barge | - | + | - | - | - | - | + | | |
| skateboard | + | - | - | - | - | + | - | | |
| bus | + | - | - | - | + | + | + | | |
| | | | | | | | | | |
| | | | | | | | | | |
| | | | | | | | | | |
| | | | | | | | | | |
| | | | | | | | | | |
| | | | | | | | | | |

FEATURES —>

Figure 2-5

# SFA Grid

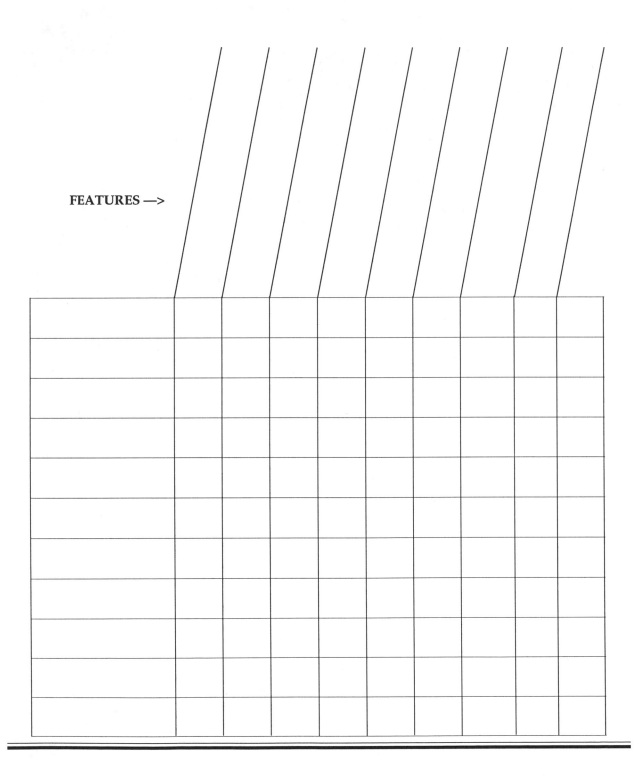

## Reflective Sharing Technique

The Reflective Sharing Technique demonstrates the interrelationships that naturally exist between the language arts **and** specific curricular areas. This strategy stimulates children to use language as a basis for learning across the curriculum. The Reflective Sharing Technique encourages students to share and discuss ideas that are important to them while, at the same time, reacting in positive ways to each other.

1. Choose a book or story appropriate to the interests of your students or their developing reading abilities. Select the general subject area of the story and record it on the chalkboard.

2. For approximately 3-5 minutes invite students to brainstorm for as many ideas, concepts, or items that could be included in that subject area (see below). These items can be recorded on the chalkboard. Brainstorming should stimulate a free flow of ideas, irrespective of their quality. The emphasis should be on generating a quantity of ideas and a wide range of responses.

3. Ask each student to select one of the brainstormed ideas from the list on the board. Invite each student to write about his/her selected item for about five minutes (this time limit can be adjusted according to the age or ability levels of students).

4. Sharing what each person has composed is the most important part of this activity.

   a. Students are divided into groups of four (it is very important to have groups of four for the sharing process). In each group of four, members take specific roles:

      (1) Person 1 — Reads what he/she wrote.

      (2) Person 2 — Summarizes what Person 1 read.

      (3) Person 3 — Tells what he/she liked about what Person 1 read.

      (4) Person 4 — Tells something else he/she would like to know about the subject Person 1 wrote about.

   *Note 1:* This completes Round 1

   *Note 2:* If you can't get four students in every group (even with you as a participant) eliminate role 3 or 4 in one or two groups.

   b. After one round of sharing, the process is repeated until four rounds are completed and everyone has taken on all four roles (see the chart below).

| Role | Round 1 | Round 2 | Round 3 | Round 4 |
|------|---------|---------|---------|---------|
| Reads what he/she wrote | Person 1 | Person 2 | Person 3 | Person 4 |
| Summarizes reader's story | Person 2 | Person 3 | Person 4 | Person 1 |
| Tells what he/she liked | Person 3 | Person 4 | Person 1 | Person 2 |
| Tells something else he/she wants to know | Person 4 | Person 1 | Person 2 | Person 3 |

5.   Provide the groups with an opportunity to share some of the ideas discussed in their sessions(s) with the entire class (it is not necessary to have every group share because some ideas will be redundant). Point out to students the wealth of information they already have about the subject of the book or story even before they begin to read it. You may wish to invite students to discuss how their backgrounds of experience melded with ideas in the book.

6.   At this point you may wish to invite students to read the book independently or share the book with them in an oral format.

     *Note:* With younger students you may wish to conduct the Reflective Sharing Technique as an oral activity. Designated students are selected to talk about special interests. The entire class takes on the roles of summarizer, positive reactor, and those asking about other things they would like to know.

## During Reading

### *Directed Reading-Thinking Activity (DRTA)*

The <u>DRTA</u> (Stauffer, 1969) is a comprehension strategy that stimulates students' critical thinking about text. It is designed to allow students to make predictions, think about those predictions, verify or modify the predictions by referring to text, and stimulate a personal involvement with many different kinds of reading material.

DRTA's are guided by three essential questions that are inserted throughout the reading and discussion of a book. These include:

"What do you think will happen next?" (using prior knowledge to form hypotheses)

"Why do you think so?" (justifying predictions; explaining one's reasoning)

"How can you prove it?" (evaluating predictions; gathering additional data)

Vacca and Vacca (1989) outline a series of general steps for the DRTA.

1.   Begin with the title of the book or with a quick survey of the title, subheads, illustrations and so forth. Ask students, "What do you think this story (or book) will be about?" Encourage students to make predictions and to elaborate on the reasons for making selected predictions ("Why do you think so?").

2.   Have students read to a predetermined logical stopping point in the text (this should be located by the teacher before students read). This point can be a major shift in the action of the story, the introduction of a new character, or the resolution of a story conflict.

3.   Repeat the questions from step 1. Some of the predictions will be refined, some will be eliminated, and new ones will be formulated. Ask students "How do you know?" to encourage clarification or verification. Redirect questions to several students (if working in a group situation).

4.   Continue the reading to another logical stopping point. Continue to ask questions similar to those above.

5.   Continue through to the end of the text. Make sure the focus is on large units of text, rather than small sections that tend to upset the flow of the narrative and disrupt adequate comprehension. As students move through the text, be sure to encourage thoughtful contemplation of the text, reflective discussion, and individual purposes for reading.

*Asking Divergent Questions*

Use of some of the following questions throughout the discussion of text can help students appreciate the diversity of observations and responses they can make to literature. The intent is not to have all the students arrive at "right answers," but rather to help them look at the diversity of thinking that can take place concerning a piece of literature.

Initially, you will want to ask students these questions as part of a whole class discussion of a children's book. The basic intent is to have students begin asking themselves these questions as they become more accomplished readers.

1.   List all the words you can think of to describe _____.

2.   What are all the possible solutions for _____?

3.   List as many _____ as you can think of.

4.   How would _____ view this?

5.   What would _____ mean from the viewpoint of _____?

6.   How would a _____ describe _____?

7.   How would you feel if you were _____?

8.   What would _____ do?

9.   You are a _____. Describe your feelings.

10.  How is _____ like _____?

11.  I only know about _____. Explain _____ to me.

12.  What ideas from _____ are like _____?

13.  What _____ is most like a _____?

14.  What would happen if there were more _____?

15.  Suppose _____ happened, what would be the results?

16.  Imagine that _____ and _____ were reversed. What would happen?

Prior to and during the reading of the book *Oceans* by Seymour Simon (New York: Morrow, 1990), Chris Terriman shared some of the following questions with her students. As Chris stated, "It was not my intent to force students into right or wrong answers. Rather, I wanted to help them think about the information we were learning from the book, how it related to their own lives, and how selected facts could be looked at from a number of viewpoints." Here are some of Chris's queries:

*   Make a list of all the words you can think of that describe an ocean.

*   How would a seagull describe an ocean? How would a shark describe that same ocean?

*   How would you feel if you were a piece of driftwood floating on the surface of the ocean?

- How are ocean currents like a river?

- You are a sea urchin. Describe your feelings about the rise and fall of tides.

- What do you think would happen if there were more salt in the oceans of the world?

- Suppose all the icebergs melted. What do you think might happen?

- Imagine that you had to live on a boat in the ocean for the next year. What habits would you need to change?

Chris's intent was to assist her students in becoming active thinkers during the reading of selected literature throughout the thematic unit. While her initial focus was to provide students with books and activities on "Oceanography," a secondary goal was to help her students use reading as a vehicle for learning in any area or endeavor. The use of divergent questions helps students process information instead of just committing it to memory.

### *Self-Questioning*

Providing students with opportunities to initiate their own questions throughout the reading process can be a valuable goal of reading instruction. Table 2-3 includes a list of questions that accomplished and mature readers tend to ask themselves. Here is a modeling procedure you may wish to follow:

1. Select a piece of children's literature.

2. Ask yourself (out loud) some of the *Pre-Reading* questions and provide answers for yourself (again, out loud).

3. Read the book aloud to the class.

4. Periodically through the reading continue to ask yourself questions (this time from the *During Reading* list.

5. Complete the oral reading and once more ask yourself a sampling of questions from the *Post-Reading* section.

6. After several readings, ask a student to come forward and model similar processes for the entire class.

7. Invite several students to demonstrate the steps outlined above.

8. Encourage students to select several questions from each of the three sections and respond to them in writing in their journals. After the reading of a piece of literature, use their questions and responses as discussion points in individual conferences.

Table 2-3

## Self-Initiated Reading Queries

PRE-READING

_____ Is this similar to anything I have read before?

_____ Why am I reading this?

_____ Why would this information be important for me to know?

_____ Do I have any questions about the text before I read it? If so, what are they?

DURING READING

_____ Am I understanding what I'm reading?

_____ What can I do if I don't understand this information?

_____ Why am I learning this?

_____ Are these characters or events similar to others I have read about?

_____ How does this information differ from other things that I know about?

_____ Why is this difficult or easy for me to understand?

_____ Is this interesting or enjoyable? Why or why not?

_____ Do I have any questions about this text that have not been answered so far?

_____ What new information am I learning?

_____ What information do I still need to learn?

AFTER READING

_____ Can I write a brief summary of the story?

_____ What did I learn in this story?

_____ Where can I go to learn some additional information on this topic?

_____ Did I confirm (or do I need to modify) my initial purpose for reading this text?

_____ Is there anything else that interests me and that I'd like to find out about this topic?

_____ Do I have some unanswered questions from this text?

### *Cooperative Learning*

One of the ways students can be supported in their literature adventures is through cooperative learning. Following are some brief examples of cooperative learning methods. It will be important to note how these methods can become integral elements of thematic units. Indeed, when students are provided with opportunities to learn from each other in the pursuit of mutual goals then the vitality and purpose of thematic units is enhanced and strengthened.

1. **STAD (Student Teams - Achievement Divisions)**

   Students are assigned to four-person teams, each of which is mixed according to ability, gender, and ethnicity. After the presentation of a teacher-directed lesson, students work in their teams to master the lesson. Individual quizzes are given to each team member.

2. **TGT (Teams-Games-Tournaments)**

   This is similar to STAD; however, quizzes are replaced with weekly tournaments in which teams compete against each other. Teammates help one another prepare for the tournaments through instruction, sharing, and coaching techniques.

3. **Cooperative Integrated Reading and Composition**

   Teams are composed of individuals of varying ability levels. Groups work to read through an assignment and engage in productive activities (see the sections above) that capitalize on all the language arts. Students do not take quizzes until other team members determine that they are ready.

---

As a result of the initial semantic web created by David McManus's students at the beginning of their thematic unit on "Communities" (see page 35), David decided to divide the class into six individual groups of four and five students each. Each of the groups was given one of the original topics (for example, "Urban," "Rural," "Ethnic Communities," "Animal Communities," "Jobs," and "Oregon Communities"). Each group was encouraged to investigate a variety of library resources and other printed materials to collect data and information related to their assigned topic. After collecting the necessary data, each group proposed a method of preparing and sharing the information with the whole class. Methods of presentation included:

- Preparing a group diary of essential information collected over a period of time.

- Writing a series of letters to students in another class about information learned.

- Putting together an informational brochure to be contributed to the school library.

- Creating a videotape and accompanying information packet to share with other classes in the school.

- Writing their own reader's theater script for presentation to one of the first grade classes.

- Assembling a "Big Book" of important facts and data related to their topic.

Each of the groups was responsible for collecting, evaluating, and presenting the information related to their assigned topic. In so doing, each group was able to work together on a clearly defined topic and assist other class members in comprehending that aspect of the larger theme.

4. **Jigsaw**
   Students are assigned to six-person teams to work on material that has been divided into sections. Team members read and study their respective sections. Next, members of different teams who have studied the same material meet in "expert groups" to share their findings. Then the students return to their team and teach their teammates about the information.

5. **Web Weavers**
   Three or four students work together prior to reading or discussing a story. A large piece of poster paper or chart pack paper is given to each group. Each member of the group is provided with a different color pen or felt tip marker. A preliminary semantic web for the story is drawn on the paper by the teacher and each student (in turn) records his or her background knowledge or prior experiences around the categories designated on the web. Students discuss any similarities and/ or differences. As the story is read, new data is recorded on the web.

6. **Prediction People**
   Students are organized into groups of three or four and are provided with a prediction "map" (a large sheet of paper). Each member of the group is encouraged to write a prediction (for a forthcoming story) on the map and discuss his/her reasons for recording that information. The group talks and arrives at a common prediction. As the story is read, students are invited to stop at selected spots and change, modify, or rewrite their initial predictions. The groups' prediction is also changed, modified, or rewritten.

7. **Reader's Roundtable**
   The class is divided into several small groups and assigned the same piece of reading. Each group is responsible for dividing the reading into several parts (as in "reader's theater") and assigning readings to individual members of the group. Afterwards, each group can share their interpretation with other members of the class. It would be important to discuss the differences in interpretation with class members.

## After Reading

### *Continuums*

The Character Continuum (Figure 2-6) is a delightful post-reading strategy that helps students discuss information related to the qualities and characteristics of selected characters in a story. With some minor modifications (see below), this strategy can also be used to help students focus on the setting of a story.

A. Ask students to brainstorm for all the words they can think of that can be used to describe one or more characters in a story. Write all the words on the chalkboard or overhead projector.

B. Invite students to suggest antonyms for most or all of the recorded words.

C. Place each word pair at opposite ends of a continuum (see Figure 2-6). For primary level youngsters 6-8 lines are sufficient; for intermediate students 8-12 lines are adequate.

D. Invite students to work in pairs, small groups, or as a whole class to place an "X" on each line, indicating the degree to which an identified character exhibits a particular trait (there are no right or wrong answers).

E. Encourage students to discuss their rationale for placement of the "X's." Rereading of portions of the book may be necessary to verify information or assumptions.

F. Students may wish to create a "Master Continuum" that can be duplicated and used repeatedly with other characters in other stories. Separate continuums also can be developed for story settings.

---

### Figure 2-6

# Character Continuum

Book Title: _____

Character: _____

| | |
|---|---|
| Friendly | Unfriendly |
| Happy | Sad |
| Popular | Unpopular |
| Wise | Foolish |
| Outgoing | Shy |
| Unselfish | Selfish |
| Sociable | Unsociable |
| Ambitious | Lazy |
| Neat | Messy |
| Honest | Dishonest |
| Brave | Cowardly |
| Kind | Cruel |

Figure 2-7 is a Character Continuum that Taro Yoshida's students created for the book *Why the Sun and the Moon Live in the Sky* by Elphinstone Dayrell (Boston: Houghton Mifflin, 1968). [This is an African folktale that explains how the sun and the moon came to live in the sky.] One of the major characters is the sun, and the following continuum about the sun was created after Taro had read the first half of the book to the class.

---

## Figure 2-7

# Character Continuum

Book Title: _____Why the Sun and the Moon Live in the Sky_____

Character: _____The Sun_____

Friendly.X .................................................................................................Unfriendly

Happy.X .........................................................................................................Sad

Popular.....................................................................X ...........................Unpopular

Wise.............................................................X .......................................Foolish

Outgoing............X ............................................................................................Shy

Unselfish.X ...............................................................................................Selfish

Sociable...X .............................................................................................Unsociable

Ambitious.........X ............................................................................................Lazy

Neat.........................X .............................................................................Messy

Honest.X ...............................................................................................Dishonest

Brave...................X ............................................................................Cowardly

Kind...X ...................................................................................................Cruel

---

After students had completed the Character Continuum, Taro read the rest of the book to them. She then invited them to consider repositioning any of their "X's" on the Continuum as a result of hearing the second half of the story. In this way, Taro helped her students understand that characters change, grow, and develop throughout a story.

Figure 2-8 is an example of a Setting Continuum that can be used with students. The words and their antonyms have all been suggested by students in a second grade classroom. You are encouraged to invite your students to suggest their own words (and their opposites) for continuums used in your classroom.

Figure 2-8

# Setting Continuum

Book Title: _____

Setting: _____

Hot ...........................................................................................................................Cold
Urban......................................................................................................................Rural
Friendly ..............................................................................................................Hostile
Flat ........................................................................................................................Hilly
Near Ocean ..............................................................................................Far from Ocean
Colorful.................................................................................................................Plain
New ........................................................................................................................Old

A modification of the Character Continuum is the "Facts/Attitude Continuum," which is appropriate for use with non-fiction material. The procedure is similar to that outlined above, except that students are encouraged to suggest <u>facts</u> about a topic as well as their <u>attitudes</u> or perceptions of that topic. These items (and their accompanying antonyms) are arranged on continuum lines as above. Students are invited to complete these after reading a book. [*Note*: This is also appropriate as a pre-reading strategy, with students suggesting ideas based on their background knowledge of a forthcoming topic.]

Figure 2-9 is an example of a Facts/Attitude Continuum created by Chris Terriman and her students in preparation for reading the book *Animals at the Water's Edge* by Charles P. Milne (Minneapolis, MN: Raintree, 1988).

Figure 2-9

# Facts/Attitude Continuum

Book Title: _____ Animals at the Water's Edge _____

Topic: _____ Mussels _____

Author: _____ Charles P. Milne _____

Publisher: _____ Raintree, 1988 _____

Strong..X ..............................................................................................................Weak
Neat ...............................................................................................................X..Yuccy
Useful..................................................................X ..........................................Harmful
Eat Meat....................................................................X ..................................Eat Plants
Important ...................................................................................................X......Worthless
Live Birth......................................................................X ........................................Eggs
Not Poisonous....X ...............................................................................................Poisonous
Fun .....................................................................................................X............Boring
Industrious...............................................................................................X.....Lazy
Underground .......................................................................................X...Above Ground

### *Plot Graph*

The Plot Graph allows students to design a graphic representation of the plot of a story. In so doing, they are able to use selected math skills in concert with a pictorial display of the sequence of events in a story or book. This post-reading strategy is particularly useful in helping students understand the utility of charts and graphs in realistic situations as well as comprehend the "flow" of a story from beginning to end.

A. Provide students with graph paper and invite them to select four or five of the major events of a story to record (in sequence) at the bottom of the sheet.

B. Encourage students to record numbers up the left-hand side of the graph indicating degrees of intensity.

C. After a story has been completed invite students to plot each of the selected events on the graph according to the way (and intensity) each event reflects an element of the story (for example, specific personality character) (see Figure 2-10).

D. Students may wish to use their Plot Graphs as an aid to journal writing or summarization activities.

## Figure 2-10

## Plot Graph

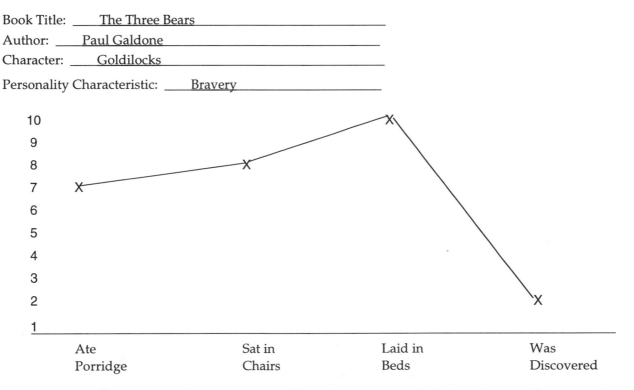

Book Title: ____The Three Bears____

Author: ____Paul Galdone____

Character: ____Goldilocks____

Personality Characteristic: ____Bravery____

Summary: ____When Goldilocks ate the porridge at the Three Bears house she was fairly brave. When she sat in the chairs she was even braver. When she laid down in the beds she was at her bravest. But, when the Three Bears came home Goldilocks and her bravery went right out the window.____

## Literature Log

A Literature Log provides students with opportunities to think about what they have read and to organize that information into a systematic piece of writing. These should not be interpreted as "worksheets" because there are no right or wrong answers to any literature log. They can be used by individuals or small groups of students as a way to record information and thoughts about a particular book. As such, you may find them important to use as assessment tools or as summary sheets to be maintained in each student's portfolio.

The first Literature Log (Figure 2-11) is appropriate for use at the conclusion of a book or story. The second Log (Figure 2-12) can be used by students prior to, during, and after the reading of a book.

---

### Figure 2-11

## Literature Log — I

Name: _____

Date: _____

Title: _____

Author: _____

My favorite part was _____

_____

My least favorite part was _____

_____

The central problem was _____

_____

_____

Some important words were _____

Words I need to learn are _____

My favorite character was _____

My least favorite character was _____

I didn't understand _____

I will never forget _____

I would recommend this book to _____ because _____

_____

_____

---

Figure 2-12

# Literature Log — II

Name: _____

Date: _____

Title: _____

Author: _____


**Before Reading**

Why I want to read this book: _____

_____

What do I know about this topic: _____

_____

What questions would I like to ask before I read: _____

_____

_____

What I think the book is about: _____

_____


**During Reading**

What I am learning as I read this book: _____

_____

What I did when I didn't understand something in the book: _____

_____

Will I want to finish this book? _____

Why? _____

_____

Am I finding answers to some of my questions? _____

Is the main character(s) similar to any other(s) I have read

about? _____

How? _____

_____

**After Reading**

Why did the author write this book? _____

_____

Am I satisfied with this story? _____

Why? _____

_____

Can I write a brief summary of the story _____Here

it is: _____

_____

_____

_____

Would I want to read this story at another time? _____

What questions do I still need answers to? _____

_____

How can I find that information? _____

_____

Here's how the author could have made this a better book: _____

_____

## CREATIVE *Questioning*

CREATIVE Questioning is a framework that stimulates children to think about common occurrences and events in creative and unusual ways. It is set up in the form of a paradigm that uses each of the letters in the word "CREATIVE" as a key to questions or writing activities that help students use traditional forms of grammar in different ways. The intent is not to have all youngsters reach the same conclusions, but rather to provide students with thinking activities that support their creativity and allow them to "play with" language in a new and different way.

Figure 2-13 illustrates types of writing activities, discussion questions, and literary concepts that enhance childrens' appreciation of the varied uses of language.

Figure 2-13

# CREATIVE Questioning Paradigm

**C** — *Combine:* Blend two or more details together
"What would be the consequences if Snow White and the witch had the same personality?"

**R** — *Rearrange:* Change the order of events
"What would change if the enchanted frog had been a princess instead of a prince?"

**E** — *Eliminate:* Remove one or more details
"How would 'Curious George' stories (by H.A. Rey) be different if George didn't have a tail?"

**A** — *Adapt:* Use data from another source
"What if Robin Hood had a gun instead of a bow and arrow?"

**T** — *Take advantage of:* Use story details in a different way
"What would have happened if Goldilocks had eaten all of the porridge?"

**I** — *Insert something else:* Substitute new ideas
"What would have happened if Mary had taken an elephant to school one day?"

**V** — *Vary:* Make changes in factual information
"What would have been the consequences if Charlotte (in *Charlotte's Web*) had been a tarantula?"

**E** — *Exaggerate:* Magnify events or details
"What would you have to change around your house if your dog was as large as Clifford (the Big Red Dog)?"

## Cloze Technique

In the cloze technique, the teacher prepares sentences or paragraphs in which selected words have been omitted. The teacher may wish to delete every fifth or every tenth word, for example. Or, the teacher may wish to delete all the nouns or all the adjectives from a written piece of work. The written piece could be a student paper or a selection from a popular book.

When the teacher has decided on the words to be deleted from the piece, it is retyped leaving blank spaces for the deleted words (it is suggested that each blank be the same length so that students cannot infer words based solely on their length). The retyped piece can then be used with students as part of a group lesson or individual activity. The advantage of cloze is that it allows you to focus on specific grammatical concepts within the context of a familiar and contextually appropriate piece of writing. Students are then encouraged to work together or by themselves to replace the missing words with words that "sound right" or that make sense in the selection.

Following is a cloze piece developed by David McManus for his students. He took a portion of text from the book *Miss Rumphius* by Barbara Cooney (New York: Puffin, 1982) and retyped it onto a sheet of acetate for projection on an overhead projector. As he prepared the piece, he deleted selected nouns and replaced each one with a blank ten spaces long. He then projected the story sample onto the screen and invited students to contribute nouns that would help restore a sense of meaning to the original story (David was not interested in having students replicate the exact words he had deleted from the text, but rather wanted them to focus on a specific part of speech as it was used within a familiar book).

> *Then my Great-aunt Alice set out to do the three things she had told her _____ she was going to*
>
> *do. She left _____ and went to live in another _____ far from the sea and the salt _____.*
>
> *There she worked in a _____, dusting books and keeping them from getting mixed up, and helping*
>
> *_____ find the ones they wanted. Some of the _____ told her about faraway _____.*

## Story Frames

A story frame (Fowler, 1982) is a basic outline of a story that is designed to help the reader or writer organize his or her thoughts about a story. A "frame" consists of a series of extended blanks (similar in nature to the cloze procedure) which are linked together by transition words or phrases. Story frames differ from cloze in that students are provided longer blanks to complete and are given more latitude in selecting appropriate words or phrases. Following is a story frame that could be used in helping students focus on a particular character in a story.

This story is about _____

_____

who is an important character. _____

tried to _____

_____

_____

_____

_____ .

The story ends when _____

_____ .

Story frames, when completed, can serve as discussion starters for the components of good stories as well as an outline for students who need a support structure for the creation of their own stories. Obviously, the intent is not to have all students arrive at an identical story, but rather provide them with the freedom they need to create stories within appropriate grammatical contexts. The following examples offer additional story frames you may find appropriate for your classroom.

## Plot Frame

In this story the problem starts when _____
_____
_____ . After that _____
_____ .
Next, _____
_____
_____ . Then, _____
_____ . The problem is finally
solved when _____
_____
_____ .

## Information Frame

This story was written to teach us about _____
_____ One important fact
I learned was _____ . Another fact I
learned was _____
_____ . A third important fact I learned was _____
_____
_____ .

## Character Analysis Frame

_____ is an important
character in this story. _____ is important
because _____
_____ . Once, he/she _____
_____ .
Another time, _____
_____ .
I think that _____ is _____
because _____
_____ . He/she is also _____
_____ because _____
_____ .

The strategies you select for use with the literature within a thematic unit can assist youngsters in becoming accomplished and interested readers. We do not mean to suggest, however, that every book you share with your students should be used as a part of a reading/language arts lesson. It is equally important that students be exposed to a wide variety of literature simply for the sheer enjoyment of reading a book independently or hearing you read aloud to the entire class. Thematic units provide a framework in which literature can be shared in a host of venues, situations, and instructional settings. Be sure to blend pleasurable book experiences with instructional experiences, too.

# CHAPTER 3

# Authentic Assessment

Bright sunlight peeked around the shades in Kenny Bachman's third grade classroom, reflecting off the walls and dancing across the posters, murals, triramas, and hand-made books that hung from every corner. A casual observer would have a difficult time locating Kenny among the groups of students who covered the floor, crowded into two of the corners of the room, or congregated around the classroom library or the ten-gallon aquarium on the science table. In fact, that same visitor would have a difficult time locating the walls of the classroom — a true print-rich environment on which and from which every manner of student work and creation hung. It would be interesting to note that not a single teacher-created bulletin board display or announcement was displayed on any surface — each entry bore the unmistakable signature of one or more of Kenny's third graders.

There was a constant hum in the room — not loud, but at a level signaling a great deal of activity and animation as students shared ideas, discussed strategies, or debated the merits of a shared book. Erin, Marcia, and Karyn were discussing the tribulations faced by Emmeline in *Prairie Songs* (by Pam Conrad [New York: Harper and Row, 1985]); Peter and Kwasi were working on a salt map of the American midwest; Lawrence, José, and Katrina were preparing a series of letters to be sent to the Department of Tourism in selected midwestern states; and William, Arthur, Natalie, and Kwan were working on a reader's theater adaptation of *Grasshopper Summer* (by Ann Turner [New York: Macmillan, 1989]). The room was buzzing with enthusiasm as students actively participated in self-selected activities related to their thematic unit on "Midwestern America."

Kenny himself was sprawled out on the floor under the display table near the closet. In front of him was Hector, a large manila portfolio, and an assortment of papers, charts, hand-made books, letters, and other items.

"Tell me, Hector," Kenny asked, "why did you want to include this book you wrote on Native American life in your portfolio?"

"Well, you see, Mr. Bachman, I did a lot of research in the books you got from the library and I interviewed Maria's mother after she showed us some of her weavings and I spent a long time writing the story about Lone Bear…well, anyway, Mr. Bachman, I think it shows all my hard work. It sort of sums up a lot of what I learned."

"So what you're saying to me then, Hector, is that this entry in your portfolio is there because it's a good representation of some of the independent work you did in our unit."

"Yea, that's right, Mr. Bachman."

"O.K., then what would you like to write on your 'Reflection Sheet' for your portfolio?" Kenny asked.

"I'm going to say that I'm including this because I learned a lot about the hardships the early settlers had in the midwest. I also learned about some of the customs and traditions faced by Native Americans in that area, something that I never knew before. I would also like to put down that I found some new books to read that I didn't know about before."

"That sounds fine," Kenny replied, "and I think I'll record that your self-made book shows that you have learned several new things about the midwest, especially about its climate; you developed an interest in the ceremonies of Native Americans, which you researched through letters to my sister in Iowa; and you are going to read some new books from the classroom library and share some of them with the class. How does that sound, Hector?"

"That's great, Mr. Bachman. Now I'm going to work with Julie and Bryan on that mural about different houses on the prairie. See ya later!" And off he scampered.

"See you, Hector," Kenny replied to the disappearing figure.

The conversation between Kenny and Hector was not by chance — it was systematic and planned. It had been scheduled on the large "I'm Ready for a Conference" chart (a laminated sheet of poster board on which students affix Post-it® notes with their names on them whenever each feels the need to conference with the teacher). But, most important, that conversation was indicative of a new perspective on assessment — one which is student-driven, reflective, and holistic. Kenny sincerely believes that students should have input into the methods and procedures by which they are evaluated. He also believes that portfolio assessment encourages children to take personal responsibility for their individual progress and achievement within and throughout the language arts program. Kenny has discovered that this approach to assessment not only expands the variety of ways in which student progress can be gauged, but also allows Kenny opportunities to take a more facilitative role in the thematic projects, activities, and discussions in which his students participate. Kenny believes that the information collected in each student's portfolio becomes a more accurate representation of involvement and growth than end-of-chapter quizzes and standardized tests. Significant, too, is the fact that students view assessment as an on-going process in which they are a participant, rather than an event controlled by the teacher and administered at the conclusion of a unit of study.

## The Nature of Assessment

To be effective, evaluation must be a continuous process. It must also engage students in the design of their own learning objectives and provide both teachers and students with useful data that can be used to enhance learning opportunities. In that light, evaluation is much, much more than the traditional pen-and-paper tests of yesterday; rather, it is more a process of reaction, reflection, and redirection. It is certainly much more than the simple administration of a test and the recording of resultant scores. It is a combination of factors and forces that should have a positive impact on children's literacy growth and development.

Let's take a moment and look at some of the purposes of assessment, particularly as they relate to thematic units. We believe that effective assessment:

- is a cooperative activity between teachers and students. In other words, assessment is not something done *to* students, but rather an activity done *with* students.

- provides opportunities for students to assume a sense of responsibility for their own learning. When actively engaged in evaluation, students become less teacher-dependent and more student-independent.

- respects the child and preserves and enhances the self-esteem of every child.

- should be used to improve instruction and gauge progress, not simply assign numerical scores to academic achievement.

- offers teachers and students viable opportunities to examine the learning process and make individual modifications as necessary.

- provides opportunities for teachers and students to work toward common curricular goals — both short-term and long-term.

Effective assessment is integrated into all aspects of a thematic unit, providing both teachers and students with data useful in gauging progress and determining the effectiveness of materials and procedures. In that light, it is important to consider assessment as a positive feature of thematic units — one woven into all its dimensions. This means that assessment is important during the initiation of a thematic unit, during the sharing of the unit, and even at the end of a unit.

Here are some considerations you may wish to keep in mind as you start designing your own units, use the ones provided for you in this book, or introduce commercial units. We like to think of these as the "Success Factors" — factors that can make assessment a positive feature of any thematic unit.

---

- Assessment should be continuous and ongoing — a constant process of evolution.

- Effective assessment utilizes a variety of evaluative measures — both formal and informal.

- Meaningful assessment should be child-centered.

- Successful assessment offers students active opportunities to engage in self-evaluation throughout all aspects of a thematic unit.

- A well-designed assessment program promotes a collaborative spirit between teacher and students and between students and students.

- Assessment should emphasize students' strengths and how students can build upon those strengths to become better learners.

- Good assessment is authentic in nature — it emanates from the literacy activities pursued by students, not from the artificial tests designed by large publishing houses.

- One of the most effective assessment tools is teacher observation — the interpretation of what children do, how they do it, and what they learn from their activities can be the cornerstone of a successful assessment program.

- Student portfolios (see below) are an efficient and effective way of tracking student progress over time and responding to the instructional needs of students in a variety of contexts.

---

It should be evident that effective assessment is more complex than writing a test, giving it to a group of students, scoring it, and handing it back with a numerical grade. It involves a combination of procedures and designs that gauge students' work while helping them grow in the process.

There are many forms of assessment that can be used with thematic units in this book or units you design on your own. Consider the following as suggestions for use in your classroom. Obviously, we do not mean to imply that you use all of these within the context of a single thematic unit; rather, the intent is to provide you with an assortment from which to choose according to the nature of a particular thematic unit, your own philosophy of teaching, the needs and interests of your students, and the data you and your students believe will be most useful in fostering academic progress.

## Portfolio Assessment

Most professional artists have portfolios — collections of their best work which can be shown to galleries and art dealers. A portfolio is a coordinated assembly of past and present work which provides the viewer with a definitive and representational look at the artist's work and talent. Through a portfolio an artist can collect a variety of work to reveal the depth and breadth of his or her talent.

Portfolios are also useful in thematic units. They exhibit the talents and skills of individual students and demonstrate their growth and progress over a period of time. Portfolios are accurate and informative collections of students' work and academic development, presented in a systematic assembly.

## Types of Portfolios

There are three basic types of portfolio designs that you should consider for classroom use. Well-rounded portfolios will include elements from all three of these designs in order to achieve a balance in design and function.

- *Showcase.*   This type of portfolio focuses on work selected exclusively by the student. As such, the student has an opportunity to choose his/her best and most representative work for inclusion in the portfolio.

- *Descriptive.*   The items included in this variety of portfolio include a majority chosen by the classroom teacher. The work represents selections predetermined by the teacher and measured against standards established primarily by the teacher.

- *Evaluative.*   All of the items in an evaluative portfolio are scored, rated, ranked, or evaluated. This is a very directed type of portfolio and is indicative of a quantitative approach to assessment.

It seems practical and logical to create portfolios that embody elements of all three designs. In that way you and your students will be able to assemble materials that highlight different aspects of academic growth and development and are instructive as well as illustrative.

## Contents of Portfolios

A portfolio can be as simple as a single file folder or accordion file for each student. They can be as complex as a series of mailbox compartments set up in a corner of the classroom or painted soda pop boxes stacked along one wall of the classroom. Included in each portfolio can be some of the following:

### Anecdotal Records

By their nature, anecdotal records are subjective assessments of students. However, they have the advantage of "tracking" students over many occasions and many learning opportunities. In this way, they serve as an accurate record of performance that can be shared with administrators and parents. We would like to suggest the following guidelines in using anecdotal records:

1. Identify four or five youngsters and concentrate on those individuals for a day.

2. Keep your comments short and to the point.

3. Maintain separate file folders on each student.

4. Plan time at the end of the day to discuss your observations and anecdotes with each identified student.

### Checklists

Use of a pre-designed checklist allows you to gauge students' progress against a pre-determined set of observational criteria. In other words, as you watch students participate in a project or activity you can check off items on a checklist according to how those students perform or behave. This data is similar in some respects to the information gleaned via anecdotal records; however, it does provide a series of constants against which all students can be assessed.

Figure 3-1 is a checklist which can be used to assess listening, reading, speaking, and writing performance.

## Figure 3-1

# Developmental Inventory - Speaking, Writing

Name: _____ Grade: _____ Dates: _____

Observation and evaluation of   SPEAKING     WRITING   (circle one)
Instructions: Circle the appropriate letter to describe how each statement fits this student during your most recent period(s) of observation. U = Usually, O = Occasionally, R = Rarely

**Guides Audience Through Text**

1.  Uses language markers to identify the beginning, middle and end of
    spoken or written accounts                                          U   O   R
2.  Develops and elaborates ideas                                       U   O   R
3.  Uses descriptive names for objects and events                       U   O   R
4.  Provides adequate information for audience understanding of
    events, ideas, arguments, accounts                                  U   O   R

**Knows How Text Works**

5.  Demonstrates knowledge of common text elements and patterns         U   O   R
6.  Relates information in a logical sequence                           U   O   R
7.  Uses language and sentence structures appropriate to text type
    and age/grade level                                                 U   O   R
8.  Demonstrates fluency and confidence while speaking and writing      U   O   R

**Understands Social Aspects of Meaning Construction**

9.  Understands and appreciates various speech and writing styles       U   O   R
10. Adjusts language to clarify ideas (spontaneously or over time)      U   O   R
11. Participates in interactions to negotiate meaning construction and
    develop elements of text and style                                  U   O   R

**Uses Range of Strategies While Speaking/Writing**

12. Uses ideas and language effectively to show sequence of events,
    cause-effect relationships, and to support main ideas               U   O   R
13. Revises extemporaneous speech or first draft writing to arrive at
    a more polished product                                             U   O   R
14. Develops cohesion through idea organization and language use        U   O   R
15. Explores topics with some degree of breadth and depth              U   O   R
16. Develops graphic, spoken and written text that illuminates meaning  U   O   R

The Development Inventory may be reproduced for classroom use.

## Figure 3-1 (con't)

# Developmental Inventory - Listening, Reading

Name: _____ Grade: _____ Dates: _____

Observation and evaluation of    LISTENING    READING    (circle one)
Instructions: Circle the appropriate letter to describe how each statement fits this student during your most recent period(s) of observation. U = Usually, O = Occasionally, R = Rarely

### Guides Self Through Text

1.  Makes predictions                                                        U   O   R
2.  Supports predictions with logical explanations                           U   O   R
3.  Uses both prior knowledge and text information to support predictions    U   O   R
4.  Changes and refines predictions as reading proceeds                      U   O   R

### Knows How Text Works

5.  Demonstrates knowledge of common story/text elements and patterns        U   O   R
6.  Draws inferences from spoken and written text                            U   O   R
7.  Understands similarities and differences between spoken and written
    text; narrative and expository text                                      U   O   R

### Understands Social Aspects of Meaning Construction

8.  Is aware and tolerant of others' interpretation of spoken and written text  U   O   R
9.  Supports and maintains own position in face of opposition                U   O   R
10. Engages in interactions to negotiate meaning construction                U   O   R

### Uses Range of Strategies While Listening/Reading

11. Raises questions about unknown information                               U   O   R
12. Uses illustrations and/or other environmental information to construct
    meaning                                                                  U   O   R
13. Relocates and uses specific information to support predictions,
    inferences, and conclusions                                             U   O   R
14. Revises meaning as new information is revealed                           U   O   R
15. Uses a functional system to gain meaning for unknown words
    (for example, context-structure-sound-reference)                        U   O   R

*Source*:    Ruddell, M.R. (1993). Teaching content reading and writing. Boston: Allyn and Bacon.

*Examples of the student's work in progress*

Each piece is stamped with a "Work in Progress" notation (rubber stamps can be made up at most stationery stores or local printing firms) and included in a separate file folder.

*Dated observational notes written by the teacher*

These can include brief notes by the teacher on a special form (see Figure 3-2) or a series of anecdotal comments recorded throughout the length of a thematic unit.

## Figure 3-2

## Teacher Observation Sheet

Student Name: _____ Date(s): _____

|  | (low) 1 |  | (high) 10 |
|---|---|---|---|

1. Active Participation:
   Comments:

2. Interaction With Others:
   Comments:

3. Level of Enthusiasm:
   Comments:

4. Making Progress:
   Comments:

Student's Comments and/or Reactions:

Future Goals (designated by student):

_____          _____
Student's signature                                      Teacher's signature

*Dated progress notes written by the student*

Self-evaluative questionnaires, checklists, and narrative summaries would be important to include in any portfolio. The form shown in Figure 3-3 offers students an opportunity to track reading materials throughout a thematic unit.

Figure 3-3

## Books I Have Read, Shared, and Written About

| Date | Book Title & Author | Read | Shared | Written About |
|------|---------------------|------|--------|---------------|
|      |                     |      |        |               |
|      |                     |      |        |               |
|      |                     |      |        |               |
|      |                     |      |        |               |
|      |                     |      |        |               |
|      |                     |      |        |               |
|      |                     |      |        |               |
|      |                     |      |        |               |
|      |                     |      |        |               |
|      |                     |      |        |               |
|      |                     |      |        |               |

*Work samples selected by the student*

Students are encouraged to include work with which they are especially proud and which they feel is illustrative of their progress. Along with each piece selected, students may elect to attach a Reflection Sheet, as illustrated in Figure 3-4.

---

### Figure 3-4

## Student Reflection Sheet For Portfolio Entries

Student Name _____ Date:_____

Thematic Unit Topic _____

Type of product or assignment _____
_____

I have chosen to place this item in my portfolio because _____
_____
_____
_____

From this assignment I have learned: _____
_____
_____
_____

One thing I want to tell you about this assignment/project is: _____
_____
_____
_____

*******************************************************************************************

Teacher Comments:




_____
Teacher signature

### Photographs/illustrations of completed projects

Take photographs of student work (a display, bulletin board creation, clay model, and so forth) and include them in a portfolio. This provides students (and their parents) with a permanent record of the activities and projects completed during a thematic unit.

### Audio-or videotapes of selected work

Students may wish to tape-record speeches, dramatic presentations, or choral readings to demonstrate their progress in oral reading activities. Audiotapes also have the added advantage of indicating reading progress, especially if recordings are made periodically throughout the year.

### Thematic Logs

As students begin a thematic unit, encourage them to record their predictions and background knowledge about the topic on a special form (see Figure 3-5). The Thematic Log can also be used to record information used and data learned upon completion of the unit.

---

## Figure 3-5

# Thematic Log

Name: _____ Date:_____

Topic: _____

Some things I already know about this topic: _____
_____
_____

Where I learned that information: _____
_____

Some questions I have about the topic:_____
_____
_____

Things I would like to know: _____
_____
_____

*************************************************************************************************

What I learned from participating in this unit: _____
_____
_____

What I still need to find out: _____
_____
_____

Where I can go to get the answers: _____
_____
_____

### Tests, quizzes, and/or exams

The teacher and student should work together in selecting formal evaluation measures for inclusion in a portfolio. Although you may not be using a large number of the more traditional forms of evaluation (that is, standardized tests, basal reader progress tests, skills tests) they can be included as *one element* of a student's portfolio.

### Writing samples

It is not necessary (nor is it practical) to include everything a student has written in his or her portfolio. A representative sampling of compositions selected by the teacher and student together should be considered, however. Included could be:

- Selected journal entries
- Content area writing samples
- Diary entries or personal logs
- Student-initiated questionnaires, surveys, forms
- Literature extension activities
- Teacher-student conference records

### Cooperative group assignments

Whenever students work together in cooperative groups, it may be appropriate for a designated member of each group to complete a survey form similar to the Journal Entry Sheet shown in Figure 3-6. Copies of completed sheets can be included as entries in each group member's portfolio.

The major criterion for items that can be included in a portfolio is that they be representative samples of each student's work over time. It is equally important that the selection of portfolio items be the result of a joint decision between teacher and student. It is ultimately valuable that "ownership" of the portfolio remain with the student.

Figure 3-6

# Journal Entry Sheet

Topic/Subject: _____

Date: _____

What we knew: _____

_____

_____

_____

_____

_____

What we discovered: _____

_____

_____

_____

_____

_____

Books or media where information was found: _____

_____

_____

Would we like to learn more?          Yes          No          ?

The most interesting fact we learned: _____

_____

_____

Signed _____ (Group/Class Secretary)

## Suggestions for Portfolio Management

The following ideas will assist you in managing your portfolio assessment program. You should feel free to modify or alter these suggestions according to the design and dynamics of your own language arts curriculum, the specific needs and abilities of your students, school or district policy, and your own level of "comfortableness." These ideas are not presented in any particular order, but they can assist you in the design and development of a systematic and functioning portfolio project.

- Limit the portfolio contents to two to three items of each kind.

- Review, with each student, the contents of his or her portfolio on a regular basis.

- Include samples from a specific academic area (that is language arts) or examples from a variety of curricular areas.

- Date all samples and arrange them chronologically within the portfolio or within designated sections of the portfolio.

- Invite students to participate in the identification and selection of work samples to be included in the portfolio.

- Retain only those items (over a designated period of time) that demonstrate growth over that period of time (for example, marking period, a whole year).

- Encourage students to self-evaluate the contents of their individual portfolios on a periodic basis.

- Invite students to review selected portfolio entries periodically with a *Portfolio Progress Sheet* (see Figure 3-9).

- Return work to a student as soon as it is no longer needed for assessment purposes.

- Invite parents to review the contents of a student's portfolio on a regular basis. Have portfolios available for parents at parent-teacher conferences.

- Use portfolios as an adjunct to report card grades. Use portfolio entries to clarify grades, identify student strengths, point out areas of concern, or note progress.

- Invite students to clarify any entries and add explanatory comments when necessary.

- Include an appropriate balance of formal and informal measures of academic achievement and progress. You may wish to use the "Evaluation Portfolio Contents" shown in Figure 3-7.

Figure 3-7

# Evaluation Portfolio Contents

| Contents | Comments |
|---|---|

Tests

_____          _____

_____          _____

_____          _____


Student Inventories

_____          _____

_____          _____

_____          _____


Checklists

_____          _____

_____          _____

_____          _____


Reading Log/Book Report

_____          _____

_____          _____

_____          _____


Student Writing Samples

_____          _____

_____          _____

_____          _____


Other

_____          _____

_____          _____

_____          _____

- Portfolio entries should provide answers to the following three questions:
  - Where did the student begin?
  - Where is the student going?
  - Is the student achieving success?
- A student's portfolio should center on his or her individual accomplishments rather than on comparisons with the class.
- Consider whether students' portfolios will be shared with the next year's teachers or presented to each child's parents.

## Rationale for Portfolios

Below are two "Top Ten " lists for you to consider in deciding on the utility of portfolio assessment for thematic units or for any other aspect of your language arts curriculum. You may wish to duplicate these lists and share them with colleagues, parents, or administrators who are curious about your use of portfolios.

---

**Top Ten Reasons Why Teachers Use Portfolios**

Teachers use portfolios because doing so

1. Respects student ownership of their work
2. Facilitates discussion that reflects student strengths, versatility, interests, and efforts
3. Shows development over time
4. Establishes a safe place to store collections that support student interests, decision making, and collaboration
5. Invites parents to be involved
6. Asks students to explain their reasons for including particular works
7. Provides an update at regular intervals
8. Gives teachers time to review progress
9. Showcases work for parents and peers
10. Demonstrates aspects of student work for discussion with parents and district personnel

---

**Top Ten Reasons Why Portfolios Help Students**

Portfolios help students

1. Make a collection of meaningful work
2. Reflect on their strengths and needs
3. Set personal goals
4. See their own progress over time
5. Think about ideas presented in their work
6. Look at a variety of work
7. See effort put forth
8. Understand their versatility as a reader and a writer
9. Feel ownership
10. Feel their work has personal relevance

The advantage of portfolios is that they provide teachers, students, administrators, and parents with a concrete representation of student growth over a designated period of time. They also offer a forum to discuss that growth as well as procedures and processes that might stimulate further growth. Although portfolios are useful in parent/teacher conferences, they are even more beneficial in teacher/student conferences. Portfolios personalize the evaluation process, making it dynamic and relevant to the lives of children and useful in the planning and design of future thematic units.

# Student Self-Assessment

We strongly believe that an effective thematic unit is one that involves youngsters in each and every aspect of that unit — including assessment. When students can participate in evaluating their own progress within a thematic unit they begin to develop an internal sense of responsibility that helps them assume some degree of control over their own learning. A thematic unit that promotes student self-assessment is one in which teachers and students can work in harmony to promote and evaluate activities and processes on an individual basis.

Self-evaluation can take many forms. The simplest type of all would be that which takes place within the context of student/teacher discussions. Teacher/student conferences allow you to pose several types of questions which provide opportunities for students to "look inward" and gauge their learning. Wasserman and Ivany (1988) have provided several examples of these types of questions:

1. Tell me about the way you worked.
2. Tell me about some discoveries you have made.
3. Tell me about some of the things that did not go well for you.
4. Tell me about some of the things that gave you trouble.
5. What comments would you like to make about your behavior?
6. What were some of the things you could do for yourself?
7. What were some of the things you needed help with?
8. Where do you think you need help from me?
9. What did you discover about the materials you worked with?
10. What were some of the decisions you made, and how did they work for you?
11. What questions do you have about what happened?
12. Tell me how you think this thematic unit is going for you.

Another format for self-evaluation includes data sheets or self-report forms. There are many varieties of these that you can design and use in your classroom. Figures 3-8 and 3-9 show two examples that would be appropriate in a variety of settings and situations.

## Figure 3-8

# Student Self-Report Form

Name: _____ Date: _____

Thematic Unit Topic: _____

*Directions:*   Please complete this report about your activities in our thematic unit this week. Your comments will form the basis for a discussion with me later.

1. These are some of the things I learned this week:

_____

_____

_____

_____

2. These are some of the things that gave me trouble this week:

_____

_____

_____

_____

3. I believe I have improved this week. Here's why:

_____

_____

_____

_____

4. Here are some things I'd like to learn more about:

_____

_____

_____

_____

5. Here is how I would rate my performance this week:

_____

_____

_____

_____

6. This is what I'd like to do next week:

_____

_____

_____

_____

## Figure 3-9
# Portfolio Progress Sheet

Name: _____  Date:_____

Some things I have learned since the last "visit" to my portfolio include: _____

_____

_____

_____

My favorite entry is: _____

_____ Because: _____

_____

My work shows that I have: _____

_____

_____

But, I still need to: _____

_____

_____

I want to learn more about: _____

_____

_____

Here are some additional items I'd like to include in my portfolio before my next "visit": _____

_____

_____

Listed below are some additional ideas and activities that you can use to help students assume some degree of self-evaluation within thematic units.

- Provide opportunities for students to establish their own goals for an activity. Afterward, encourage them to decide if those goals were attained.

- Design a formal evaluation instrument for a thematic unit. Instead of having students respond with answers, ask them to indicate (for each question) whether they: (a) positively know the answer; (b) are mostly sure of the answer; (c) have some idea of the answer; or (d) have no idea what the answer is. Discuss and share reasons (via individual conferences) why students responded as they did.

- Ask students to evaluate the questions in the Teacher's Edition of the textbook. Encourage them to design a system that rates the queries in terms of difficulty, appropriateness, level of cognition, or any other criterion.

- Encourage students to explain their reasons for selecting answers to specific questions.

- Stimulate the development of student-generated questions throughout any activity or experiment.

- Model your own metacognitive processes as you share information with students.

- Provide opportunities for students to explain the reasons why they understood or did not understand parts of an activity.

- Allow students to state their own expectations or criteria for assignments.

- Provide opportunities for students to write lists of things they learned from a unit as well as things they did not understand. Take time to discuss those lists.

- Permit students to rate any one of your thematic units in terms of *their* level of comprehension. In other words, did the unit promote understanding and interest? Discuss *your* reactions in terms of *their* perceptions.

- Provide a variety of self-correcting assignments within each unit.

# Criterion Checks

Providing children with opportunities to become personally involved in the dynamics of a thematic unit and to sense their active role in that unit can be accomplished through the use of criterion checks. A criterion check is a question, situation, or mini-activity placed periodically throughout a unit that allows children to assess their progress and the teacher a chance to monitor student progress.

Inform students that these checks are not for grading purposes, but instead provide you and them with guideposts with which the progress of a lesson can be gauged. Here are some possibilities:

1. Ask students several open-ended questions, such as the following:

   "What have you learned so far in this unit?"

   "Why is this information important?"

   "How does this information relate to any information we have learned previously?"

   "How do you feel about your progress so far?"

   "What do you think might happen next?"

   "How do you think this will turn out?"

   "Is there something you don't understand at this point?"

2. Have students provide a brief summary (in 25 words or less) about what they have learned up to a specific point of time.

3. Direct students to prepare a brief written summary. Direct them to keep a record of these summaries in a journal for review after the lesson is over.

4. If small group work is being done, have each group appoint a reporter who briefly summarizes the work of the group.

5. Have students make a preliminary sketch of one major piece of information they have learned.

6. Ask students to describe what information they would need at a particular point if they were teaching or tutoring another student about the unit concepts.

Criterion checks should be "dropped into" a lesson periodically. In so doing you provide yourself as well as your students with several checkpoints that indicate whether the thematic unit is progressing smoothly and is in line with your stated objectives.

# Multiple Options

In order to give you a flavor for the many types of evaluative measures you may wish to consider for your thematic units, we suggest some of the following options. You will need to decide which of these (or any others not on this list) would be appropriate for a specific unit. Of course, as you become more practiced in the design of thematic units, you will develop personal preferences as well as other options not listed here. Once again, we would encourage you to invite your students to take an active role, not only in the evaluative process, but in deciding on the assessment measures that could be considered for any developing unit.

- Students can determine beforehand an established number of books that should be read throughout the unit.
- Each student should create an original language arts product to include in a play, skit, narrative, diary, or other appropriate creation.
- Each student can create a bank of five to eight questions to be placed in a central location. All students can draw from this bank and respond to the questions of their classmates.
- Small groups of students can each create an original quiz on the information shared in class. Duplicate and randomly distribute these quizzes to the groups for completion.
- Have each student prepare a simple outline of the significant points covered in the unit. Post these on the bulletin board.
- Have each student make a tape recording of the four or five most important pieces of information they learned in the unit. The tapes can be evaluated according to predetermined objectives.
- Read student journal entries to determine how students are organizing their thoughts, integrating new data, and drawing important conclusions.
- Schedule frequent conferences with students or groups of students. Provide them with opportunities to share and discuss the information they are learning and using.
- Direct students to act as interviewers of other students. What has been learned? What are the implications? What else would you like to know?
- Have students write a letter to their parents summarizing what they have learned during various parts of the unit.
- Have a small group of students present a mini-lesson to another class.
- Direct students to write a critical review of one of the segments in the unit, including what they think would have made it a better lesson.
- Have an "Expert Day" and let students report to the class about various and specific aspects of a unit.
- Have students create their own bulletin boards using relevant and pertinent material from a unit.
- Encourage students to make a "ratings list" of the concepts they felt were most critical to the entire unit.
- Direct students to create a certain number of research folders summarizing the concepts learned throughout the unit.

- Actively "kidwatch" and evaluate each student's progress in group and individual work.

- Have students construct a book or booklet about what they would want to teach other students about the concepts within the unit.

Table 3-1 illustrates an assortment of assessment options categorized according to function. Consider these, too, in the development of your thematic units.

## Table 3-1

### Assessment Strategies

**Building Background**
  quick write
  think-pair-share
  story mapping
  prediction chart
  knowledge chart
  graphic organizer
  teacher observation
  student resource book
  discussions
  brainstorming
  word web

**Reading the Literature**
  guided reading
  monitoring comprehension sheet
  oral reading
  teacher observation
  audiotaping of oral reading
  shared reading
  discussions
  cooperative reading
  Reading Notes in journal
  use of strategies
  checklists

**Responding to Literature**
  story frame
  monitoring comprehension sheet
  literature log
  teacher conferences (individual,
    small group, casual)
  discussing and sharing
  peer response group
  journal pages
  story retellings
  story summary
  character map
  Venn diagram
  dramatic activities
  story pyramid
  writing samples
  teacher observation
  plot relationship charts
  story chart
  anecdotal records of observation
  think-pair-share
  K-W-L chart
  Literature Discussion Circles
  personal responses

**Developing Strategies and Skills**
  journal pages
  writing samples
  students resource pages
  discussions
  self-evaluation
  peer evaluation
  monitoring comprehension sheet
  students modeling
  teacher observation
  teacher conferencing

Assessment should be an integral part of the learning process and an important part of the thematic units you design and use in your classroom. As such, assessment must be sensitive to the needs, attitudes, and abilities of individual students as well as the class as a whole. Be careful that you do not over-rely on one or more forms of assessment just because they are easy or convenient for you. In other words, what you evaluate is just as important as how you evaluate! The "Assessment Data Planning List," Figure 3-10, will help you select and use a variety of authentic assessments.

## Figure 3-10

## Assessment Data Planning List

Student's Name: _____

Theme: _____

| | Type/Example | Comments |
|---|---|---|
| _____ Anecdotal Records | | |
| _____ Checklists | | |
| _____ Portfolio | | |
| _____ Student Self-Evaluation | | |
| _____ Others | | |

# CHAPTER 4

# Parent and Community Involvement

Boyd Ransom has been teaching fifth grade in a school district in southeastern Illinois for almost six years. An active and energetic teacher, Boyd is a strong believer in the value and impact of thematic teaching. While in college, his professors had prepared him by requiring him to create several thematic units and to "test" those units during his student teaching placement. What Boyd discovered was an exciting way to involve students in all the dynamics of learning by using children's literature as the primary vehicle.

During student teaching, Boyd also discovered that the local community offered a plethora of opportunities for extending and expanding thematic units. While presenting a unit on Native Americans, Boyd discovered that the parents of one of his students' had spent several years on an Indian reservation in Oklahoma; another had an extensive collection of arrowheads, and still a third had been a volunteer curator for a museum in New Mexico. Boyd also discovered that there were some community resources he could use in the development of his unit — including the local historical society, records from city hall, and documents held by one of the founding families of the town. The librarian at the town library recommended some books for Boyd's unit, including *Death of the Iron Horse* by Paul Goble (New York: Bradbury, 1987); *Arrow to the Sun* by Gerald McDermott (New York: Penguin, 1974); *Before You Came This Way* by Byrd Baylor (New York: Dutton, 1969); and *Pocahontas and the Stranger* by Clyde Bulla (New York: Crowell, 1971). What had begun as a class assignment for a course on "Teaching Elementary Language Arts" had mushroomed into a multifaceted thematic unit that continued to grow and expand throughout Boyd's twelve weeks of student teaching.

Boyd also saw the impact and power of parents and community involvement in the design of thematic units for his own classroom. For example, while developing a science unit on "The Environment," Boyd was able to enlist (1) several parents for a field trip to a local game preserve, (2) members of a chapter of The Sierra Club to speak to the class, (3) parents who were willing to create a listening library of tape-recorded books, and (4) a teller at the local bank who was an amateur wildlife photographer to present a selection of her photographs to the class. The reference librarian at the public library provided Boyd with the addresses of several environmental groups (for example, Alliance for Environmental Education, Environmental Defense Fund, and the World Wildlife Fund). A nearby senior citizen center had two residents who had worked for the U.S. Forestry Service as park rangers/guides and were able to share their experiences with students. A parent of one of the students contributed a selection of environment-related books (purchased by her older children) including *Global Warming: Assessing the Greenhouse Threat* by Laurence Pringle (New York: Arcade, 1990); *Pollution and Wildlife* by Michael Bright (New York: Gloucester Press, 1987); *Tropical Rain Forests Around the World* by Elaine Landau (New York: Franklin Watts, 1990); and *Endangered Animals* by National Wildlife Federation Staff (Washington, DC: National Wildlife Federation, 1989).

It became clear to Boyd that the creation and implementation of an effective thematic unit was based, in large measure, on the involvement of individuals outside the school—namely, parents and other community members. While Boyd often struggled with the creative aspects of designing a thematic unit from scratch, he quickly found that when the resources of others in the local area were included as factors in any thematic unit, the design of that unit could be facilitated considerably. Parents and community members provided a wealth of resources, activities, designs, documents, and experiences that Boyd could not provide on his own. In essence, Boyd was able to extend and expand the impact of any thematic unit simply through the use of the experiences and expertise of other adults in the community. So, too, Boyd was able to make learning much more than a classroom event — it became an experience to be shared and enjoyed by those outside the four walls of his classroom. Quite naturally, when parents were offered genuine opportunities to become active participants in the development of any unit, they were more aware of the types of experiences their children were participating in as well as ways in which they could actively support those experiences. In short, parent involvement became much more than overseeing the completionof workbook pages and drilling multiplication tables — it became an opportunity for the entire family to take an active role in the whole learning process.

In the design of your own thematic units, you will want to consider the role of parents and other community members. So, too, you will want to provide opportunities for students to learn from the community and environment outside the classroom — encouraging students to develop relationships between classroom work and "real-life" situations. In the , sections that follow, we offer some ideas regarding parent involvement and community field trips — valuable "ingredients" of any thematic unit.

# Involving Parents

Inviting parents as partners in the education of children presents many interesting possibilities for educational enrichment. Soliciting parent involvement not only opens up lines of communication between home and school, it also provides a vehicle through which parents and educators can work hand-in-hand towards the scholastic success of all youngsters.

(Fredericks & Rasinski, 1990)

Developing a successful outreach effort to solicit parent involvement within and throughout your thematic units is not always an easy proposition. It demands some planning and attention to specific factors that can ensure the success of those efforts. Following are some principles that can aid you in the development of successful outreach efforts and equally successful thematic units:

- *Regular Daily Time.*   It is important that parents be provided with activities and designs that will help them take an active role in the learning process on a regular and consistent basis.

- *Purpose and Motive.*   Parents and children must understand the relevance of any home-based activities. That is, how does a particular unit relate to the day-to-day lives of youngsters? Completing workbook pages may have little relevance to childrens' lives — collecting water samples from a nearby stream or interviewing one's older relatives can!

- *Support and Encouragement.*   Parents should understand that the activities and ideas you suggest to them are backed up by a system of support. Parents like to know that, should they have any concerns or questions, they are free to contact you to resolve any problems. Simply giving parents a project to complete with their children is not the best way to solicit their support.

- *Informality.*   Spontaneity should be a prime consideration in any parent-involvement effort. Parents should realize that learning happens in any number of informal situations as well as formal ones. For example, when parents and children talk about the eating habits of a family pet they are involved in an informal science activity. So, too, when parents and children discuss their ethnic heritage, they are involved in informal learning activities that can have far-reaching and positive effects.

- *Interaction.* Whatever activities or projects you suggest to parents as extensions of your classroom program, keep in mind that there should be a maximum of parent-child interaction built into those activities. Parents should not be asked to *tell* their children what to do, but rather *encouraged* to interact with their children in meaningful discussions and conversations.

## Successful Tips for Parent Involvement

Following is a compilation of additional ideas that can be made part of any thematic unit — strategies that ensure sustained family involvement throughout a unit. Garnered from a host of effective thematic units from around the country, this is a collection of ideas that you can consider in developing your thematic units.

- Outreach efforts need to offer life-like activities that capitalize on the natural and normal relationships between parents and kids. In other words, don't offer suggestions that are a repetition of school-like activities, but rather provide opportunities for families to interact in mutually supporting pursuits.

- Encourage parents to participate continuously throughout the length of a thematic unit.

- Be patient with parents. Some may be reluctant to get involved with your efforts due to any number of extenuating circumstances. Keep trying and never give up on ANY parent.

- Encourage parents to participate in the affairs of the unit through volunteering, observing, or sharing their hobbies, vocations, or vacations. Keep this process as non-stressful as possible and provide a host of sharing opportunities throughout the year.

- Make a regular effort to communicate with parents through a brief phone call or short note (this is particularly appropriate for those parents who do not participate regularly).

- Parents must know that your outreach efforts are a natural and normal part of the unit.

- Get kids involved in any thematic unit — use them as "recruiters" for their own parents. Solicit their ideas as much as possible.

- You must be a good role model for parents — that is, be enthusiastic and committed to the idea of parent engagement. That desire will rub off on families and stimulate greater participation.

- Communicate to parents the fact that their involvement in a thematic unit is ultimately for the benefit of their children.

- Whenever possible, try to get any and all family members involved in a thematic unit. Moms, dads, grandparents, siblings, and extended family members can all lend an air of credibility to a project and help promote its benefits.

- Make sure parents are rewarded and/or recognized for their efforts, however small. Everyone likes to receive some form of recognition and parents are no exception. Giving out certificates, awards, letters of commendation, or blue ribbons are all possible ways of rewarding parent participation.

- Coordinate your outreach efforts with some local community agencies (religious, social service, fraternal). They can be most effective in creating "contacts" for materials or resources.

- When sending any written information to parents, be careful that you do not use educational jargon. Keep your tone informal and to the point — don't talk down to parents and don't insult their intelligence.

- It is vitally important that you be friendly, down to earth, and truly interested in parents and their children. A sincere interest in working together will provide the fuel for any type of outreach effort.

# Ideas to Implement

Helping parents understand their roles and enlisting them to actively participate in the dynamics of a thematic unit can be a significant (if not overwhelming) task for many teachers. Terms such as "whole language," "integrated curriculum," and "literature-based reading program" may leave many parents confused and frightened. Yet, when we demonstrate to parents that many of the activities and interactions they naturally share with their children each day can support the goals and objectives of any thematic unit, we can then help them appreciate their valuable and significant role in the total scholastic development of their children. In doing so, we can assist parents in becoming supporters of whole language classrooms through regular daily activities in a relaxed and comfortable learning environment — the home.

Following are a variety of activities that involve parents. Most of them can be suggested to parents as extensions of many thematic units.

- Set up a special series of workshops on the topic of a scheduled thematic unit.

- Write a letter to the editor of the local newspaper requesting resources and information about a thematic topic.

- Hold a monthly "Parent Tea" after school hours to share ideas with parents and discuss various parts of a thematic unit.

- Call one parent each week to relay some good news about what their child is doing in a thematic unit.

- Set up a lending library of resource books and extra theme-related materials for parents to check out and use at home.

- Provide parents with lists of theme-related books and literature that they can share with their youngsters at home. Also provide sources (library locations, teacher supply stores, bookstores, and so forth) for obtaining that information.

- Invite parents into the classroom to share their theme-related interests, recent trips, or hobbies.

- Encourage parents to schedule "Family Field Trips" in which all members of the family can travel together to a particular site or exhibit. Consult local agencies or the yellow pages for locations of special places in the local community.

- Provide parents with a periodic newsletter (see example on pages 90-91) updating them on unit activities and projects. [The sample provided could be used as part of a thematic unit on "Communication."]

- Keep abreast of upcoming TV shows related to a particular theme and provide parents with information on those programs.

- Have students prepare a calendar of upcoming events in the unit. These can be sent home on a regular basis — once a week or once a month.

- Interview parents about some of their theme-related interests, hobbies, activities, or vacations. Prepare this information in the form of a special classroom newsletter.

- Many popular magazines frequently carry theme-related articles. You may wish to clip these and distribute them to parents.

- Every two weeks or so have your students prepare special "homework packets" consisting of theme-related articles, games, pertinent worksheets, upcoming TV programs, museum exhibits, and the like.

- Have parents tape-record a book (related to a theme) or portion of a book so that the child can listen to it again and again.

- Parents and children can make a collage of important events related to a theme. Pictures from old magazines can be cut out and pasted onto sheets of construction paper.

- Encourage parents to have their children write a letter to a friend about what they're learning in a unit.

- Encourage parents to read several different books on the same theme.

- Ask parents and children to make up a fictitious newspaper about a thematic unit.

- Parents can help their children adapt thematic events into a news report or TV program.

- Parents and children can create a glossary or dictionary of important words related to a theme.

- Encourage parents and children to create a scrapbook about important places, people, and events discovered as part of a thematic unit.

- Encourage parents and children to interview outside "experts" in the local community about information or data related to a theme.

- Have parents and children create time lines of thematic events.

- Have parents work with their children as they put together a time capsule of objects mentioned in a thematic unit.

- Families can set up a "museum" of theme artifacts in one corner of the living room.

- Parents can help their children design and create a diorama of significant events in a unit.

- Ask parents to take photographs of scenes (similar to those from selected thematic unit books) within the local community and arrange them into an attractive display.

What makes any thematic unit successful is the creative vision of educators and parents working together in a spirit of mutual cooperation and support. Strong thematic units are those which not only integrate all aspects of the elementary curriculum, but also integrate parents into the designs and delivery systems of those units, too. The bonds established between home and school can be powerful ones in terms of the effectiveness of any thematic unit. When parents are "employed" as partners in a thematic unit, students are afforded a wealth of exciting educational possibilities.

# Parent Newsletter

## Questions and Answers about Thematic Units

Dear Parents:

There's an exciting "revolution" taking place in schools today. It's called *Thematic Teaching or teaching with thematic units* and it offers youngsters exciting possibilities in terms of their reading growth and development. Your child may have been talking about some of the exciting activities taking place in our classroom and you may have some questions about this approach to teaching and learning. Here are some of the questions (and accompanying answers) parents are asking:

**What is a thematic unit?** A thematic unit is a series of lessons developed around a single theme — usually a theme in science or social studies. The unit encourages students to use their language arts skills (reading, writing, speaking, and listening) in a host of stimulating and supportive activities. Units are built around an abundance of children's literature related to the theme and whole language activities that encourage youngsters to investigate all the dynamics of that theme. Thematic units are a way in which regular writing activities, an abundance of children's literature, and a host of communication activities are used in all subject areas. Thematic units focus on the individual learning needs of each child in the classroom and offer a natural learning environment in which students can begin to assume some responsibility for their own learning.

**What do students do?** In a thematic unit, students are given choices to explore aspects of a particular theme through the use of one or more of the following: daily writing time, silent reading time, book sharing experiences, read-alouds by the teacher, sharing opportunities between students, teacher-modeled writing, lots of children's literature in every subject area, reading conferences and small group cooperative work, and frequent book-oriented discussions. Thematic teaching provides opportunities for the teacher to concentrate on the individual learning needs of each student and opportunities for the students to examine and explore several aspects of a selected topic or theme, thereby gaining a broad-based exposure to, and appreciation of, a particular subject area.

**What about skills?** In a thematic unit skills are presented to children in a context that is meaningful to them. Typically, children do not fill in a lot of workbook pages or skill sheets. Instead, the teacher uses children's language (what they have said or written) and children's literature to focus on the skills needed by each individual child. For example, the teacher may have children write a journal entry about some of their favorite plants (as part of a science-related theme). The teacher may decide to focus on each child's use of capital letters and punctuation (as part of an English lesson). Each child's writing then become his or her own "lesson materials" for the identified skills. The skill lessons the teacher designs can then be supplemented with quality literature and textbook materials.

**What can I do?** The success your children achieves in all subject areas can be maximized by your support and involvement. In fact, you are probably already doing many things at home that support your child's involvement in a particular thematic unit. These include:
- sharing with your child (for example, reading aloud) books related to a certain theme.
- talking with your child about the ideas and concepts that are discussed in class.

- buying books for your child or visiting the local public library to locate additional books related to a particular theme.
- listening carefully as your child tells you about events related to a thematic unit.
- helping your child maintain a journal, notebook, or diary of thoughts and ideas related to a theme.
- encouraging your child to create puppets, models, posters, or dioramas of characters and events from selected books.
- inviting your child to become an author and create some original stories related to a theme and display them in the family library.
- taking your child on field trips or excursions to sites in the local community that are related to a current theme.
- encouraging your child to talk with experts and other community people about concepts and facts related to a certain theme.

Thematic units are a wonderful opportunity for your child to explore and examine a particular topic through a host of positive learning experiences. By taking an active role in your child's discoveries you will be helping him or her become an accomplished learner and an active participant in a variety of scholastic opportunities.

# Community Field Trips

Field trips provide youngsters with marvelous opportunities to expand and enlarge concepts taught within a particular thematic unit. In addition, field trips can enhance and promote your entire curriculum, providing students with important new information that is often unobtainable in textbooks. Most important, however, is the fact that students begin to see any subject as something more than a textbook topic or collection of "memorizeable" facts. Field trips can be a positive and dynamic part of the entire curriculum—particularly when they are considered as an important element of any thematic unit

There is no limit to the places and sites that should be considered for a thematic unit field trip. The possibilities for field trips are only limited by a teacher's imagination. The following list provides you with some possibilities to consider for the curricular areas of science, social studies, math, and language arts:

| **Science** | **Social Studies** |
|---|---|
| hospital | different neighborhoods |
| forest | social service agency |
| lumber yard | city hall |
| garden center | local/county government agency |
| pet store | manufacturing plant |
| dairy farm | chamber of commerce |
| natural history museum | cultural organization/club |
| aquarium | museum |
| nature center | historical display |
| college biology department | college geography department |
| river, stream, swamp | police/fire station |
| police crime lab | Red Cross Center |
| generating station | volunteer recruitment center |
| machine shop | newspaper |
| music store | state department of transportation |

| | |
|---|---|
| service station | telecommunications center |
| fix-it shop | graveyard |
| manufacturing plant | shipyard |
| water treatment plant | festivals |
| dumps | church/temple/synagogue |
| recycling center | historical site |
| hydroelectric plant | nursing home |
| planetarium | ethnic restaurants |
| radio station | sanitation areas |
| hobby store | train station/airport |
| local astronomy club | |

**Math**

precision instrument company
cartographer
surveying company
bank, credit union
bakery
any small business
pizza parlor
music store
meteorologist
weather station
college math department
high school computer lab
manufacturing plant
architect
pool hall
artist or art studio
flea market
supermarket
hospital
hardware store
symphony/orchestra

**Language Arts**

book store
library
author
book binding plant
stationary store
paper manufacturer
newspaper or magazine publisher
computer store
live plays/theater
printers
post office

### Guidebooks

You can enhance any field trip by working with your students in preparing a guidebook. A guidebook becomes a creative, "real-life" extension of any language arts-based thematic unit. This guide book not only provides students with some relevant information on the site they are to visit, but also allows them to record impressions and information gathered during the trip. Just as important, it can become an valuable record of one or more field trips taken during the year — a record that can be referred to throughout the year. The guidebook should be prepared well in advance of any field trip and can be done individually by students or in small groups. You may wish to have students construct a separate guidebook for each field trip or a permanent guidebook for all field trips taken during the year. The following items can be included in a guidebook prior to a field trip:

- Brochures or other printed materials available from the field trip site (write in advance for these)

- Students can write a brief capsule description of the site and the reasons for visiting that place.

- Student-generated questions about the site and what might be seen (have students provide space under the questions for responses).

- A list of safety rules and the expected manner of behavior during the trip.

- Blank pages for students to record observations and illustrations of significant points or observations.

- A summary page for students to write a brief wrap-up of the trip (this should be done prior to boarding the bus back to school).

## Tips for a Successful Field Trip

Any teacher who has taken a class of kids on a field trip knows that field trips are much more than loading students onto a school bus, traveling to some distant site, having "an expert" dispense a variety of facts and figures, wolfing down a semi-stale peanut-butter-and-jelly sandwich, and trying to make it back to school with one's sanity still intact. Successful and effective field trips take planning and preparation — they do not come about as the result of an overnight flurry of activity. Teachers should consider the following items as important elements in any meaningful field trip.

### Before

What is done prior to the actual field trip often determines the success of the trip itself. Planning involves much more than sending out parental permission slips and arranging for bus transportation. Consider these activities as part of the preparation process, too.

- If possible, obtain some brochures or other literature about the site you are visiting or the topic(s) that will be discussed. Many museums, planetariums, and the like have all sorts of printed materials that you can obtain and share with students prior to the trip.

- Discuss with students the reasons for the trip, what they can expect to discover, and any additional highlights. Talk about how the planned trip is correlated with information discussed in a thematic unit.

- Provide students with examples of children's literature in advance of the scheduled field trip. Use of children's literature before a field trip can provide students with the necessary background information they need to fully understand and appreciate what actually takes place during the field trip.

- If possible, visit the site yourself in advance of the scheduled field trip. Talk to the people in charge, pick up some literature, and ask some questions. This "dry run" will provide you with important points and observations that can be shared with students prior to the trip.

### During

To be successful a field trip must provide students with opportunities to become actively engaged in learning new information or in reinforcing previously learned material. The following guidelines provide kids with opportunities to become participants rather than just observers.

- Invite students to discuss the questions they generated before the trip. Encourage students to generate additional questions throughout the trip, too.

- Help students understand the relevance of the exhibit, display, or venue to the materials and information they are studying in a thematic unit.

- Invite students to record their thoughts, impressions, or drawings of important information or concepts. It is advisable to stop every so often to review what has been seen and allow children to make notations on newly learned information.

*After*

After a field trip, invite students to participate in a "debriefing" session during which important points are discussed, misconceptions are cleared up, and relationships are drawn between the outside world and the concepts in a thematic unit.

- Invite students to share their perceptions of the field trip, the important or unimportant points, and how specific features relate to the thematic unit.

- Encourage students to create drawings, models, dioramas, posters, or some other artistic (and permanent) display of the information they learned during the trip (see Table 4-1).

- Integrate the field trip into the thematic unit by providing students with opportunities to create plays, stories, dances, poems, lyrics, and video or audio recordings of portions of the field trip.

- Invite students to review the purposes for the trip and ask them to decide if those purposes were met.

- Provide opportunities for students to understand the relevance of the field trip to all areas of the curriculum (for example, how the information gathered during the trip can be used in social studies, reading, art, or physical education).

---

### Table 4-1

### Post-Field Trip Activities

| | |
|---|---|
| class newspaper | newsletter |
| bulletin board display | map |
| collage | thank you notes |
| videotape summary | brochure on trip site |
| class survey on favorite items | song with new lyrics |
| photo album | mini lesson |
| picture book (share with | "Jeopardy!" game |
| younger class) | word puzzles |
| field trip magazine | poetry |
| "Flip book" | skit or play |
| news broadcast | big book |
| book of "world records" | showcase display |
| letter to the editor | cartoon strips |
| read follow-up literature | school experts |

---

We like the idea of mini field trips. These are field trips you can take around the school or in the immediate community. They require little planning, no money, and a host of possibilities for students to integrate classroom information with the world around them.

Design several short (10-20 minutes each) investigations of the environment around the school. Each of these ideas should be recorded separately on individual index cards and kept in a card file in the classroom. The activities can be used for individuals, small or large groups, or as "homework" assignments. Here are some mini field trip ideas, each of which could be embedded in a relevant thematic unit:

Plants

Go outside and see how many different leaves you can collect in ten minutes. What are some similarities? What are some differences?

Weather

Go outside and record the temperature, wind speed, and humidity. Do this during the day at one-hour intervals. What do you notice?

Measurement

Go home and collect three different measurement instruments from the kitchen, the garage, or your bedroom. Make a list of the similarities and differences between the instruments.

Geometry

Use several different grocery bags and collect objects representing each of several basic geometric shapes. For example: sphere - baseball, cube -block, rectangle - letter.

Writing

Ask selected adults in your family or neighborhood to contribute selected examples of writing ("To do" lists, order forms, grocery lists, etc.) that they use in their everyday work. Categorize the writings by types and purpose.

Communication

Take a walking field trip around the school and list all the ways in which people communicate with each other (for example, signs, billboards, letters, etc.).

Families

Interview three different adults and obtain their definitions of the word "Family." What similarities are there in the definitions?

Geography

Pretend you are an ant and have to travel from one end of the playground to the other. Record all the geographical features you would encounter on your trip.

Effective thematic units offer students unique opportunities to work with their parents and other community members in enhancing and expanding their knowledge base. When families and the local environment are intertwined into the dynamics of a thematic unit, students are then afforded learning opportunities that far exceed the objectives of textbooks or curriculum guides. We sincerely hope that the units you create for your classroom will include a host of individuals, organizations, and situations, with all of them helping students understand the relevance of classroom experiences to those experiences beyond the classroom.

# References

Fowler, G.L. (1982). Developing comprehension skills in primary grades through the use of story frames. *The Reading Teacher*, 36(2), 176-179.

Fredericks, A.D. & Rasinski, T.V. (1990). Factors that make a difference. *The Reading Teacher*, 44(1), 76-77.

Fredericks, A.D., Meinbach, A., & Rothlein, L. (1993). *Thematic units: An integrated approach to teaching science and social studies*. New York, NY: HarperCollins Publishers.

Ogle, D. (1986, February). K-W-L: A teaching model that develops active reading of expository text. *The Reading Teacher*, 564-570.

Pincus, M. (1986). Unpublished manuscript. Philadelphia, PA.

Rosenblatt, L. (1978). *The reader, the text, the poem*. Carbondale, IL: Southern Illinois University Press.

Stauffer, R. (1969). *Directing reading maturity as a cognitive process*. New York: Harper & Row.

Vacca, R. & Vacca, J. (1989). *Content area reading*. New York: HarperCollins.

# PART II:

Thematic Units

# PART II: Thematic Units

The thematic units included in this section emphasize key concepts in Science, Social Studies, Language Arts, and Mathematics. In addition, the activities included within each unit integrate skills from a variety of areas to ensure a unique, multidisciplinary, interdisciplinary unit of study with strong literature component.

The chart that follows lists the focus for each thematic unit, along with the various mini-themes that have been developed for each unit. These mini-themes, which can be used alone or in conjunction with other mini-units, extend the focus and concepts developed through the main thematic unit. Each mini-theme includes activities, questions, and related works of literature to provide you with a variety of choices through which to develop specific content objectives and skills.

The wide scope of activities developed for each unit illustrates the tremendous possibilities from which you can select to provide students with a framework that best meets their individual needs and interests. While each unit also develops a number of literary works, you may choose to use only one or two selections or you may wish to substitute other titles.

As students become involved in the various units, we suggest that you guide them in developing other activities based on classroom dynamics and teaching/learning styles. For learning to be meaningful, it must have relevance. We urge you to adapt the activities included in the units and mini-units to create a challenging learning environment that will arouse each student's natural curiosity and encourage students to pursue new ideas and formulate their own connections.

The scope of activities in the thematic units and the outcomes developed will allow you to employ a wide variety of assessment techniques that not only gauge students' work but also help them grow in the process. Journals, anecdotal records, portfolio assessment, checklists, conferences, student self-evaluations, and so forth (all described in Chapter 3) provide authentic assessments that will provide an accurate evaluation of students' learning and progress. We hope you will encourage your students to take an active role in both the assessment process and in determining the assessment measures
for any developing unit.

# Thematic Units: Themes and Mini-Themes

## PRIMARY UNITS:

| | Unit | Focus | Mini-Themes |
|---|---|---|---|
| I. | **Insects**<br>(Science) | Students will learn some of the common characteristics of insects and spiders. | Caterpillars, Butterflies, and Moths<br>Bees<br>Ants<br>Spiders |
| II. | **Growing Up**<br>(Social Studies) | Students will identify feelings about aging and recognize that growing up is individualistic and developmental | Growing Up with Separation and Divorce<br>Death and Dying<br>Growing Up as Part of a Family<br>Growing Up with Brothers and Sisters |
| III. | **Folktales from Around the World**<br>(Language Arts) | Through the readings and discussion of folktales from countries around the world, students will gain an appreciation for this literary form and become familiar with a variety of cultures. | Folktales of Native Americans<br>Afro-American Folktales<br>Tall Tales |
| IV. | **Measurement and Sizes**<br>(Math) | Students will become familiar with the various aspects of measurement and how it relates to mathematics. | Time<br>Months and Seasons<br>Days of the Week<br>Temperature |

## INTERMEDIATE UNITS:

| Unit | Focus | Mini-Themes |
|------|-------|-------------|
| I. **Space: The Final Frontier** (Science) | Students will journey through our Solar System and share in many discoveries that are the results of human's quest for knowledge of our world and our universe. | Men and Women in Space<br>Space Technology<br>The Night Sky: The Constellations<br>Third Planet from the Sun: The Earth |
| II. **The Wild, Wild, West** (Social Studies) | The Wild West comes alive as students travel through time to one of the most colorful and romanticized periods of American history | Legends of the Wild West<br>The Native Americans of the Wild West<br>Wagons Ho: The Trails West<br>Today's Cowboys |
| III. **Poetry: The Words and the Music** (Language Arts) | To create in children a delight for poetry and an understanding of the elements that make poetry so appealing to the senses | Curricular Connections<br>Poems of Everyday Life<br>Humorous Poems<br>Mother Goose for Older Children |
| IV. **Geometry** (Math) | Students will develop an understanding of the usefulness of geometry in their daily lives | Architecture<br>Paper Folding<br>Lines and Angles<br>Non-Geometric Shapes |

# PRIMARY UNITS

## Primary Unit: Insects

**Theme:**  INSECTS

**Focus:**   Students will learn some of the common characteristics of insects and spiders.

**Objectives:**   On completion of this thematic unit, students will be able to:

1.  Recognize and describe a variety of insects.
2.  Describe the difference between spiders (arachnid and insects. (Spiders have two body parts and eight legs. Insects usually have six legs; one or two pairs of wings, and three body parts.)
3.  Describe where insects live and what they eat.
4.  Identify how some insects are helpful and how some are harmful.
5.  Demonstrate how insects move.

**Initiating Activity:**    Create a semantic web about insects by first asking the children to share with you what they know about insects as you record it on the web. After you have recorded what they know about insects, add the following facts and information about insects to the web, such as:

- There are more than a million species of insects on the earth.
- All insects hatch from eggs.
- Bodies of insects have three parts: head, thorax, and abdomen. (Show a diagram, if possible.)
- Insects are food for birds, reptiles, some mammals, and other insects.
- Insects have no bones. They have an outside skeleton that protects their bodies.
- The mouth of an insect has teeth, a tongue, and a sucking tube used for eating.
- Most insects have two sets of eyes.

EXAMPLE:

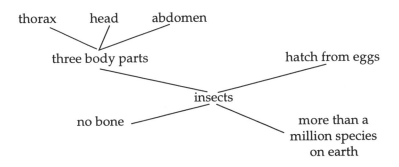

## General Activities

1. Provide the students with some clay and an assortment of pipe cleaners in various sizes and colors, toothpicks or straws. Ask the students to make an insect or spider of their choice, using a picture as a guide. The clay can be used to represent the bodies and the pipe cleaners, straws or toothpicks the legs and antennae. Provide an area where the insects/spiders can be displayed. Ask the students to label their insects/spiders by placing a small piece of paper beside it with the name of the insect and the student's name.

2. Obtain a medium-sized, wide-mouth jar that you can secure by placing a piece of netting or nylon stocking over the opening and holding it in place with a rubber band. Then take a nature walk outside to look for insects. The jar can become the habitat for an insect that the students find (for example, a caterpillar, ant, etc.). Once the insect is caught, be sure to put a twig, leaves, and other materials appropriate for that particular insect's environment in the jar and put the cover over the top. Allow the children to observe the insect for a few days, record findings, and then carefully return it to it's original environment.

3. Ask the children to select an insect or spider whose movement they can demonstrate. (For example, for a bee, they could extend their arms and buzz around the room; for a caterpillar, they could slither on the floor.) Allow other children to guess what the insect/spider is. The child who guesses correctly gets to act out the next movements.

4. Provide the children with an assortment of magazines that contain pictures of insects and spiders. Encourage them to bring in old magazines from home. Then ask the children to make a class collage by pasting pictures of different insects/spiders on an insect graffiti wall.

5. As a class, write to *Ranger Rick's Nature Magazine*, National Wildlife Federation, 1412 - 16th Street, N.W., Washington, DC 20036, asking them to send you information about the materials they have available about insects and spiders. You may be able to obtain some free and/or inexpensive pictures and books that can be displayed and used in the classroom. If you do not subscribe to *Ranger Rick* or *Your Big Backyard,* ask for sample copies. Both magazines would be an excellent addition to your library.

6. Invite an entomologist to visit the class. Explain to the children that an entomologist is someone who studies insects. Many entomologists have collections of insects and spiders. Ask the entomologist if he/she has a collection of insects/spiders and would be willing to share it with the class. Also, ask the entomologist to explain why entomologists study insects/spiders and how they do it. Encourage the children to ask questions. *Note*: Many museums also have insect collections.

7. Have the children help make an "Insect Concentration Game." This can be done by purchasing two sets of insect stickers, putting one sticker of each insect on two sets of cards so that you have a pair of each insect laminating the cards, and then turning the cards face down. Next, a player turns over two cards. If they match, he/she keeps the pair. The game continues until all cards are matched. The person with the most matched pairs is the winner. Matching cards can also be made by making sets of animals/insects and the food they eat (turtles eat bugs, bees get their food from flowers, etc.) or by combining habitats with insects (bees with hive, ants with hills, caterpillars with cocoons). Pictures for cards can be drawn by children or cut from magazines.

8. Provide inked stamp pads and ask the children to use their thumb prints to make insect/spider bodies and then draw legs and antennae. Tell the children to also illustrate the environment in which you would find that particular insect(s). Display the illustrations.

9. Send a letter to the parents telling them that the children in your class are learning about insects and spiders. Ask them for their cooperation in helping their child find an insect/spider to bring to the class. Caution them about how they need to be sure the insect/spider is harmless and to

be careful scooping it into a jar. Small plastic containers with small holes punched in the lid are safe containers to put insects/spiders in to transport to school. Be sure to remind them to include dirt, grass, leaves, and twigs to create an appropriate environment. Ask the children to bring in the different insects/spiders, identify them, place them on a "Science Table" that has magnifying glasses available, and allow the children time to observe them. Have a sheet on the table where each child can write out observations.

10. Create a Semantic Feature Analysis (SFA) Grid (see Chapter 2, pages 42-44) in which the children list insects with which they are familiar along the left-hand side of the grid and some features of insects across the top of the grid. The SFA Grid below illustrates this strategy:

## SFA GRID

If a word matches up with a feature, place an "x" in the row where a row and a column intersect. If it doesn't match, place a "—".

|          | colorful | eates plants | eates other insects | helpful | harmful |
|----------|----------|--------------|---------------------|---------|---------|
| FIREFLY  |          |              |                     |         |         |
| LADYBUG  |          |              |                     |         |         |
| APHID    |          |              |                     |         |         |

When the grid is completed, encourage children to discuss insects that have common features.

## Discussion Questions

1. What is the different between a spider and an insect? (Most insects have three body parts, six legs, one or two pairs of wings. Spiders have two body parts and eight legs).

2. How can insects/spiders be helpful to humans?

3. How can insects/spiders be harmful to humans?

4. If you could be an insect/spider, what kind would you be? Why?

# Literature Related Activities

| Title: | *Fireflies in the Night* |
|---|---|
| Genre: | Nonfiction |
| Author: | Judy Hawes |
| Illustrator: | Ellen Alexander |
| Bibliographic Information: | HarperCollins Publishing, New York, 1991 |
| Summary: | A young girl visiting her grandparent's home in the country finds out how and why fireflies make light and how to catch and handle them. She also finds out several uses for the light made by the fireflies. |
| Interest Level: | Grades K–3. |

1. Pre-Reading Activity:

Read the title of the book, *Fireflies in the Night*. Then turn to the first two pages (pages 4 and 5) and show the children the illustrations as you read the text. Then initiate the K-W-L three-step framework (see Chapter 2, pages 37-39) by creating the following columns on the chalkboard and asking the children to respond to the headings.

| What I <u>K</u>now | What I <u>W</u>ant to Learn | What I <u>L</u>earned |
|---|---|---|
| | | |
| | | |
| | | |
| | | |

Record what the children tell you they already know about fireflies and what they want to learn. Read the story and record what they learned.

2. Learning Activities:

   a. Obtain other books about fireflies, such as J. Brinckloe's *Fireflies!* Compare and contrast these books.

   b. As a group, write an experience story about a night with some fireflies. Ask the children to pretend they are somewhere, like the little girl in the story was. What would they see? What would they do? How would they feel? When the story is completed, divide the text into different parts. Assign different parts or even one sentence to a small group of children to illustrate. Finally, put the text and the illustrations together and make a class book about fireflies.

   c. Allow the children time to look at the illustrations. Then ask them to work in cooperative learning groups to write a Haiku poem about the firefly. Haiku is a form of Japanese poetry consisting of three lines. The first line has five syllables in it, the second line seven syllables, and the third line five syllables. Usually the topic of the poem has to do with nature.

|   | 1 | 2 | 3 | 4 | 5 |   |   |
|---|---|---|---|---|---|---|---|

For example:  Fire/flies light  at  night

|   | 1 | 2 | 3 | 4 | 5 | 6 | 7 |
|---|---|---|---|---|---|---|---|

Beau/ti/ful and bright  as stars

|   | 1 | 2 | 3 | 4 | 5 |
|---|---|---|---|---|---|

Will you  light  my  way

d.  Help the children create a crayon resist picture by drawing fireflies all over a paper and then coloring their tails bright yellow, their wings brown and white. Remind them to press very hard with the crayons. Then, using very thin black tempera paint, paint over the fireflies. The fireflies will look as if they are lighting up in the dark. Display pictures.

3.  Discussion Questions:

a.  Do you think the little girl likes to visit her grandparents or not? Why?

b.  What part of this story did you like best? Why?

   What part of this story did you like least? Why?

c.  What were some of the uses made of the light from the fireflies?

d.  Do you think the little girl wanted to let the fireflies out of the jar? Explain. What do you think would have happened to the fireflies if they had not let them go?

e.  Do you believe a doctor in Cuba used a firefly lamp in the operating room?

―――――――――――――――――――

| | |
|---|---|
| Title: | *The Very Quiet Cricket* |
| Genre: | Picture Book |
| Author: | Eric Carle |
| Bibliographic Information: | Philomel Books, New York, 1990 |
| Summary: | A beautifully illustrated book about a very quiet cricket who wanted to make a sound. He meets many other insects that do make sounds. Finally, he meets another cricket and he is able to make a beautiful chirping sound. |
| Interest Level: | Grades Pre S–2. |

―――――――――――――――――――

1.  Pre-Reading Activity:
Show the children the book and read the title. Ask the children to tell you what they know about crickets. Ask what kind of noises they make. Then read them the introduction about crickets. If possible, share additional information and pictures of crickets that you have collected.

2. Learning Activities:

   a. As a group, review all the different insects that are introduced in this book. Then ask them to make a large illustration of that insect and label it. Display the illustrations on a bulletin board that is labeled, "Our Insect Collection."

   b. Divide the class into cooperative learning groups and assign each group an insect that was introduced in the book. Ask this group to work cooperatively to find out more about their insect. (For example: What do they eat? Where do they live? Are they helpful to humans?) Are they harmful to humans? Resources such as the encyclopedia, *Ranger Rick,* and Your Big Backyard magazines may be helpful. The children may be able to find some of the insects (except for the bumble bee!) and put them in jars. Finally, allow time for the groups to share what they found out about their assigned insect.

   c. As a group, discuss what you think will happen now that the cricket has met another cricket and he can chirp. Then write a language experience story as a sequel to *The Very Quiet Cricket* and illustrate it.

   d. Obtain other books by Eric Carle, such as *The Very Hungry Caterpillar; The Grouchy Lady Bug; The Very Busy Spider; The Honeybee and the Robber.* Allow time for the children to read these books. Then discuss the style of this illustrator/author. Also, discuss the different insects introduced in these stories and how Mr. Carle's presentations of the insects are similar or different. As a culmination of looking at Eric Carle's books, write him a letter telling him what you like about his books, and send it to him via his publisher.

3. Discussion Questions:

   a. What would be a good name for the cricket in this story? Why?

   b. What do you think the other crickets thought when they said "Hello" and the cricket said nothing? How do you think the cricket felt?

   c. Which of the insects that the cricket met would you like to meet?

   d. Why was the cricket able to make a sound when he met the other cricket and not before?

---

Title:              *Insects*

Genre:              Informational

Author:             Keith Brandt

Illustrator:        Robin Brickman

Bibliographic Information:        Troll Associates, Mahawah, NJ, 1985

Summary:            This book provides an introduction to some of the more than 800,000 insects that inhabit the world.

Interest Level:     Grades 2–5.

---

1. Pre-Reading Activity:

   Write the word insects on the chalkboard. Ask the children to name some insects as you list them. After insects have been named, ask the children to describe what all these insects have in common (most of them are small, they have six legs, three body parts, etc.). Read the book and compare what the children said to the information provided in the book.

2.  Learning Activities:

    a.  Provide the children with an assortment of arts and crafts materials (paper, glue, yarn, pipe cleaners, glitter, small plastic moveable eyes, sequins, etc.). Ask the children to create an insect and label what it is. Display the insects.

    b.  Reread the last paragraph of the book (page 30). Ask the children to create a make-believe insect that is yet to be discovered. The make-believe insect should be illustrated, named, and a brief paragraph written telling where the insect would live, what it would eat, if it is helpful or pesty, etc. Allow time to share.

    c.  Demonstrate the stages of a butterfly by making the following sock puppet out of two socks. You will need one knee sock (preferably brown) and a small paper butterfly. Place the butterfly in your hand and pull the brown knee sock up over one arm. The long knee sock is the caterpillar. Next, pull the knee sock down over your hand and hold your hand down (looks like a cocoon hanging from a tree). Finally, shed the knee sock and in your hand will be the final stage: the butterfly. The students will be amazed and will want to try it themselves.

    d.  As a class, brainstorm (both positive and negative) about what the planet earth would be like if there were no insects. For example, imagine no more mosquito or bee bites, no more honey, no more flowers, no more butterflies, etc. Categorize these into "Positive effects of insects" and "Negative effects of insects" and list them on the chalkboard. Then write and illustrate a short story about the planet if it had no insects.

3.  Discussion Questions:

    a.  Are spiders insects? (No) Explain. (Spiders have eight legs instead of six and their bodies are divided into two parts instead of three.)

    b.  What is meant by a complete metamorphosis? (It is the process whereby insects go through four stages of life to become an adult.) Name one insect that goes through four stages.

    c.  What are the four stages a butterfly goes through? (egg, larva, pupa, butterfly)

    d.  How do insects help us?

    e.  What do insects eat?

| | |
|---|---|
| Title: | *Ladybug* |
| Genre: | Informational |
| Author: | Barrie Watts |
| Bibliographic Information: | Silver Burdett Press, Morristown, NJ, 1987 |
| Summary: | This book follows the stages of development of the ladybug, from mating and hatching of the larvae to the growth of the larvae into an adult ladybug. It contains realistic photographs and drawings. |
| Interest Level: | Grades K–6 (The text is written in two different levels.) |

1.  Pre-Reading Activity:

    Read the title of the book and show the children the cover. Ask the children if they have ever seen a ladybug. If so, ask them to tell you about it. If not, ask them to tell you what they think a ladybug is like. Before reading the story, you may want to introduce some of the key words found on page 25 of the book.

2.  Learning Activities:

    a.  Have the children fold a piece of paper or draw lines so they have 6 boxes. Tell them to number the boxes 1 to 6. Ask the children to illustrate the life cycle of the ladybug. Pages 24 and 25 in the book will help them. This paper could be cut apart and stapled to make a booklet that the children could take home.

    | 1 | 2 |
    |---|---|
    | 3 | 4 |
    | 5 | 6 |

    b.  Collect other books about ladybugs such as, *Ladybug, Ladybug* by K. N. Daly; *My Lady Bug* by Herbert Wong and Matthew Vessel; *The Grouchy Ladybug* by Eric Carle. Allow time for the children to compare and contrast these books with *Ladybug* by Barrie Watts.

    c.  Ladybugs live on aphids. Discuss how aphids suck juice from leaves and then the leaves die. Help the children find out more about aphids. Encyclopedias or other insect books can provide information. *The Grouchy Ladybug* by Eric Carle would be a good book to share with the children while you are discussing aphids.

3.  Discussion Questions:

    a.  What do ladybugs like to eat? (aphids) How many do they eat in a day? (about 30)

    b.  How do you think the ladybug got its name? Do you think it is a good name? Why or why not?

    c.  What is the most interesting thing you learned about ladybugs from reading this book?

    d.  Why can't ladybugs fly when they first come out of the pupa? (Their wings are wet.) Describe how a ladybug flies. (They climb up a grass stalk to take off. They can't fly very fast. They open up their wing cases and beat their wings rapidly up and down).

**Culmination:**   Ask each of the children to each write three questions about spiders and insects for which they *do or do not* know the answer. Cut the questions apart, fold the strips of paper, and put them into a container. As a group, pull one question at a time from the container and see if anyone knows the answer. If someone does, go to the next question. If no one knows the answer, assign two or three children to research the answer at a later time. Once all the questions have been dealt with, allow a few days for the researchers to find answers for those questions not answered. Then reconvene the group and allow researchers to report their findings. Finally, compile all the questions with answers into a class booklet entitled "Everything We've Ever Wanted to Know About Spiders and Insects."

## Supplemental Literature

### Primary (Grades 1–3):

Aardema, Verna. (1978). *Why mosquitoes buzz in people's ears.* New York: Dial Books.
   A beautifully illustrated African tale that explains the origin of mosquitoes buzzing in people's ears.
Brinckloe, J. (1985). *Fireflies!* New York: Macmillan.
   A beautiful story that captures the freedom of the fireflies on a summer night.
Carle, E. (1985). *The grouchy ladybug.* New York: HarperCollins.
   A braggart becomes a better-behaved bug as it learns something about getting along with others.
Caudill, R. (1964). *A pocketful of crickets.* New York: Holt.
   A young farm boy's affection for the world around him is beautifully expressed in this appealing story that tells how he loved the sights and sounds of everything around him.

Hornblow, L., and Hornblow, A. (1989). *Insects do the strangest things.* New York: Random House.

This book describes nineteen insects that have peculiar and strange characteristics, such as the camouflage of the walking stick, bugs that row themselves like boats on the water's surface, and so forth.

Jeunesse, G., and de Bourgoing, P. (1989). *The ladybug and other insects.* Illustrated by Sylvie Perols. New York: Scholastic, Inc.

The brightly painted transparent pages allow the reader to watch a ladybug lay eggs on a leaf, see larvae turn into mature insects, and more.

Lavies, B. (1991). *Wasps at home.* New York: Dutton.

This book is a study of social wasps, paper wasps, and baldface hornets from a colony's beginnings in spring to its demise in autumn.

Oxford Scientific Films. (1982). *Mosquitoes.* Photos by George Bernard and Dr. John Cooke. New York: G.P. Putnam's Sons.

Presents the biology and life history of mosquitoes. It also discusses the dangers of diseases carried by mosquitoes.

Parker, N.W., and Wright, J.R. (1987). *Bugs.* New York: William Morrow.

Includes general information, jokes, and brief descriptions of the physical characteristics, habits, and natural environment of a variety of common insects.

Pringle, L. (1990). *The golden book of insects and spiders.* Racine, Wisconsin: Western Publishing Company.

Beautifully illustrated book that includes diagrams and information about various insects and spiders.

Watts, B. (1987). *Ladybug.* Morristown, NJ: Silver Burdett Publishing.

Photographs, drawings, and text on two different levels of difficulty follow the stages of development of the ladybug.

# Supplemental Literature

## Intermediate (Grades 4–6):

Althea, A. (1990). *Insects.* Mahwah, NJ: Troll Associates.

A book that describes characteristics common to all insects.

Graham, A. and F. (1978). *Bug hunters.* Illustrations by D.D. Tyler. New York: Delacorte.

Good explanations of the use of some insects to save crops from other insects.

Johnson, S. (1986). *Chirping insects.* Illustrations by Yuko Sato. Minneapolis, MN: Lerner Publications.

Describes how insect songs are produced and used.

Julivert, A. (1991). *Bees.* Illustrated by Carlos de Miguel. Hauppauge, NY: Barron's Educational Series.

This book describes the appearance, life cycle, activities, and social habits of bees. It also provides information on beekeeping.

Kaufman, J. (1972). *Insect travelers.* New York: William Morrow Publishing.

This book covers such topics as how and why insects move, their use of the sun for navigation, and their storage of fat for fuel.

McGavin, G. (1989). *Discovering bugs.* Illustrated by Wendy Meadway. New York: Bookwright Press.

Describes the physical characteristics and behavior of a variety of bugs. It also presents their life cycle, lifestyles, defenses, and other interesting information.

Morris, D. (1987). *Insects that live in families.* Milwaukee, WI: Raintree Childrens Books.

A well-written book describing the behavior of bees, ants, and other insects that live in colonies.

Taylor, R. (1975). *Butterflies in my stomach, insects as human nutrition.* Santa Barbara, CA: Woodbridge Press.

Insects as a human food source.

# MINI-THEMES

## Caterpillars, Butterflies, and Moths

Butterflies and moths come in many shapes, colors, and sizes. The adult butterfly and moth are not harmful. They mostly suck the nectar of flowers and particularly like juice from fruit, sap, and honey. They taste with special organs on the bottoms of their feet. Most butterflies fly during the day; whereas moths mostly fly at night. The children will enjoy learning about how butterflies and moths change in form and structure — how they go through the stages of metamorphosis: Egg, larva, or caterpillar, pupa, and finally emerge as a butterfly or moth.

## References

Arvetis, C. (1987). *What is a butterfly?* Chicago, IL: Childrens Press.

Brin, R. (1974). *Butterflies are beautiful.* New York: Lerner Publications.

Brown, M. (1981). *All butterflies.* New York: Macmillan.

Carle, E. (1969). *The very hungry caterpillar.* New York: Putman.

Cox, R.K. and Cork, B. (1980). *Butterflies and moths.* Tulsa, OK: EDC Pub.

Curry, P. (1983). *The caterpillar.* New York: Scholastic.

French, V. (1993). *Caterpillar, caterpillar.* Cambridge, MA: Candlewick Press.

Heller, R. (1985). *How to hide a butterfly and other insects.* New York: Grosset and Dunlap.

Hines, A.G. (1991). *Remember the butterflies.* New York: Dutton.

Hooker, Y. (1982). *Little green caterpillar.* New York: Putnam Pub. Group.

Howe, J. (1992). *I wish I were a butterfly.* Illustrated by Ed Young. San Diego: Harcourt Brace Jovanovich.

Reidel, M. (1981). *Egg to butterfly.* Minneapolis, MN: Carolrhoda Books.

Rowan, J.P. (1983). *Butterflies and moths.* Chicago, IL: Children's Press.

Selsam, M. and Hunt, J. *A first look at caterpillars.* New York: Walker & Co.

## Activities

1. Read Eric Carle's, *The Very Hungry Caterpillar* or *Egg to Butterfly* by Marlene Reidel and then discuss four stages of a butterfly: egg – caterpillar – pupa – butterfly. If possible, find a caterpillar and put it in a large jar that has nylon or netting secured over the top. Place leaves in the jar for the caterpillar to eat, and put in a twig or branch on which it will hopefully build a cocoon. Tell the children to be patient, because it takes several months for the metamorphosis to take place. *Note*: Silkworm metamorphosis takes less than two months.

2. Cut large sheets of paper into a simple butterfly shape. Then ask the children to write a brief paragraph that begins, "If I Were a Butterfly I..." Allow children to share their stories and then compile them into a class booklet.

3. Some people collect butterflies. Try to locate someone with a butterfly collection who will bring it into your class to share. If this is not possible, obtain a copy of *Butterflies Are Beautiful* by Ruth Brin, or similar books that contain excellent illustrations of butterflies. Allow time for the children to look at the different kinds of butterflies. Discuss the differences and similarities of the butterflies.

4. As a follow-up to Activity 3, collect the appropriate materials and plan a creative art time in which children make butterflies. Demonstrate how they can make butterflies by putting a pipe cleaner

around the middle of a sheet of tissue paper. The butterfly can then be decorated, if desired. Another method is to shave old crayons onto wax paper, lay another sheet of wax paper over it, and press with an iron set on low heat (use caution with iron). Then mount the melted crayon under a butterfly-shaped mat opening. Display the butterflies.

5. Cut egg cartons in half, lengthwise. Tell the children to paint the egg carton. When it is dry, make a face on one end and then insert pipe cleaners for feelers and you have a caterpillar!

6. Butterflies can be grown in the classroom by obtaining a "Butterfly Garden" from Nasco Co., 901 Janesville Avenue, Ft. Atkinson, WI 53538 (1-800-558-9595).

# Bees

There are several varieties of bees found around the world. The two found in the United States are the honeybee and the bumblebee. Bees live together in colonies called nests or hives and do special dances that communicate messages to each other. They gather pollen and nectar from flowers which, when combined, make honey. Many bees produce honey in their natural habitat, whereas others produce their honey in what is called an apiary, where an apiarist, or beekeeper, harvests the honey to use or sell. Children will enjoy learning more about the types of bees and their responsibilities.

## References

Baraw, T. (1971). *Bees.* New York: Grosset.

Barton, B. (1973). *Buzz, buzz, buzz.* New York: Macmillan.

Carle, R. (1981). *The honeybee and the robber: A moving picture book.* New York: Putnam Pub.

Ernst, L.C. (1986). *The bee.* New York: Lothrop.

Heller, R. (1983). *The reason for a flower.* New York: Putnam Pub.

Migutsch, A. et al. (1981). *From blossom to honey.* Minneapolis, MN: Carolrhoda.

Pluckrose, H. (1981). *Bees and wasps.* New York: Gloucester Press.

Polacco, P. (1993). *The bee tree.* New York: Philomel.

Russell, F. (1967). *Bees.* Illustrated by Colette Portal. New York: Knopf.

## Activities

1. Read the book, *From Blossom to Honey* by Ali Mitgutsch. Then, if possible, obtain a honey comb and explain that, in most cases, the bees build this structure out of wax and then fill it with the honey. If honeycombs are not available, buy jars of honey. Allow the children to taste the honey and the beeswax. Provide a piece of toast or cracker for the honey.

2. Prepare the following recipe for a snack.
   <u>Honey Bees</u>
   2 cups peanut butter
   4 tablespoons honey
   1-1/3 cup nonfat dry milk
   8 tablespoons toasted wheat germ
   unsweetened cocoa powder
   sliced almonds

In a mixing bowl, mix peanut butter and honey. Stir in dry milk and wheat germ until well mixed. Lay waxed paper on a baking sheet. Using 1 tablespoon at a time, shape peanut butter mixture into ovals to look like bees. Put on baking sheet. Dip a toothpick in cocoa powder and press lightly across the top of the bees to make stripes. Stick on almonds for wings. Chill for 30 minutes. Makes 20 honey bees.

*Source*:    Adopted from recipe found in *Better Homes and Gardens Kids Snacks* (Des Moines, Iowa: Meredith Corporation, 1979).

3.    Invite an apiarist, or beekeeper, to come to the class and ask him/her to explain how bees make honey, what the beekeeper does and what kind of equipment is needed. If it is feasible, visit an apiary and let the beekeeper do a demonstration there.

# Ants

Ants are known as social insects and they live together in organized communities called colonies. The female members of the ant colonies are workers, except for the queen who lays the eggs. The workers jobs are to search for food, build the nest, care for the young, and fight off enemies. The male ants' only job is to mate with the young queens; they die soon after. Each queen starts her new colony after mating. Children will enjoy reading the recommended books and doing the suggested activities to find out more about how ants live.

## References

Brenner, B. (1973). *If you were an ant...* Illustrated by Fred Brenner. New York: Harper & Row.

Chinery, M. (1991). *Ant*. Mahwah, NJ: Troll Associates.

Clay, P. (1984). *Ants*. Global Library Marketing Services.

Dorros, A. (1987). *Ant cities*. New York: Harper & Row.

Hooker, Y. (1984). *The Little Red Ant*. New York: Putnam Pub.

Myrick, M. (1968). *Ants are fun*. New York: Harper & Row.

Pluckrose, H. (1981). *Ants*. Illustrated by Tony Weaver and David Cook. New York: Watts.

Van Allsburg, C. (1988). *Two bad ants*. New York: Houghton Mifflin.

## Activities

1.    Ant farms are available in some commercial catalogs as well as in many toy, hobby, or pet stores. Purchase an ant farm and allow children to observe the ants as they dig tunnels, build roads and rooms, eat and store food, and so forth. If you would rather create your own ant farm, directions are provided in *Ant Cities* by Arthur Dorros.

2.    After a few days of careful observation of the ant farm (or an outdoor ant hill) ask the children to write and illustrate a story in which they put themselves into the life of an ant. Ask them to title their stories, "My Life As An Ant." Allow time to share the stories and then compile them into a class booklet.

3.    Ants have no voice and do not communicate with sounds. They give messages through secretions that they pass throughout the colony by touching each other. They also leave a trail of secretions to help other ants find food. Provide stamp pads, tempera paints, markers, and paper. Then ask the children to create an "ant message" by "secreting" any kind of trail they want. After they have finished secreting their message, ask the children to explain their message either verbally or in writing. Ask the children questions such as, "What are you trying to tell the ants? What will the ants find at the end?"

4.   After reading books such as *Ant Cities* by Arthur Dorros, provide the children with a large sheet of paper. Then ask them to pretend that they are inside an ant farm or hill and to draw a map of what it would look like. Tell them to label or illustrate the various rooms, for example, room for queen to lay eggs, rooms for larva and pupae, rooms for food, etc. Allow time to share.

# Spiders

Spiders are not insects. They are called arachnids. Spiders have two body parts and eight legs, whereas insects have three body parts and six legs. Spiders have no backbones or antennas. They spin webs for their homes, for their young, and to help catch insects for food. Most spiders have poison glands and fangs that they use for killing prey and protecting themselves. They are not usually dangerous to humans because they do not attack unless they are cornered or provoked. Children should be cautioned not to touch black widow, tarantula, or cinnamon brown spiders because they are poisonous and their bites can have serious effects. Children will enjoy learning more about spiders as they read the recommended books and do the suggested activities.

## References

Back, C. (1986). *Spider's web*. Photos by Barrie Watts. Norristown, NJ: Silver Burdette.

Carle, E. (1984). *The very busy spider*. New York: Philomel.

Chinery, M. (1991). *Spider*. Mahwah, NJ: Troll Associates.

Lane, M. (1982). *The spider*. New York: Dial Books.

Podendorf, M. (1982). *A new true book — Spiders*. Chicago, IL: Children's Books.

Selsam, M. and Hunt, J. (1983). *A first look at spiders*. New York: Walker.

White, E.B. (1952). *Charlotte's Web*. New York: Harper and Row.

## Activities

1.   To emphasize that spiders have eight legs, have the children make spiders. Use a black circle for the body and glue on eight strips for legs. Paste on two circles of yellow construction paper for the eyes, attach a string, and hang the spider somewhere in the room.

2.   Use caution as you and the children hunt for a spider to put in a jar. Carry the jar with you. When you find a spider do not pick it up with your hands. Use a piece of wood or cardboard to shove it into the jar. Put tiny holes in the lid for air. The bottom of the jar should be covered with dirt. Also put a small leafy branch that has smaller branches coming off of it into the jar. Put a small piece of moist sponge in the jar for water. Small dead insects could be dropped in the jar for food, if they are available. Keep the spider for approximately two weeks and allow the children to observe it. Then free the spider.

3.   Read *Charlotte's Web* by E.B. White to the children. The children will not only learn a lot about the life cycle of the spider, but also about friendship. As a group, write a continuation (sequel) of what will happen next in the lives of Wilbur and Charlotte's spiderlings.

# Primary Unit: Growing Up

**Theme:**   GROWING UP

**Focus:**   Students will be able recognize that the feelings they have about aging, and the changes they experience are all part of growing up. The students will also be able to understand that growing up is individualistic and developmental.

**Objectives:**   On completion of this thematic unit, students will:

1.   Explain some changes people go through while growing up.

2.   List various issues faced while growing up.

3.   Explain feelings experienced while growing up.

4.   Understand that growing up is individualistic and developmental.

**Initiating Activity:**   Ask the children to bring in photographs of themselves when they were babies and at various age intervals up to their current age. Display the pictures. Then discuss the changes that have occurred over the growing years, both physically and mentally, and what changes will occur in the future.

## General Activities:

1.   Have students take their fingerprints by using a stamp pad. Discuss the individuality and uniqueness of each child's fingerprints and mention the fact that fingerprints do not change as one grows up.

2.   Have the students interview their grandparents to find out what it was like when they were growing up. For example, did they have television, radios, dishwashers, and so forth? What were their schools like? What kinds of transportation did they have? After the students have completed gathering the information, allow time for them to compare and contrast growing up during their grandparents' day with growing up today.

3.   Ask the students to bring in something that has been or was important to them (for example, a stuffed toy, favorite blanket, bedtime story, etc.). Have the students share these items and explain their personal importance.

4.   Read the poem "Sarah Cynthia Sylvia Stout Would Not Take The Garbage Out" to the class. (This poem is located in *Where the Sidewalk Ends*, by Shel Silverstein, on pages 70–71 in the hardback copy.) Have a discussion with the class on the importance of doing chores, a responsibility of growing up. Have the students write a journal entry, in poetry form, about the chore they dislike the most. A sharing time may be optional for students who want to share their poem.

5.   At the beginning of the year, help the students construct their own height chart by using a yard stick to mark each inch on a 2-inch-by 5-foot strip of paper. Students can roll the strip up, secure it with a rubber band, and keep it in their desks. Have the students measure each other, twice a month, using the strip, which can be taped on a wall. Record the date of measurement on the tape at the appropriate height. Continue to record heights until the end of the year, and then send the growth chart home to the parents as a record of their child's growth during that school year. (If possible, laminate the charts to help preserve them.)

6.   Discuss different cultures and what is important to each culture as their children grow up. For example, the Japanese keep students in school almost year-round and for very long school days. This suggests that education is valued as a most important aspect of growing up in Japan. Have the students do some independent or partner research into a specific culture's values concerning

growing up. Have them write a brief report on the culture's values related to growing up. Have the students or the team present the report to the class.

7. Discuss with children the importance of self-esteem and growing up. Ask why it is important to feel good about oneself in order to grow up into a healthy, happy person. Have children make a list of positive attributes about themselves. When they are finished with their lists, the children can come up to the front of the room and write on a huge piece of white paper, in different-colored markers, one of their positive attributes. As the children write these down on the paper, the class can discuss whether or not they agree with the attributes that are written down. This could be a great way to bring out the positive things about the children in the class.

8. Children can design their own T.V. show about growing up for the class. They can use a cardboard box and cut a T.V. window in the front of the box. Different pictures can be drawn by the children about what it is like to grow up in their house, neighborhood, or town. They can put their name on these pictures. Each child can make two pictures. When all of the pictures are finished, they are taped together. At the top of the box a spool can be connected around which the taped-together paper would be turned wound. A handle could be placed on either side of the box to turn the spool. As the spool is turned, the pictures will come through the window in the box. As they appear, children can explain their creations to the class and take turns being the narrator of the TV show.

9. With the permission of the principal, the teacher can invite someone from a pet store to come to the classroom and bring animals of different sizes and ages. Some may be puppies and kittens and others grown-up dogs or cats. Have them talk about the growth of the animals. How fast do they grow? What is the significance of their years in comparison to human years? Children can learn the similarities and differences of growing up as animals as compared to humans. Having dogs, cats, or birds, for example, would be significant because many children have these animals for pets. The book, *My First Book About Nature: How Living Things Grow* by Dwight Kuhn would be a good book to share at this time.

10. Children can design a guidebook for parents. This would explain to parents the important things that they need to know about their child growing up. For example, the text could read, "When I was a baby I needed diapers, a bottle, and a rattle. Now that I am seven years old, I need love, food and attention. When I am a teenager I will need..." The children would include pictures with this guide book. When it is finished, they can show it to their parents either by taking it home or during an open-house night when the parents come to the school.

11. Ask the students, with the help of their parents, to complete the following statements:

    When I was 1 year old my favorite thing to do was _____.

    When I was 2 years old my favorite thing to do was _____.

    When I was 3 years old my favorite thing to do was _____.

    When I was 4 years old my favorite thing to do was _____.

    When I was 5 years old my favorite thing to do was _____.

    When I was 6 years old my favorite thing to do was _____.

    After students have completed this assignment, give each student a code number to put on his/her paper instead of a name. Collect the papers and randomly distribute them to other students. The children will then have to find the person whose interest paper they have by asking questions. When the children are finished, these can be put into a book entitled "Our Second Grade Class Interest Book."

**Discussion Questions:**

1.  What are some things that you like about growing up?

2.  What are some things that you do not like about growing up?

3.  Do you think everyone grows up in the same way? Explain your answer.

4.  Who is your favorite grown-up person, and why?

5.  If you could be any age you wanted to be, how old would you be, and why?

6.  What do you think are the hardest things about growing up?

7.  If you could change places with any living person, who would it be, and why?

8.  What do birthdays mean to you? to society?

9.  What if you were growing up in Japan? in Africa? in Australia?

10. What one thing would you tell children younger than you about growing up?

11. What are some of the similarities between the way you were when you were five years younger and the way you are now?

**Culmination:**   The culminating activity will be a "Growing Up Day." This day could include all or some of the following activities:

1.  Have the students write three brief summaries. The first summary tells about important events they remember about growing up during their first five years. These can be happy events or sad events. For the second summary, ask the students to describe how they feel about growing up now, and for the third what they think growing up in the future will be like.

2.  Invite guest speakers from a day care center, a retirement home, and a juvenile center. The speakers can be representatives of the facilities or residents. Ask guests to discuss growth as it relates to the individuals who live in their facilities. Have the students prepare questions for the speakers prior to their visits.

3.  Play charades. Have the students guess which stage of development their classmate is acting out, (for example, infant, adult, elderly, etc.).

4.  Children can dress up in outfits of people of all ages. For example, one child might have a toddler outfit on. This might include a diaper and shirt. Another child may be dressed as a teenager. He or she might wear a pair of jeans and a t-shirt. The children can design their own outfits and bring the materials to put this outfit together from home. A child dressed as an older man or woman might want to wear a tie or a dressy hat. The children can decide beforehand what outfits they are going to wear, but an attempt should be made to have an equal distribution of each age bracket. The children can wear these outfits all day. They may want to put on a skit to go along with the outfits they have on.

5.  Children could design their own comic strip or comic book on how to survive from birth through whatever grade they are in. This could be a funny comic strip or comic book based on the child's viewpoint of growing up. For example, parents often call two-year-olds the "terrible two's." The children could draw illustrations and include words describing what they thought they were like during the terrible-two's. These comics could be placed together on a bulletin board or big piece of oaktag, and either placed up in front of the room or designed as a book. The children might want to take them home to show their parents.

6.  The children could make a video on growing up in their school. They could take a video camera around the school and tape all of the children from kindergarten through fifth or sixth grade, depending on the type of school. The children could pretend that they are the interviewers or

newscasters and ask the other children the questions. For example, What do you think about being in your grade? What grade do you wish you were in? The children could show this video to the whole school when they are finished. All of the children would get to see themselves on the videotape.

## Literature Related Activies

| | |
|---|---|
| Title: | *Now One Foot, Now the Other* |
| Genre: | Picture Book |
| Author: | Tomie DePaola |
| Bibliographic Information: | G.P. Putnam's Sons, New York, 1980 |
| Summary: | This is a heart-touching story about a boy named Bobby and his best friend, his grandfather. They do everything together until one day Bobby's grandfather has a stroke. Bobby must reverse roles with his grandfather and help him learn how to do all of the things, such as walking, that his grandfather once taught him to do. |
| Interest Level: | Grades 1–4. |

1.  Pre-Reading Activity:

Children can go to a nearby nursing home and adopt a grandparent. If this is not possible, ask them to adopt a neighbor, grandparent, friend, or someone else who is older. Have them design their own adoption certificates that they can give to a person at the nursing home, which says something on it like, "My adopted grandparent is _____ and he or she is helping me to be happy and grow up to be the best person that I can be." The children can visit the nursing home periodically and do various activities with the residents.

2.  Learning Activities:

    a.  In the story, the first word Bobby said was Bob, the name of his grandfather. Ask the students to find out what their first word was and what age they were when they said it. Allow time for the students to share their first word and the ages when they spoke it.

    b.  Bobby liked to play with blocks when he was growing up. Display the sentence, When I was growing up I liked to play _____ , and ask the students to copy it onto an 8" x 11" sheet of paper. Then tell them to complete the sentence and create an illustration to accompany it. Put the pages into a class book titled "Things We Liked to Play While Growing Up."

    c.  First Bobby said a word and then he learned how to walk. Ask the students to divide a piece of paper into eight boxes. Then tell the students to illustrate eight steps of their growing up. Allow time to share.

    d.  Read Tomie de Paola's companion book, *Nana Upstairs and Nana Downstairs*, which deals with the subject of death and dying. Then lead a discussion on the similarities and differences between that book and *Now One Foot, Now the Other*.

3.  Discussion Questions:

    a.  Who do you think did the greater service: Bob, because he loved and helped Bobby when he was little, or Bobby, because he loved and helped Bob when he was old and sick? Why do you think that way?

b. Can you remember the people in your family who helped you learn how to walk? Why is it important that we have loving protection around us to help us learn things like this while we are growing up?

c. What is the most important thing you know about having a loving relationship with another person, such as a grandparent? How does this make you feel inside?

d. What do you think was the significance of the blocks that Bobby and his grandfather built in the story?

e. Do you think Bob would have recovered from his stroke without Bobby's help? (Probably not.) What makes you think that? (Bob was making no progress until Bobby started working with him.)

f. Like Bobby, everyone enjoys hearing stories about what they did when they were little. What is your favorite story about yourself?

g. If you had to tell what this story was about in just one word, what word would you choose? (Love, caring, help, devotion).

---

| | |
|---|---|
| Title: | *Love You Forever* |
| Genre: | Picture Book |
| Author: | Robert Munsch |
| Bibliographic Information: | Firefly Books, Ontario, Canada, 1986 |
| Summary: | This is the story of a young boy who grows up through all the stages of childhood until he becomes a man. It shows the enduring love that a parent in the story continues to show her child and how this love can cross the generations. |
| Interest Level: | Grades 1–3. |

---

1. Pre-Reading Activity:

   Children can do a semantic web on the word *love* and the importance of this word. Ask them to think of anybody or anything they love. For example:

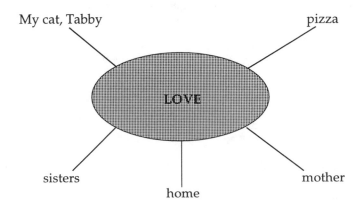

After they have listed all the people or things they love, ask each of them to think, to themselves, which of the these are most important to them and why.

2.  Learning Activities:

    a.  Write the words for the song that the mother sings to her son on the chalkboard. Ask the children to think of a tune or make up a tune to go with the words. Then, as a group, sing the song.

    b.  Create a time line on the chalkboard of the stages of growth the boy went through in this story and the things he did at each stage. For example:

    pulled books off shelf                              never wanted a bath

    pulled food out of refrigerator                   said bad words

             2 years                                       9 years

    Then ask the children to create their own time line of their yearly growth up to their current age. They may need to get information for the time line from their parents.

    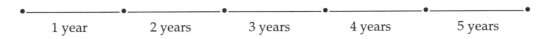

          1 year          2 years          3 years          4 years          5 years

    c.  As a group, write a sequel to *Love You Forever*. Ask the children to think about what kind of father the boy who grew up and now has a baby daughter will be. How will he treat his daughter and how will she treat him from now until she grows up?

    d.  Discuss with the children how the boy did things that upset his mother in *Love You Forever*. The things he did were things most children his age might do. Ask the children to think of things they have done that might have upset their parents or others who take care of them. Ask each of the children to create a page that includes the sentence "I remember when I _____ (finish sentence with something "naughty" he/she did) and an illustration to go with it. Allow time to share.

3.  Discussion Questions:

    a.  Who do you know that you think you'll love forever, no matter how old you get? Who do you know that you think will love <u>you</u> forever, no matter how old you get?

    b.  Sometimes we forget how important our parents are to us while we are growing up. Was there ever a time when you felt badly about something you might have done or said to one of your parents? What happened?

    c.  Why do you suppose the mother in the story said that the boy would always be her baby as long as she was living, even when the boy was all grown up?

    d.  What did you like best about this story? What did you like least?

Title:          *Ira Sleeps Over*

Genre:          Picture Book

Author:         Bernard Waber

Bibliographic Information:      Houghton Mifflin, New York, 1972

Summary:      Ira is very excited about staying overnight with his friend Reggie; however, he has never spent a night without sleeping with his teddy bear, Tah Tah. He is afraid his friend will laugh at him if he brings his teddy bear so he leaves it at home. After playing and having a great time, Reggie begins to tell a scary ghost story. In the middle of the story he goes to a drawer, pulls out a teddy bear, and brings it back to bed. When Ira finds out about Reggie's teddy bear he goes home and gets his teddy bear.

Interest Level:      Grades K–3.

1. Pre-Reading Activity:

   Tell the students that this book is about Ira, a young boy who is invited to spend the night with his friend Reggie; however, Ira has never spent a night without sleeping with his teddy bear. Divide the students into small groups and allow time for them to discuss the following questions: Have you ever spent a night with a friend? If so, what was the first night away from home like? If you haven't spent a night away from home, would you like to? Explain.

2. Learning Activities:

   a. Reggie had a junk collection in his room. Discuss the different items he had in his collection — picture postcards, bottlecaps, chewing gum wrappers, rubber stamps, etc. Then ask the children to share collections they may have by providing a space in the classroom and asking them to bring in their collections and displaying them.

   b. Reggie's teddy bear was named Foo Foo, and Ira's teddy bear was named Tah Tah. Both of these names may appear silly to others. Discuss how pets and toys get their names. Then ask the children to share the names of their pets and toys and list them on the chalkboard. Ask children to also share how they decided on the names of their pets and toys.

   c. Play the ABC game, in which the first student says, "I'm going to a friend's house to stay overnight and I will take _____ ." A child provides something that begins with a letter "a". (for example, an apple, alligator, aspirin, etc.). Then the next player must repeat the same line and the "a" word provided and then add a "b" word. The next player adds a "c" word, and so forth.

   d. Most children have something they like to sleep with. Have a sharing day during which all children bring in an item with which they like to sleep. Provide a time for the children, if they want, to tell how they started sleeping with the item.

   e. Declare a specific week as "teddy bear" week. During this time, invite the students to bring in their stuffed teddy bear. Provide a shelf or table of books related to bears, such as: *Teddy Bears Go Shopping* by Suzanna Getz (New York: Macmillan, 1982); *Teddy Bear, Teddy Bear* by Michael Hague (New York: Morrow Jr. Books, 1993); *Beady Bear* (1982), *Corduroy* (1968), and *Corduroy's Day* (1985), all three by Don Freeman (New York: Viking). Allow time for the children to peruse the bear books and to share their bears.

   f. Create a Character Continuum (See Chapter 2, pages 52-53) by asking the children to brainstorm all the words they can think of that can be used to describe one or more of the characters in *Ira Sleeps Over*. Record these words in a column on the chalkboard. Invite the children to think of opposites for all the recorded words. Place the opposites at either end of a continuum. For example:

Book Title: _Ira Sleeps Over_

Character: __Reggie__

Giving _____ Selfish

Nice _____ Mean

Fun _____ Boring

Friendly _____ Unfriendly

Kind _____ Cruel

Sociable _____ Unsociable

Ask the students to put an "x" on the line to indicate the degree to which an identified character exhibits a particular trait. Allow time for them to discuss their rationale for placing the "x" where they did.

3.  Discussion Questions:

    a.  Why do you think Ira's sister kept insisting that Reggie would laugh at Ira if he took his teddy bear?

        Ira's mother and father tried to make Ira feel that it was all right to take his teddy bear to Reggie's house. Why do you think their advice was different than his sister's?

    b.  Why didn't Ira want to take his teddy bear with him to Reggie's house? (Because he was afraid Reggie would laugh at him if he brought his teddy bear.)

    c.  Why didn't Reggie answer Ira when he asked him what he thought about teddy bears? (Answers may vary, but might include: Because Reggie thought Ira might laugh at him if he told him about his teddy bear.)

    d.  What were some of the things that Ira and Reggie did before they told the scary ghost story? (Answers may vary, but might include: They looked at Reggie's junk collection, played office with rubber stamps, had a wrestling match, and had a pillow fight.)

    e.  Why do you think Reggie kept his teddy bear in the dresser drawer? (Answers may vary, but might include: So that Ira wouldn't see it.)

    f.  How do you think Ira felt when he found out that Reggie sleeps with a teddy bear too?

    g.  What do you think will happen when Ira and Reggie wake up in the morning?

    h.  What do you think might have happened if Reggie hadn't taken his teddy bear to sleep with him?

| | |
|---|---|
| Title: | _Leo the Late Bloomer_ |
| Genre: | Picture Book |
| Author: | Robert Kraus |
| Illustrator: | Jose Aruego |
| Bibliographic Information: | Simon & Schuster Books, New York, 1971 |
| Summary: | Leo was a little tiger cub who could not do things other young animals could do such as read, write, draw, and speak. Leo's parents recognized that he was a late bloomer, although his father worried about him and kept anxiously watching him all year long. Finally, one day Leo "blooms" and everyone is happy. |
| Interest Level: | Grades K–3. |

1.  Pre-Reading Activity:

    Leo, a little tiger cub, could not do things other young animals could do. He couldn't read. He couldn't write. He couldn't draw. He never spoke a word. He was even a sloppy eater. Leo felt as if he couldn't do anything right. Sometimes we all feel like Leo because there are some things that are very difficult for us to do. What are some things that you find difficult to do? How do you feel about not being able to do them?

2.  Learning Activities:

    a.  People learn different skills (such as talking, walking, and so forth) at different rates. Ask the children to find out from their parents such information as the age at which they said their first word, started to walk, got their first tooth, and the like. Once this information is obtained, make a chart like the one below on the chalkboard, and enter tally marks in the appropriate columns.

    |                  | 3-6 mo. | 6-9 mo. | 9-12 mo. | 12-15 mo. | 15-18 mo. |
    |------------------|---------|---------|----------|-----------|-----------|
    | Started to walk  |         |         |          |           |           |
    | First word       |         |         |          |           |           |
    | First tooth      |         |         |          |           |           |

    Discuss with the children the differences and similarities among the group members in terms of the age when they did the specific things.

    b.  Make available a flowering plant or bouquet of flowers so that the children can observe how all flowers on the same plant do not bloom at the same time. This provides a good example of the fact that even though all the buds on this plant received the same amount of water and light, they still did not all bloom at the same time, just as all children do not grow and "bloom" at the same time. Discuss other observations children have made in regard to differences among people, plants, and/or animals.

    c.  In the book, *Leo the Late Bloomer*, the animals all wrote their names differently — one with dotted lines, one with double lines, one with triple lines, and so forth. Provide construction paper, paint, glue, sand, yarn, markers, and other media. Ask the children to be creative and write their names using a media different than the usual pencil or crayon. Display the names.

    d.  Ask the children to write a journal entry about how they would feel if they were Leo before he "bloomed" and after he "blooms." Allow time to share.

3.  Discussion Questions:

    a.  What things couldn't Leo do that other young animals could do? (read, write, draw, speak, eat properly, etc.)

    b.  Explain what is meant by being a late bloomer. (Answers may vary, but may include: Not doing certain things at the expected time.)

    c.  Do you think Leo's father was worried about Leo's not being able to read, write, draw, and speak? Why or why not? (Answers may vary, but may include: Yes, he was worried, because he kept watching Leo.)

d.   How do you think Leo felt about not being able to read, write, draw, and speak like the other animals?

e.   What happened that finally made Leo bloom?

# Supplemental Literature

### Primary (Grades 1–3):

Allen, M.N., and Rotner, S. (1991). *Changes.* New York: Macmillan.
> The authors describe in rhymed text and with illustrations how things in nature change as they grow and develop.

Cork, B.T. (1989). *Going to school.* New York: Derrydale Books.
> This is the story of a little boy named Sam who is going to school for the first time. It tells of his preparation for his first day and then of the exciting adventures he has when he finally gets to school.

dePaola, T. (1978). *Nana upstairs, nana downstairs.* New York: Penguin.
> Describes a boys visits with his ill great-grandmother

Hazen, B.S. (1992). *Mommy's office.* New York: Atheneum.
> As part of growing up and learning what her mother does at work, Emily accompanies her Mommy to her downtown office.

Hoberman, M.A. (1992). *Fathers, mothers, sisters, brothers: A collection of family poems.* New York: Scholastic.
> Through this collection of poems, readers can identify with what it is like to grow up in all kinds of families — extended, nuclear, foster, fractured, and adoptive.

Jukes, M. (1984). *Like Jake and me.* New York: Alfred A. Knopf.
> With the help of a loving family, Alex grows closer to his stepfather.

Kuhn, D. (1993). *My first book about nature: How living things grow.* New York: Scholastic.
> This book provides an introduction to growth, explaining how it occurs in the line of such everyday things as dogs, apples, trees, guppies, and humans. It contains beautiful, realistic photos.

Moss, T. (1993). *I want to be.* Illustrations by Jerry Pinkney. New York: Dial Books.
> A young girl describes, in poetic terms, what kind of person she wants to be when she grows up.

Russo, M. (1993). *The trade-in mother.* New York: Greenwillow Books.
> A young child gets frustrated with all his mother's "no's," so at bedtime he expresses his wish to trade-in his mother for a new one.

Silverstein, S. (1964). *The giving tree.* New York: Harper & Row.
> This is the story of a young boy who loved a tree and was loved by the tree. The tree gave and gave to the boy. As the boy grew older, he began to want more and more from the tree. This story is about the gift of giving and the acceptance of another's capacity to love in return.

Silverstein, S. (1974). *Where the sidewealk ends.* New York: Harper & Row.
> A collection of contemporary and often quite humorous poems by Silvrstein.

### Intermediate (Grades 4–6):

Abercrombie, B.M. (1981). *Cat-Man's daughter.* New York: Harper & Row.
> Kate, a thirteen-year-old, sees herself as a pawn in her divorced parents' struggle for power. She wishes her life could return to "normal," but in the meantime she relies heavily on her grandmother, with whom she has a very special relationship.

Adler, C.S. (1979). *The silver coach.* New York: Coward, McCann and Geoghegan.
> As a result of being away from her mother for a summer plus an eye-opening visit from her father, Chris, a twelve-year-old, gains a new perspective on her parents' divorce and a deeper understanding of and appreciation for her mother.

Angell, J. (1981). *What's best for you.* New York: Bradbury Press, Inc.
> This is a story about brothers and sisters who are split up because of their parents' divorce. The reader is given candid insights into the convictions and misgivings of each family member as each struggles to adapt to the divorce.

Fassler, D., Lash, M., and Ives, S.B. (1988). *Changing families: A guide for kids and grown-ups.* Burlington, VT: Waterfront Books.
> A guide to help children and their families cope with the many changes that can occur in a family unit.

Hermes, P. (1982). *You shouldn't have to say goodbye.* San Diego, CA: Harcourt Brace        Jovanovich.
> Robin, a thirteen-year-old, is faced with her mother's death from cancer. The reader will appreciate the courage and gallantry with which Robin's mother confronted death.

Kramer, P. (1991). *The real you.* New York: Rose Publishing Group.
> This book demonstrates how heredity, environment, and personality and character traits all combine to make each person a unique individual with his or her own special sense of self-worth.

Little, J. (1984). *Mama's going to buy you a mockingbird.* New York: The Viking Press.
> This is a very tender, compassionate story of how the members of a family cope with their day-to-day lives as they face the pain of their father's dying.

MacLachlan, P. (1985). *Sarah, plain and tall.* New York: Harper & Row.
> This is the story of a motherless family, living on the prairie. Sarah, a prospective mail-order bride, comes and decides to stay.

Mann, P. (1977). *These are two kinds of terrible.* New York: Doubleday and Company.
> This sad, but not melodramatic, story portrays a child's loneliness and grief after his mother dies of cancer. It is through her death that he and his father really become a family.

McHugh, E. (1983). *Raising a mother isn't easy.* New York: Greenwillow Books.
> Karen, a Korean orphan who was adopted by a single parent, begins to understand that her mother will make her own decisions about marriage.

Pearse, P. (1988). *See how you grow.* London, England: Frances Lincoln.
> This book portrays how a baby is conceived, and how it grows up. The book discusses what makes a person grow, how your body knows to grow, and other things that keep on growing, such as hair. The book ends by expressing what old age is and what happens when a person gets old.

Pearson, G. (1986). *Fish Friday.* New York: Atheneum.
> Although thirteen-year-old Jamie has an unhappy summer, she comes to better understand herself, her separated parents, and her little brother.

# MINI-THEMES

## Growing Up With Separation and Divorce

Dealing with separation and/or divorce can be a very traumatic experience — it creates change in our lives and we must learn how to cope with these changes. Hopefully, by giving children an opportunity to relate to others going through separation/divorce and an opportunity to discuss the changes affecting them and their feelings related to those changes, they will be better prepared to accept and adjust to their own situations in a more positive way.

### References

Ballad, R. (1993). *Gracie.* New York: Greenwillow Books.

Boegehold, B. (1985). *Daddy doesn't live here anymore.* Racine, IL: Western. Christiansen, C.B. (1990). *My mother's house, my father's house.* New York: Puffin Books.

Drescher, J. (1986). *My mother's getting married.* New York: Dial.

Girard, L.W. (1987). *At daddy's on Saturday.* Chicago: Albert Whitman & Co.

Ives, S., Fassler, D., and Lash, M. (1985). *The divorce workbook: A guide for kids and families*. Burlington, VT: Waterfront Books.

Lash, M., Loughridge, S.I., and Fassler, D. (1990). *My kind of family: A book for kids in single-parent homes*. Burlington, VT: Waterfront Books.

Okimoto, J.D. (1979). *My mother is not married to my father*. New York: G.P. Putnam's Sons.

Steel, D. (1989). *Martha's new daddy*. New York: Delacorte Press.

Vigna, J. (1987). *Mommy and me by ourselves again*. Niles, IL: Albert Whitman & Co.

Watson, J., Switzer, R.E., and Hirschberg, J.C. (1988). *Sometimes a family has to split up*. New York: Crown.

## Activities

1.  Ask the children to take the position of one of the main characters from a book they have read on divorce and write an autobiography of this character. Tell them to write the autobiography in diary format, documenting the events of the book and how they felt about each.

2.  After reading some of the recommended books for this unit, discuss the finding that there is usually one character who feels that he/she is the only one hurt and/or inconvenienced by a separation/divorce. As a group, select one of the books and make a list of all of the characters. After you have listed the characters, ask the children what advice they would give to help each of them overcome some of the problems they had or thought they had.

3.  Tell the children to pretend that they are a main character in one of the books they have read about separation/divorce. As that character, ask them to write a "Dear Ann Landers" or "Dear Abby" letter asking for advice. Next, tell them to give the letter to a friend and ask him/her to write a response and return it to them. When they get their responses, allow time to share the letters and to compare them with what actually happened in the book.

4.  Allow time for the children to read some of the recommended books for this unit. Then discuss the similarities and differences among the families in these books. You may want to expand this discussion to cover similarities and differences among the families in these books and the children's families.

5.  Invite an attorney and a psychologist to come to the classroom. The attorney can discuss the many legal concerns and ramifications of a separation/divorce, such as financial arrangements, custody of the child(ren), living arrangements, and so forth. The psychologist can discuss some of the emotional problems that are common to most people who experience a separation/divorce. In addition, ask him/her to suggest how and where to obtain help in solving some of these problems.

6.  Discuss with the children the fact that when there is a separation and/or divorce in a family, certain changes do occur. For example, both parents are no longer living in the same house; new family members — stepmothers, stepfathers, stepbrothers, or stepsisters — may become part of the new family; a move to a different house, city, and/or state may become necessary; it may become necessary to give up some items of furniture and other belongings; and so forth. Ask the children to draw three houses and to do the following: In the first house illustrate and/or write about the way you see a family before a separation/divorce. In the second house, illustrate and/or write about the way you see the family after a separation/divorce. In the third house, illustrate and/or write about what they see as a perfect or ideal family. The children may use their own family, a fictitious family, or one of the families about which they have read.

# Death and Dying as Part of Growing Up

Accepting death is naturally one of the most difficult life situations with which we all must deal. In recent years, educators have acknowledged the importance of educating children about death. For too long children have been sheltered from the reality of death and this has caused them even greater fear and anxiety. Children must be given the opportunity to discuss death and to express their feelings related to death. Writers in the field of death education have noted the importance of this kind of openness in order to help children put their fears about death into proper perspective. As paradoxical as it may seem, death education leads to a greater appreciate of life.

## References

Brown, M.W. (1938). *The dead bird.* New York: Young Scott Books.

Buscaglia, L. (1982). *The fall of Freddy the leaf.* New York: Holt Rinehart & Winston.

DePaola, T. (1978). *Nana upstairs, Nana downstairs.* New York: Puffin Books.

Douglas, E. (1990). *Rachel and the upside down heart.* Los Angeles, CA: Price Stern Sloan.

Viorst, J. (1971). *The tenth good thing about Barney.* New York: Atheneum Publishing, Inc.

Whelan, G. (1992). *Bringing the farmhouse home.* Illustrations by Joda Rowland. New York: Simon & Schuster.

## Activities

1.  Tell the students to pretend that they have just gotten word that their best friend has an incurable disease and will not live for more than one year. This friend does not need to be in bed or in the hospital at this time. In fact, it is hard to believe that anything is wrong. Ask the children what they would do in this situation? What would they say? Would they act differently toward him/her? Allow time for the children to react and discuss this situation.

2.  Plan a field trip to an old graveyard. Allow the students time to "browse" through the graveyard looking at tombstones. Tell them to notice some of the following:

    Birthdates and dates of death

    Epitaphs

    Relationships

    Symbols and designs engraved on the tombstones

    Names of people

    Provide the children with a sheet of paper and ask them to design a tombstone.

3.  Invite a funeral director to come to the class to answer the children's questions about funerals. Prior to his/her visit, have the students write questions for him/her on index cards.

4.  Ask the children to work in pairs or small groups and research the customs related to death in a particular culture (Native Americans, Mexican Americans, Black Americans, Cubans, Jews, and so forth). Allow time for each group to share their findings with the class.

5.  Make available some newspapers that contain "Death Notices." Here you will find obituaries that highlight pertinent information about a person who has died. Read at least three of these obituaries to the class, pointing out the kind of information that is provided. Point out that close friends or relatives are often asked to write the obituaries for the person who has died. Ask the children to work in small groups, and to select a person (living or dead) and pretend that they have been asked to write his/her obituary. Tell them to use the newspaper obituaries as a guide, and to write an obituary for the person they have selected.

## Growing Up as Part of a Family

There are many different types of what is called a family. A family may consist of a mother, a father, and sibling(s), wheras other families may be made up of a single parent, step-parents, two mothers, two fathers, grandparents, aunts or uncles, foster parents and other types of guardians. It is important to recognize that "family" refers not only to the immediate family (those sharing a single household), but also to all persons sharing a common ancestry. Children will enjoy reading about different families and their experiences together.

## References

Berry, J. (1987). *Teach me about mommies and daddies*. Chicago: Children's Press.
Bond, F. (1985). *Poinsetta and her family*. New York: Harper & Row.
Carlson, N. (1985). *The perfect family*. Minneapolis, MN: Carolrhoda Books.
Drescher, J. (1980). *Your family, my family*. New York: Walker.
Garza, C.L. (1990). *Family pictures: Cuadros de familia*. Chicago: Children's Book Press.
Mayer, M. (1977). *Just me and my Dad*. New York: Golden Press.
Merriam, E. (1955). *Mommies at work*. New York: Scholastic.
Schick, E. (1970). *City in the winter*. New York: Collier Books.
Simon, N. (1976). *All kinds of families*. Chicago: Albert Whitman.

## Activities

1. Discuss the concept of a family as a team and the need to work together to accomplish what needs to be done. Talk about the various responsibilities that different family members have (taking out garbage, washing dishes, making beds, and so forth). Then ask the children to name some of the responsibilities they have at home as you list them on the board. If a responsibility is mentioned more than once, make a tally mark. Finally, make a graph of the results as you compare and contrast the different family responsibilities.

2. Ask each student to tell about the family member who has most influenced his or her life and why. This can be done orally or in written form.

3. Ask the children to draw pictures and write a brief paragraph that describes some of the things their families do together that they enjoy (a holiday celebration, picnic, playing games, and the like). Compile these into a *Class Family Album* for the children to share. Prior to initiating this activity share the book *Family Pictures: Cuadros de Familia* by Carmen Lomas Garza.

4. Explain the concept of a family tree by illustrating your own or that of a fictitious family. Then tell the children to ask family members for help in making their own family tree. Display the family trees on the bulletin board. *Note*: When illustrating a family tree, be careful to consider one-parent families, extended families, foster families, and other family types.

## Growing Up With Brothers and Sisters

Sibling rivalry is a natural phenomenon of growing up. Brothers and sisters often fight, are jealous of one another and yet love each other and share strong, inseparable bonds. The books and activities recommended for this unit will help children identify with some of the joys and sacrifices of growing up with a brother and/or sister.

## References

Alexander, M. (1971). *Nobody asked me if I wanted a baby sister*. New York: Dial Books.
Berry, J. (1987). *Teach me about brothers and sisters*. Chicago: Children's Press.
Blume, J. (1974). *The pain and the great one*. New York: Dell.
Hoban, R. (1964). *A baby sister for Frances*. New York: Harper & Row.
Keats, J.E. (1967). *Peter's chair*. New York: Harper & Row.

Lacoe, A. (1992). *Just not the same*. Illustrations by Pau Estrada. Boston: Houghton Mifflin.
Wells, R. (1973). *Noisy Nora*. New York: Scholastic.

## Activities

1.  Have the children write letters to a story character from one of the books they have read to ask questions about an incident in the book or to respond to questions. For example, after reading the story *Peter's Chair* by Ezra Jack Keats, one of the children could write to Peter and ask him how he felt after he helped his father paint his chair pink for his sister. The children can then become the character and write back, or other students can respond by taking on the role of a character.

2.  Divide the class into two groups. Ask one of the groups to take the position that it is great to have a brother and/or sister. Ask the other group to take the position that it is not good to have a brother and/or sister. Hold a debate and then summarize the points made for and against having brothers and/or sisters.

3.  Ask the children to complete one of the following statements, depending on whether they have a sibling or not.

    What I like most about having a (sister/brother) is _____ .

    What I would like most about having a (sister/brother) is _____ .

    Allow time to share.

4.  Tell the children to select a main character from one of the recommended books for this unit, then pretend to be that character as they write a brief autobiography telling how they felt, what should be done in a given situation, and so forth. Allow time to share.

# Primary Unit: Folktales From Around The World

**Theme:**  FOLKTALES FROM AROUND THE WORLD

**Focus:**  Through the reading and discussion of folktales from countries around the world, students will become familiar with a variety of cultures, and gain an appreciation for this literary form.

**Objectives:**  Upon completion of this thematic unit, students will:

1.  retell several folktales that originated in other countries.

2.  recognize that often the folktales of a culture mirror its traditions and values.

3.  relate the differences and the similarities among cultures as reflected in their literature.

4.  create their own folktales to reflect an understanding of the elements of this literary genre.

**Initiating Activity:**  Decorate a shoe box with words and phrases from the folktale *Rumpelstiltskin* as retold by Paul Zelinski (1986). Inside the box, place objects that are appropriate to the story, such as a small baby doll, a picture of a spinning wheel, pieces of straw, and the like. Show students one object at a time and ask them to try to figure out what folktale is being represented by the items. Once someone has guessed correctly, or when the class is stumped, read the folktale *Rumpelstiltskin*. After the reading, ask students to relate the significance of each object that was in the box. Discuss the story with students, asking such questions as, "Which character do you think was the most foolish?" "Which character do you like most?" "Which character do you believe is the most cruel?" "What does this folktale tell you about the qualities that were admired?" Explain to students that Rumpelstiltskin is a folktale that originated in Germany (locate Germany on a class map ) and introduce students to folktales.

## General Activities

1.  Read aloud several folktales. Have students come to a generalized understanding about the way folktales usually begin (once upon a time), how they usually end (and they lived happily ever after), and when and where folktales usually take place (long ago and far away). Ask them to brainstorm about other similarities that many folktales have in common, such as magical happenings, things occurring in threes, talking beasts, good winning over evil, good being rewarded, and so forth.

2.  Read aloud several different versions of the same folktale. Ask students why they think there might be so many versions of the same tale. Play the game "Gossip" with students (whisper a short summary of a folktale to one student, have him/her whisper it to the next, until all students have been told the tale). Ask the first student and the last student to repeat the versions they heard and compare them. Again ask students why they think there are so many versions of the same tale. Explain that most folktales were told orally, from generation to generation, and in the process details were changed, reflecting the times and skills of the storyteller.

3.  Have students select a favorite folktale from a collection of folktales from around the world. Have students create a box similar to the one in the initiating activity, and introduce others in the class to the tale. Encourage students to include a variety of objects and materials in their boxes that represent the tale and its country of origin.

4.  Divide students into groups. Assign each group several folktales from a specific country (see the references at the end of the unit). Have students select their favorite folktale from this country and

present it using some type of dramatic interpretation — storytelling, puppet show, flannel board retelling, a short skit, and the like. Have students introduce the tale to the class by identifying the country of origin, pointing out the location of the country on the map and telling five facts about the country.

5.   Folktales often reflect a culture's traditions, customs, and values. Read aloud folk tales from various cultures. After each tale is read, discuss what students have learned about the culture and together fill in a chart similar to the one below. What similarities and what differences can be found? (Several sources can be used to help you locate variations of the same basic tale, such as Margaret Read McDonald's *The Storyteller's Sourcebook: A Subject, Title, and Motif Index to Folklore Collections for Children*. The chart on page 133 lists just a sample of the versions that exist for a number of favorite folktales.)

| Title of Folktale | | | | |
|---|---|---|---|---|
| Country of Origin | | | | |
| Details about Life | | | | |
| Values and Attitudes | | | | |
| Customs | | | | |
| Other | | | | |

6.   Create an anthology of favorite folktales with illustrations by the class. The book can be divided into sections based on the folktale's country of origin. Have students illustrate each folktale with art that is appropriate to the country of origin.

7.   Many folktales lend themselves to being acted out in a mock trial. For example, Hansel and Gretel can be charged with trespassing, or the wolf in *Lon Po Po* can be charged with impersonating Grandma. Choose a folktale in which the character's motives and final actions can be questioned. Select students for the roles of judge, defendant, plaintiff, attorney for the defense, attorney for the prosecution, witness for the defense, witness for the prosecution, and jury members.

8.   Divide students into groups and give each group one or more folktale(s) that originated in different countries. Have students create a board game or floor game based on the tale(s) read.

9.   Create mobiles of folktales from all over the world. To do this, have students illustrate a favorite folktale and somewhere on the picture include the name of the folktale and the country from which it originated. Divide the pictures into groups based on the country of origin and attach them to a hangers decorated with the names of the various countries.

10.  Review the elements of a folktales. Then, review the "Creative Questioning Paradigm," Figure 2-13, page 59. Divide students into groups and have each select a favorite folktale. Have them rewrite the tale to create a version that might have originated in modern-day U.S.A., reminding them to use the strategies included in the paradigm to help them adapt their tale. For example, "What would happen

if Little Red Riding Hood had gotten lost in New York City?" Remind them that their stories and illustrations should reflect life today (that is, the clothing, forms of transportation, foods, etc.) as well as the values and attitudes of today's culture. For example, "Little Red Baseball Cap" bicycles to her grandmother 's house after hitting the winning home run for her softball team!

## A Comparison of Folktales

| Folk Tale | Country of Origin |
|---|---|
| *Rumplestiltskin* | Germany |
| *Tom Tit Tot* | England |
| *Duffy and the Devil* | England |
| *Sleeping Beauty in the Wood* | France |
| *Briar Rose* | Germany |
| *The Queen of Tubber Tintye* | Ireland |
| *Henny Penny* | England |
| *The Hare that Ran Away* | India |
| *Johnny Cake* | England |
| *The Wee Bannock* | Scotland |
| *The Pancake* | Norway |
| *Tom Thumb: His Life and Death* | England |
| *Little Tom Thumb* | Russia |
| *Le Petit Poucet* | France |
| *Little One Inch* | Japan |
| *Cinderella and the Glass Slipper* | France |
| *Little Burnt Face* | Milmac Indians |
| *Kari Woodengown* | Norway |
| *Yeh-Shen* | China |
| *The Brocaded Slipper* | Vietnam |
| *Cinderella, or the Little Glass Slipper* | England |
| *Mufaro's Beautiful Daughters* | Africa |
| *The Egyptian Cinderella* | Egypt |
| *The Maid of the Glass Mountain* | Norway |
| *Red Riding Hood* | Germany |
| *Lon Po Po* | China |

## Discussion Questions

1. Why are folktales so popular with children and adults alike?

2. What is your favorite folktale? From which country did it originate?

   What did you learn about the country based on the folktale alone?

3.  Why do you think that folktales are often called a "mirror of society"?

4.  Why have so many versions of the same basic tale originated in so many diverse countries? (Some believe that the stories came from one prehistoric group that migrated to other countries, taking their folklore with them. Others believe that the stories were independently created and came from the needs and hopes of ALL humans.)

5.  How would you define a folktale?

# Literature Related Activities

Title:              *East of the Sun and West of the Moon*

Genre:              Traditional Literature — Folktale

Author:             Scandinavian Folktales, retold by Kathleen and Michael Hague

Illustrator:        Michael Hague

Bibliographic Information:    Harcourt Brace Jovanovich, San Diego, 1980

Summary:            A handsome prince, the victim of wicked enchantment, lives as a bear by day. He must return to his castle, which lies east of the sun and west of the moon, and only true love can save him from a terrible fate.

Interest Level:     all ages

1.  Pre-Reading Activity:

    Share the title of this folktale with students. Ask each to create an imaginary land that lies "East of the sun and west of the moon."

2.  Learning Activities:

    a.  After reading the folktale, *East of the Sun and West of the Moon* have students create a semantic web (see Chapter 2, pages 34-35) in which they generate words to describe their impressions of Scandinavia. Involve students in an activity to compare their impressions with factual information about the area. First, aid students in locating the area of Scandinavia on a map. Divide the class into three groups to represent the three Scandinavian countries (Norway, Sweden, Denmark). Have each group discover five interesting facts about the country they've been assigned and present the information in a creative way. (For example, they can dress up as Vikings and tell about their homeland; they may play the music associated with Scandinavia while showing pictures they've found or created that tell about their land; and so forth.)

    b.  While the evil characters in many folktales are wicked witches and fiery dragons, the folktales of Scandinavia often include trolls. Have students create their own trolls with clay and various other materials. Encourage students to be creative and make their trolls humorous. For example, they may wish to create a troll on skis (using pieces of wood for skis), or they may wish to create a troll bride with white veil and bouquet!

    c.  Have students create a folktale based on one (or more) of the trolls created in activity "b" above.

    d.  After reading students this version of *East of the Sun and West of the Moon*, share Mercer Mayer's version (1980). Involve students in creating Venn Diagrams that illustrate the similarities and differences between the two stories.

3.  Discussion Questions

    a.  From the story *East of the Sun and West of the Moon,* what did you learn about the landscape/ climate/geography of Scandinavia? (a cold area, surrounded by water, large areas of dense forests).

    b.  What message does the tale give the reader about being too curious?

    c.  If you were the young girl in this tale, what might you have done differently?

    d.  In what ways is *East of the Sun and West of the Moon* similar to most of the folktales you have read/ heard? (It includes magical happenings, talking beasts, things occurring in threes, good triumphing over evil, and so forth.)

    e.  If you were to retell this tale, what changes would you make?

---

| | |
|---|---|
| Title: | *One Fine Day* |
| Genre: | Traditional Literature — Folktale |
| Author: | An Armenian tale, retold by Nonny Hogrogian |
| Illustrator: | Nonny Hogrogian |

Bibliographic Information: Macmillan, New York, 1971

| | |
|---|---|
| Summary: | This retelling of a favorite Armenian folktale was awarded the Caldecott Medal. The story, a cumulative tale, focuses on a red fox that stole milk from an old farm woman who, in turn, cut off his tail. In order to regain his tail, the fox spends the day bargaining with a variety of characters. |
| Interest Level: | Grades K–3 |

---

1.  Pre-Reading Activity:

    Involve students in a game in which each student must relate the responses of the students before him/her and then add his/her own response. For example, you may begin the game with the line, "I went on a picnic and brought..." The first student lists an object beginning with "A," such as "apple." The next student responds by saying, "I went on a picnic and brought an apple and a banana (B)." The game continues until each student has had the opportunity to respond. Explain that, in a way, this is similar to a cumulative tale, in which items or events are added to previous items or events and keep repeating throughout the story. Introduce *One Fine Day*, telling students that this is an example of a cumulative tale.

2.  Learning Activities:

    a.  Read the story to children and have them retell the events. Put these events on a chart, cut them apart and scramble them. Have students take turns placing the events in the proper order. Story sequencing can also be done using a flannel board and cut-outs of the various characters, with a piece of felt attached to the back of each picture. Students can retell the story as they place the characters on the board and move the fox from character to character.

b.   Once students are quite familiar with the tale, assign them different roles: the fox, the old woman, the cow, the field, the stream, the maiden, the peddler, the hen, and the miller. Reread the story, encouraging students to take the parts of the character assigned, and create a dialogue for him/her.

c.   Ask students what might happen if the story were to take place in the city instead of in the country? For example, have them imagine that a cat stole milk from a local store. What might happen next? Record their responses to this, or to a similar scenario. Next, place each event students suggest on a different piece of large, unlined chart paper, being sure to include the events that preceded it. Allow students to illustrate one of the pages to create a cumulative tale — *One Fine Day…In the City.*

d.   Help students locate Armenia on a map. Ask each child to find one piece of information about Armenia that they find interesting. As each child shares the information, add it to a class chart. However, encourage each child to repeat the facts listed on the chart before adding his/her own, thereby creating a cumulative verse.

e.   Have students imagine that the fox did not get his tail back. Have each one take on the role of the fox and explain to his friends what happened to his tail. Encourage creativity!

3.   Discussion Questions

a.   Do you think the fox's punishment fit the crime? Why or why not?

b.   If you had been the woman, how would you punish the fox?

c.   When people think of a fox, what words come to mind? How does the fox in the story compare with the idea of foxes that most people have?

d.   What do you think the fox learned from his experience? What did you learn?

e.   Does the title of the story seem to fit? Why or why not? What title would you give this folktale?

---

| | |
|---|---|
| Title: | *The Seven Chinese Brothers* |
| Genre: | Traditional Literature — Folktale |
| Author: | A Chinese folktale, retold by Margaret Mahy |
| Illustrator: | Jean and Mou-sien Tseng |

Bibliographic Information: Scholastic, New York, 1990

| | |
|---|---|
| Summary: | Seven brothers, each with an amazing power, combine their talents to fool Ch'in Shih Huang, a cruel emperor of China who was responsible for initiating the construction of the Great Wall of China. |
| Interest Level: | Grades 2–6 |

---

1.   Pre-Reading Activity:

Guide students in locating China on a map. Create a cluster of words about China by encouraging students to generate words that reflect their knowledge and understanding of the country.

2. Learning Activities:

   a. In groups, have students research the Great Wall of China. Have each group create a model of the Great Wall using items such as Legos, blocks, etc. Also, have each group write one paragraph that summarizes the information they found most interesting about the Great Wall and its creation. Display the summary along with their model.

   b. Create a Readers Theatre script for *Seven Chinese Brothers*. Assign students different parts and have them create a cover for their scripts that reflects the story in some way.

   c. Have students create an eighth Chinese brother. What would his power be? How could he use it? Have students create a sequel to the story that will incorporate the eighth brother and his amazing ability. Have students share their sequel through storytelling or in written form.

   d. Have students create a large class collage of China. They may wish to locate pictures to represent many of the words they generated in the pre-reading activity. Encourage students to include any materials and patterns that reflect the tale of *The Seven Chinese Brothers*, other folktales of China, and the country of China in general. For example, their collage might include pieces of brocaded cloth and a wallpaper border of flowers.

3. Discussion Questions

   a. What does the story tell you about the Chinese attitude toward family? (Family unity is extremely important and each member is highly respected.)

   b. What other values of the Chinese people does this tale reflect?

   c. Of all the powers displayed by the seven brothers, which do you feel was most important? Why?

   d. If you could have any one power, which would you like to have? Explain.

---

Title:        *Saint George and the Dragon*

Genre:      Traditional Literature — Folktale

Author:     An English folktale, retold by Margaret Hodges

Illustrator:    Trina Schart Hyman

Bibliographic Information: Little, Brown and Company, Boston, 1984

Summary:    In fourth-century England, Saint George battles the monstrous dragon that has been destroying the land of princess Una.

Interest Level:   Grades 2–6

---

1. Pre-Reading Activity:

   Ask students, "What is a dragon?" Have them create several lists in which they describe a dragon, compare it (with another creature), associate it (with other creatures or things), and list its parts. Have students share their lists.

2. Learning Activities:

   a. Draw children's attention to the decorated borders of the pages in this book. Among these pictures is agrimony or the fairy wand, which was used as a charm against serpents. As St. George lies wounded in the stream, the borders depict mandrake, which was considered to be an anesthetic. You can request the "Saint George and The Dragon's Guide to Flowers and Herbs," which explains the borders of the book, from Little, Brown and Co., Children's Marketing Dept., 34 Beacon St., Boston, MA. 02108. Involve students in studying the borders, making hypotheses as to the reasons why certain items are included, and in locating information to prove or disprove their hypotheses.

b.  Read aloud the description of the dragon on page 15. Have students create their own illustration of the dragon based solely on the description. Mount their pictures on construction paper and cover them with contact paper to create individual place mats.

c.  Have students create a folktale based on the dragon's point of view. Have them illustrate their story with borders that are appropriate to the tale.

d.  Read other folktales involving dragons (see general references). Have students compare the way stories that originated in Europe differ from those from Asia (for example, *The Dragon's Robe* [Lattimore, 1990]) in their treatment and attitude toward the dragon.

e.  Involve students in reading other tales dealing with dragons. Have the class create a large dragon costume into which many children can fit. Allow one child at a time to come out from under the costume and give a summary or "booktalk" about a dragon story he or she read.

f.  Saint George is the patron saint of England. He was a real person — a highly respected soldier during the crusades. Introduce students to the life and times of Saint George, who lived during the time of the crusades and knighthood. Have students create a diorama that reflects an event in the story and/or an event in his life.

g.  The illustrations in the story are quite powerful. Have each student select one illustration from the book that he/she thinks best captures the mood and meaning of the story. Tell students they must convince a team of judges (classmates) to agree with their choices.

3.  Discussion Questions

a.  Saint George was the patron saint of England. What is meant by the term "patron saint?" (The protector of the land)

b.  Why do you think George was selected as the patron saint of England? What qualities did George possess that were respected by the people?

c.  This version of *Saint George and the Dragon*, illustrated by Trina Schart Hyman, won the Caldecott Medal as the most outstanding picture book of 1984. What was so special about the illustrations that the book earned the Caldecott Medal?

d.  What does the tale tell you about the England of long ago? (People used plants and herbs for medicinal purposes; courage and bravery were respected over all else; it was a time of knights and the belief that good triumphs over evil; and so forth.)

**Culminating Activity:**   Involve students in a "fractured folktale" festival as they create new versions of folktales from around the world. In a fractured folktale, one or more elements of the story are changed. Read students the folktale "The Three Little Pigs." Then, read them the fractured version, *The True Story of the 3 Little Pigs!* by Jon Scieszka. Next, involve them in a readers theatre of "The Really, Really, Really, True Story of the Three Little Pigs," pages 139-141, (from *Frantic Frogs and Other Frankly Fractured Folktales for Readers Theatre* by Anthony D. Fredericks, Teacher Ideas Press, 1993), in which the story has been "slightly" transformed. Have students (in groups ) create a fractured version of a favorite folktale they became familiar with through this unit and present it as a readers theatre. To introduce their readers theatre, each group should create a sign with the name of the folktale, its country of origin, and decorated with items and pictures representative of the story and the culture from which it came.Combine all the scripts for a class version of *Frankly Fractured Folktales for Readers Theatre* and keep it in your class library for future reference.

# The Really, Really <u>Really</u> True Story of the Three Little Pigs

Staging:
   The narrator is at a lectern or podium near the front of the staging area. The three pigs are on stools or chairs. The wolf is standing and moves back and forth among the other characters.

|  |  |  |
|---|---|---|
| Very Smart | Average | Not Too Bright |
| Pig | Pig | Pig |
| X | X | X |

Mean and Grouchy
Wolf
X

Narrator
X

| | |
|---|---|
| **Narrator:** | A long time ago, when fairy tales used to be inhabited by animals who could talk and think, there lived these three pigs. Yeah, yeah, yeah, I know what you're saying — each of them built a house and along came this mean old wolf with incredibly bad breath who blows down the first two houses because they weren't built according to the local zoning laws and then tries to blow down the third house, which is, incidentally, made of reinforced concrete, not bricks, and he eventually falls into a big pot of boiling water and the three pigs live happily ever after, at least until their mother finds out what they've been doing and sends them to bed without their dinner. Well, that's probably the story you heard when you were a tiny tyke, but that's not the really real story. Actually, your parents couldn't tell you the really real story 'cause it was filled with all kinds of violence and a couple of bad words. Well, now that you're all grown up and very mature, we're going to tell you the really, really, <u>really</u> true story of the Three Little Pigs — but, of course, we're going to have to leave out all those bad words. |
| | So anyway, one day these three brothers who, as you know by now, were pigs — and, as you also know, they were talking pigs — were sitting in the living room of their mother's four-bedroom condominium reading some of the latest issues of *Better Pigs and Gardens* and the *New Porker*. And that's where the really, really, <u>really</u> true story of the Three Little Pigs begins. |
| **Very Smart Pig:** | Hey, brothers, you know it's about time we moved out of Mom's house. We're grown up now and ready to go out into the world to seek our fortune. And besides, Mom's getting on in years and won't be able to support us much longer. In fact, pretty soon we're going to have to think about putting her in the Old Porker's Home. |
| **Average Pig:** | You know, brother, you've got a point there. Besides, we wouldn't have much of a story if all we did was sit around Mom's living room |

|  | discussing the color of her drapes or "500 Uses for Bacon Bits." |
|---|---|
| Not Too Bright Pig: | Yeah! It sure is getting crowded in here, too. You know, because we're pigs we don't clean up after ourselves, so we track mud all over the place, and we make funny grunting noises for most of the day. I think the neighbors are beginning to wonder what we really do. We better move out while we still can. |
| Narrator: | And so it was that the three brothers decided to move out of Mom's house and buy some property in the country. The real estate agent assured them that the land was ideal — rolling hills, lots of space, and no strange or weird animals in the nearby forest. |
| Mean and Grouchy Wolf: | (insulted) Hey, wait a minute! Aren't I supposed to have a place in this story, too? |
| Narrator: | (forcefully) Hey, keep your shirt on! We'll sneak you over from the Red Riding Hood story, and no one will be the wiser. In fact, if you play your cards right, you can finish this story and get back to Grandma's house in time to hop back into her pajamas and wait for that naive Riding Hood girl to come along. |
| Mean and Grouchy Wolf: | Okay, okay. But make it quick, buster. You know what the wolf's union says about me doing double time. |
| Narrator: | Anyway, as I was saying, the three pigs began to build their dream houses along the country road that ran through their property. |
| Not too Bright Pig: | You know, I'm not very smart, so I think I'll build my house out of straw. So, who care if it blows down in the first windstorm of the season or leaks like a sieve in the winter. |
| Mean and Grouchy Wolf: | (insulted) Hey, now hold on a minute! Do you honestly think I would want to waste my time with that little porker? You know, I've got far better things to do with my time than wait until that not too bright pig builds his weak, little house of straw for me to come prancing down the lane to huff and puff and blow it down. That's got to be an absolute waste of my finely tuned acting talents! |
| Narrator: | Well then, what if we move this story along and see what Average Pig does. |
| Mean and Grouchy Wolf: | Well, okay, but this better be a lot more interesting than that little ham bone with the pile of hay in his backyard. |
| Narrator: | Settle down! Don't have a coronary! Just let me see what I can do with this part of the story. It's all yours, Average Pig. |
| Average Pig: | Thanks. While you guys were talking I was walking around my property gathering some sticks and branches and tree limbs. I think I'll build my house out of this stuff. It may not be too sturdy, but at least it won't fall down the fist time I slam the front door. Of course, the local fire marshal may have a thing or two to say about it. |
| Mean and Grouchy Wolf: | (angrily) Now just a gosh darn minute here! You want me to believe that this walking pile of pork chops is really going to build a house of sticks so that I can come along and blow it down just like I was supposed to do with his brother's house? Come on, get real! I mean, what a waste! |

Why would I even want to take the time to huff and puff my way around this stupid little structure? You know, you guys are really starting to tick me off. All I can say is, this story better get a lot better and real fast, too!

| | |
|---|---|
| Narrator: | Boy, you sure do get pushy. You know, this is supposed to be a story about the Three Little Pigs, not about some wolf with an attitude. |
| Mean and Grouchy Wolf: | Look, wise guy, how'd you like me to nibble on your face? If I want to take the lead role in this story, then I'm going to. After all, just look what my brothers and I have been putting up with in all those other stories. |
| Narrator: | *(indignantly)* Now, just hold on. We still have to see what Very Smart Pig does with this part in the story. |
| Very Smart Pig: | You know, they don't call me Very Smart Pig for nothin'. In fact, I'm the guy they call on to bring home the bacon… get it? Bring home the bacon! So, while this hotshot wolf was thinking about huffing and puffing down some flimsy houses built by my two less than brilliant brothers, I was constructing a house completely out of bricks and steel and reinforced cement. Ain't nobody going to blow this baby down! I mean this beauty is built!!! And any wolf who has any kind of smarts would do well to just keep his distance. I mean we're talkin' SOLID here! |
| Mean and Grouchy Wolf: | *(very angrily)* Look, I'm not takin' any gruff from some lard-faced pig. I'll huff and puff my way across the whole county if I want to. I'll blow down, damage, and destroy as many houses as I want. |
| Very Smart Pig: | *(angrily)* Yeah, you and whose army? |
| Mean and Grouchy Wolf: | *(angrily)* Hey, watch it, pork breath. How would you like me to turn you into a pile of ham sandwiches. |
| Very Smart Pig: | *(very angrily)* Yeah, just go ahead and try it. |
| Mean and Grouchy Wolf: | *(extremely angry)* Just watch me. |
| Narrator: | All day long Very Smart Pig and Mean and Grouchy Wolf argued about who was the strongest and who was the smartest. In fact, Wolf and Pig went far into the night with their argument, and for all we know they're still arguing away. But, of course, that would never make for an exciting story for the kiddies. So a long time ago a bunch of fairy tale writers got together and decided to spice up the story a bit and turn the wolf into a door-to-door salesperson with an asthma problem. The rest, as they say, is history. And now, you know the really, really, <u>really</u> true story of the Three Little Pigs. |

*Source:*  Fredericks, A. (1993). *Frantic frogs and other frankly fractured folktales for readers theatre.* Englewood, CO.: Teacher Ideas Press. Used by permission.

# Supplemental Literature

(*Note*: Since folktales are enjoyed by children of all ages — even though they understand them at different levels — the following literature is not divided into age groups. For single-title books, the country of origin is indicated to facilitate your lessons.)

## Collections:

Booss, C., ed. (1984). *Scandinavian legends and folk tales.* New York: Crown.

Clarkson, A., and Cross, G., compilers. (1980). *World folktales.* New York: Scribner's.
> In addition to folktales from around the world, this collection includes notes, comments, and lists of parallel stories.

Cole, J., compiler. (1982). *Best-loved folktales of the world.* Illustrated by J. K. Schwarz. New York: Doubleday.
> A collection of 200 folktales, divided by geographical location and indexed by category.

Colum, P. (1964). *The Arabian nights: Tales of wonder and magnificence.* Illustrated by L. Ward. New York: Macmillan.

Grimm, J., and Grimm, W. (1987). *Grimm's fairy tales.* Translated by J. Zipes. Illustred by J.B. Gruelle. New York: Bantam.
> Includes 210 famous original folktales, plus forty tales never before published in English.

Haviland, V. (1959). *Favorite fairy tales around the world.* Illustrated by S.D. Schindler.
> An anthology selected from a sixteen-volume series of tales from all over the world.

Impey, R. (1992). *Read me a fairy tale: A child's book of classic fairy tales.* Illustrated by I. Berk. New York: Scholastic.
> Fourteen best-loved tales, including "Jack and the Beanstalk," "The Frog Prince," and "Rumplestiltskin."

Lang, A., Ed. *The blue fairy book.* (1959) Illustrated by R. Lonette. New York: Random House.
> One of a series of collections of tales from all over the world. Each title in the series includes a different color.

Massignon, G., ed. (1968). *Folktales of France.* Chicago: University of Chicago Press.
> One in the *Folktales of the World* series.

Mayhew, J. (1993). *Koshka's Tales: Stories from Russia.* Illustrated by J. Mayhew. New York: Kingfisher Books.

Mayo, M. (1993). *Magical tales from many lands.* Illustrated by J. Ray. New York: Dutton.
> Includes tales from around the world, representing a variety of traditions, including stories from Turkey, Japan, Africa, Scotland, France, China, and Russia.

McCaughrean, G. (1982). *One hundred and one Arabian nights.* Illustrated by S. Lavis. Oxford: Oxford Univeristy Press.
> A collection of stories told to the king by his queen, Shahrezad.

Opie, I., and Opie, P. (1974). *The classic fairy tales.* Oxford: Oxford University Press.

Ozaki, Y.T., compiler. (1970). The Japanese fairy book. Illustrated by Y. Kurosaki. Rutland, Vermont: Charles Tuttle Co.

Passes, D. (1993). Dragons: Truth, myth, and legend. Illustrated by W. Anderson. Racine, Wisconsin: Western Publishing.
> Eleven dragon stories from around the world are included.

Perrault, C. (1989). *Cinderella and other tales from Perrault.* Illustrated by M. Hague. New York: Holt.

Perrault, C. (1993). The complete fairy tales of Charles Perrault. Illustrated by S. Holmes. New York: Clarion.

Sadler, C. adapter. (1982). *Treasure mountain: Folktales from Southern China.* Illustrated by C. Mung Yun. New York: Atheneum.
> Six Chinese tales illustrated with pencil drawings.

Sakade, F., ed. (1958). *Japanese children's favorites stories.* Illustrated by Y. Kurosaki. Rutland, Vermont: Charles Tuttle Co.

Singer, I. B. (1966). *Zlateh the goat.* Illustrated by M. Sendak. New York: Harper. [Poland]
   Seven tales based on middle-European Jewish stories.
Wyndham, L. comp. (1970). *Tales the people tell in Russia.* Ill. by A. Antal. New York: Messner.
Yep, L. (1989). *The rainbow people.* Illustrated by David Wiesner. New York: Harper.
   Twenty tales from China are adapted from oral narratives transcribed in Oakland's Chinatown.

## Single Titles:

Aardema, V. (1975). *Why mosquitoes buzz in people's ears.* Illustrated by L. and D. Dillon. New York: Dial.
   [Africa]
   The tale of a mosquito whose tall tales led to many problems in the jungle and resulted in the mosquito
   buzz we hear today.
Chin, C. (1993). *China's bravest girl.* Illustrated by T. Arai. Emeryville, Calif.: Children's Book Press. [China]
   The legend of Hua Mu Lan, who took her father's place as a soldier and became a general.
Climo, S. (1989). *The Egyptian Cinderella.* Illustrated by R. Heller. New York: Harper. [Egypt]
   This tale of Rhodopis and the rose-red slippers is one of the world's oldest Cinderella stories.
d'Aulaire, I., and d'Aulaire, E. (1972). *Trolls.* New York: Dell. [Scandinavia]
de Beaumont, Mme. (1988). *Beauty and the beast.* Illustrated by M. Hague. New York: Holt. [France]
   The tale of a young girl who sees the beauty beneath the skin of a prince who has been transformed into
   an ugly beast
de Beaumont, Mme. (1989). *Beauty and the beast.* Illustrated by J. Brett. Boston: Houghton Mifflin. [France]
de Beaumont, Mme. (1989). *Beauty and the beast.* Retold and illustrated by M. Gerstein. New York: Dutton.
   [France]
Grahame, K. (1938) . The reluctant dragon. Illustrated by E. Shepard. New York: Holiday. [England]
   In this reversal of the tale of Saint George, a pacifist dragon wants to help the townspeople.
Grimm, J., and Grimm, W. (1990). *Hansel and Gretel.* Retold and ill. by J. Marshall. Dial: New York. [Germany]
   Two young children get lost in the woods and discover a house made of candies and cakes.
Grimm, J., and Grimm, W. (1982). *Hansel and Gretel.* Illustrated by P. Galdone. New York: McGraw-Hill.
   [Germany]
Grimm, J., and Grimm, W. (1983). Little Red Cap. Illustrated by L. Zwerger. New York: Morrow. [Germany]
Grimm, J., and Grimm, W. (1987). *Red Riding Hood.* Retold and illustrated by J. Marshall. New York: Dial.
   [Germany]
   A young girl on the way to her grandmother's house encounters a wolf.
Grimm, J., and Grimm, W. (1983). *Little Red Riding Hood.* Illustrated by T. Hyman. New York: Holiday.
   [Germany]
Grimm, J., and Grimm, W. (1993). *Iron Hans.* Illustrated by M. Heyer. New York: Viking. [Germany]
   A mysterious wild man sends a boy out to find his way in the world.
Grimm, J. and Grimm, W. (1982). *Rapunzel.* Retold by B. Bogasky. Illustrated by T. Hyman. New York:
   Holiday. [Germany]
   The tale of a girl in a tower whose lover climbs her rope of hair.
Grimm, J., and Grimm, W. (1991). *Rumplestiltskin.* Retold and Illustrated by J. Langley. New York: Harper.
   [Germany]
   A miller's daughter spins straw into gold with the help of a strange man.
   She must learn his name or lose her first-born child to him.
Grimm, J., and Grimm, W. (1986). *Rumplestiltskin.* Retold and illustrated by P. Zelinski. New York: Dutton.
   [Germany]
Grimm, J., and Grimm, W. (1972). *Snow-White and the Seven Dwarfs.* Translated by R. Jarrell. Ill. by N.E. Brukert.
   New York: Farrar, Straus and Giroux. [Germany]
Hogrogian, N. (1988). *The cat who loved to sing.* New York: Knopf. [Russia]
   A cumulative tale of a cat who starts trading a thorn in its foot for a needle.

Kimmel, E. (1988). *Anansi and the moss-covered rock.* Illustrated by J. Stevens. New York: Holiday House. [Africa]
> Anansi, the spider, uses the power of a magic rock to steal the food of other animals.

Kimmel, E. (1991). *Baba Yaga.* Illustrated by M. Lloyd. New York: Holiday House. [Russia]
> A Russian tale with elements of Cinderella and Hansel and Gretel.

Lang, A. adapter. (1981). *Aladdin and the wonderful lamp.* Illustrated by E. LeCain. New York: Viking. [Arabia]
> The story of a poor boy whose life is changed when he discovers a genie in a magical lamp.

Lattimore, D. (1990). *The dragon's robe.* New York: Harper. [China]
> A poor weaver saves her people when she weaves a robe for the rain dragon.

Lawson, J. (1993). *The dragon's pearl.* Paintings by P. Morin. New York: Clarion. [China]
> Xiao finds a shimmering pearl that forever changes his destiny.

Leaf, M. (1987). *Eyes of the dragon.* Illustrated by E. Young. New York: Lothrop. [China]
> A Chinese painter agrees to paint a portrait of the Dragon King who controls thunder, lightning, and rain.

Louis, Al-Ling. (1982). *Yeh-Shen: A Cinderella story from China.* Illustrated by Ed Young. New York: Philomel. [China]
> A version of Cinderella from China.

McCoy, K. (1993). *A tale of two tengu.* Niles, Ill.: Whitman and Co. [Japan]
> Two Japanese goblins, called Tengu, argue constantly, each trying to better the other.

McDermott, G. (1975). *The stonecutter: A Japanese folk tale.* New York: Penquin. [Japan]
> A lowly stonecutter was happy with his work until a princess passed his way in a magnificent procession. Then he wished for wealth and his wish was heard by the spirit who lives in the mountain.

Mayer, M. (1989). *The twelve dancing princesses.* Illustrated by K.Y. Craft. New York: Morrow. [France]
> The king's twelve daughters, under an evil spell, wear holes in their dancing slippers and become ill.

Mosel, A., ed. (1968). *Tikki Tikki Tembo.* Illustrated by B. Lent. New York: Holt. [China]
> This humorous tale explains why the Chinese have short names.

Ness, E. (1965). *Tom Tit Tot.* New York: Scribner's. [England]
> A variation on the tale of Rumplestiltskin.

Pearson, S. (1989) *Jack and the beanstalk.* Illustrated by J. Warhola. New York: Simon and Schuster. [England]
> Young Jack climbs a beanstalk and comes face to face with a giant from whom he steals the magic harp and the goose that lays golden eggs.

Perrault, C. (1954). *Cinderella.* Translated and illustrated by M. Brown. New York: Macmillan. [France]
> A young girl, mistreated by her stepmother and stepsisters, goes to the ball with the help of her fairy god mother.

Perrault, C. (1985). *Cinderella.* Retold by A. Ehrlich. Illustrated by S. Jeffers. New York: Dial. [France]

Perrault, C. (1973). *Cinderella, or the little glass slipper.* Illustrated. by E. Le Cain. New York: Bradbury. [France]

Price, L. (1990). *Aida.* Illustrated by L. and D. Dillon. San Diego: HBJ. [Africa]
> Aida, the Ethiopian princess, is captured by Egyptian soldiers and forced into slavery. The story is based on the opera by Giuseppe Verdi.

Robbins, R. (1960). *Baboushka and the three kings.* Illustrated by N. Sidjakow. Boston: Parnassus. [Russia].
> The tale of a selfish old woman and the Wise Men.

Shute, L. (1988). *Clever Tom and the leprechaun.* New York: Lothrop. [Ireland]
> Tom catches a leprechaun and tries to obtain his treasure.

Steptoe, J. adapter. (1987). *Mufaro's beautiful daughters: An African tale.* N.Y.: Lothrop. [Africa]
> A version of Cinderella.

Stevents, J. (1987). *The three billy goats gruff.* Illustrated by J. Stevents. San Diego: HBJ. [Norway]
> Three billy goats attempt to cross the bridge over an evil troll.

Wade, G. (1993). *The wonderful bag.* New York: Bedrick/Blackie. [Arabia]
> Two men claim to own the same bag and must prove their ownership by identifying the contents.

Yep, L. (1993). *The shell woman and the king.* Illustrated by Y. Ming-Yi. New York: Dial. [China]
A brave woman who has the power to transform herself into large seashells outwits a greedy king in this tale of adventure.

Young, E. (1989). *Lon Po Po: A Red Riding Hood story from China.* New York: Philomel. [China]

Zemach, H. (1973). *Duffy and the devil: A Cornish tale.* Retold and illustrated by M. Zemach. New York: Farrar, 1973. [England]
A Cornish version of Rumplestiltskin.

# MINI-THEMES

The mini-themes selected focus specifically on the folktales of two groups of Americans: the Native Americans who were already here and the African-Americans who originally were brought to this land as slaves. Their tales reflect their experiences and their cultures, telling of their hopes, their tragedies, and the triumph of the human spirit. A third mini-theme focuses on those tales that reflect America itself — tales that are bold, humorous, and bigger than life — the tall tales of those who tamed our land.

## Folktales of Native Americans

More than 400 years ago, millions of Indians, comprising thousands of tribes and clans, were spread across North and South America. These diverse populations, known today as Native Americans, had their own cultures and traditions as reflected in their folklore that was handed down from generation to generation. Many of the folktales of the Native-Americans resemble creation myths — stories that explain the origin of man and beast. Each tribe had its own stories to help them make sense of the world around them.

**References**:

Bierhorst, J. (1987). *Doctor Coyote: A Native American Aesop's fables.* Illustrated by W. Watson. New York: Macmillan.

Bruchac, J. (1993). *The first strawberries: A Cherokee story.* Illustrated by A. Vojtech. New York: Dial.

Bruchac, J. (1993). *Flying with the eagle, racing the great bear.* Illustrated by M. Jacob. New York: Troll.

Caduto, M., and Bruchac, J. (1991). *Native American stories* (from keepers of the earth). Illustrated by J. K. Fadden. Golden, Colorado: Fulcrum.

Caduto, M., and Bruchac, J. (1991). *Native American animal stories* (from keepers of the animals). Illustrated by J. K. Fadden. Golden, Colorado: Fulcrum.

dePaola, T. (1988). *The legend of the Indian paintbrush.* New York: Putnam's Songs.

Esbensen, B. J. (1989). *Ladder to the sky.* Illustrated by H. Davis. Boston: Little, Brown.

Goble, P. (1978). *The girl who loved wild horses.* New York: Bradbury.

Goble, P. (1983). *Star boy.* New York: Bradbury.

Harris, C. (1979). *Once more upon a totem.* Illustrated by D. Tait. New York: Atheneum.

McDermott, G. (1984). *Arrow to the sun.* New York: Viking.

Robe, R.Y. (1979). *Tonweya and the eagles and other Lakota tales.* Illustrated by J. Pinkney. New York: Dial.

Root, P. (1993). *Coyote and the magic words.* Illustrated by S. Speidel. New York: Lothrop, Lee and Shepard.

Roth, S. (1990). *The story of light.* New York: Morrow.

Schoolcraft, H. R. (1970). *The ring in the prairie: A Shawnee legend.* Illustrated by L. Dillon and D. Dillon. New York: Dial.

Taylor, H. P. (1993). *Coyote places the stars.* New York: Bradbury.

Troughton, J. (1986). *How rabbit stole the fire.* New York: Bedrick/Blackie.

Van Laan, N. (1993). *Buffalo dance.* Illustrated by B. Vidal. Boston: Little, Brown and Co.

Yolen, J. (1990). *Sky dogs*. Illustrated by B. Moser. San Diego: HBJ.

Wood, M. (1992). *Spirits, heroes, and hunters* (from North American Indian mythology). Illustrated by J. Sibbick. New York: Peter Bedrick Books.

Young, E. (1993). *Moon mother*. New York: Harper.

**Activities:**

1.  As their folktales indicate, the Native Americans had a tremendous respect for nature. Read aloud several folktales and whenever possible give children the opportunity to experience the setting (for example, a tree, a pond, etc.) firsthand. Have students select their favorite folktale and use objects from nature — for example, a leaf, a stone, a piece of wood, etc. to create a collage or design that in some way reflects the folktale selected.

2.  The Native Americans had a special relationship with the animals that shared their lands. In many Native American tales the animals created the people. Often their tales refer to animals as their relatives and teachers. Have students select one of the animals that played an important part in the folktales of the American Indian and have students create a mini-book that relates factual information about this animal.

3.  Have students retell one of the folktales involving the animal selected in activity 2 and retell the tale using the factual information known about the animal and how it really acts. Students can create an illustration to accompany their storytelling.

4.  Discuss the origins of many things in our world as reflected in the folktales of Native Americans. Using one or more of the characters included in their folktales, have students create their own folktale to explain the origin of any natural phenomena, such as the Grand Canyon, waterfalls, rivers, and so forth.

5.  The Native Americans sang songs to honor the animals from which they received so many gifts. After reading several folktales of Native Americans, have students make a list of all the gifts *we* receive from the animal and insect kingdoms even today. Take students on a nature walk and record the voices of the birds, insects and other wildlife. Have students use these sounds to create an "Ode to Nature" and use various materials to create musical accompaniment. Students may also wish to create a dance to accompany the music.

6.  As students read various folktales of Native Americans, have them add to a chart that is divided into five areas: clothing; food; shelter; customs; crafts. Divide students into one of these five groups (or groups based on other areas you and the students would like to investigate) and involve them in the following activities, based on the knowledge and insights gained through the reading of Native American folktales. The work of each group can be combined to create a day to honor our Native Americans.

    Group 1 — *Clothing:* Students may dress up in the traditional garments worn by several of the many Native American tribes. Divide the entire class into various tribes and suggest appropriate clothing for each group.

    Group 2 — *Food:* Students may wish to bring in foods made with corn (corn chips, popcorn, corn bread, etc.), as well as other foods representative of Native American diets.

    Group 3 — *Shelter:* Students may wish to create models of the various types of housing in which Native Americans lived, such as pueblos, longhouses, and teepees.

    Group 4 — *Customs:* Students may create a reader's theatre, story theatre, puppet show, or other dramatic form to retell a folktale that includes the customs/beliefs of various tribes.

    Groups 5 — *Crafts:* Students can coordinate the efforts of the class to make one or more of the crafts popular with Native Americans.

7. As a class, create a totem pole that gives tribute to the many aspects of nature that the Native Americans honored.

# Afro-American Folktales

When the slaves of Africa were first brought to this county they continued to tell the tales of their youth, tales of talking- beasts that metaphorically offered hope and expressed the sorrow, loneliness, and fear of a people. In *The People Could Fly*, for example, Virginia Hamilton has collected the tales that "represent the main body of black folktales..." (p. xi) — stories that tell of a rich heritage and of the strength and perseverance of a people. The activities suggested will give students an understanding of the beauty, humor, and spirit of the African-Americans as reflected in their tales.

## References:

Bang, M. (1976). *Wiley and the hairy man.* New York: Macmillan.

Hamilton, V. (1993). *Many thousand gone.* Illustrated by L. Dillon and D. Dillon. New York: Knopf.

Hamilton, V. (1985). *The people could fly: American black folktales.* Illustrated by L. Dillon and D. Dillon. New York: Knopf.

Harris, J. C. (1986). *Jump! the adventures of Brer Rabbit.* Adapted by V.D. Parks and M. Jones. Illustrated by B. Moser. San Diego: HBJ.

Harris, J.C. (1987). *Jump again! More adventures of Brer Rabbit.* Adapted by V.D. Parks. Illustrated by B. Moser. San Diego: HBJ.

Harris, J.C. (1989). *Jump on over! The adventures of Brer Rabbit and his family.* Adapted by V.D. Parks. Illustrated by B. Moser. San Diego: HBJ.

Keats, E. (1965). *John Henry: An American Legend.* New York: Pantheon.

Lester, J. (1972). *The knee-high man and other tales.* Illustrated by R. Pinto. New York: Dial.

Lester, J. (1988). *More tales of Uncle Remus: Further adventures of Brer Rabbit, his friends, enemies, and others.* Illustrated by J. Pickney. New York: Dial.

Lester, J. (1987). *The tales of Uncle Remus: The adventures of Brer Rabbit.* Illustrated by J. Pickney. New York: Dial.

Rees, E. (1967). *Brer Rabbit's tricks.* Illustrated by E. Gorey. W.R. Scott.

San Souci, R. ( 1989 ). *The talking eggs.* Illustrated by J. Pinkney. New York: Dial.

Sanfield, S. (1989). *The adventures of High John the Conqueror.* Illustrated by J. Ward. New York: Orchard.

## Activities:

1. Many of the folktales of African-Americans include animals that took on characteristics of the people they found on the plantation where they were originally brought as slaves. The rabbit known as Brer Rabbit, for example, was small and helpless compared to the strong bear and sly fox, but the rabbit's intelligence and creativity enabled him to often outwit the other animals and survive. On a class chart, similar to the one on page 148, have students list the animal characters, their main qualities, and the person(s) they think the animal was supposed to represent. Next, have each student select one of the animals and create a simile in which the animal is compared to another animal or object with similar qualities: _____ (animal character from folktale) is like a _____ because _____. Have students illustrate their simile with a picture of the animal character from the folktale and the object it was compared with.

| Animal | Qualities | Person/Group the Animal Represents |
|--------|-----------|-------------------------------------|
| Brer Rabbit | Smart, clever | Slaves |
| Bear | Powerful, greedy | Slave owners |
|  |  |  |
|  |  |  |

2. Stories of John the Conqueror (John de Conquer) were popular among slaves. After the Civil War, the character of John often took the place of Brer Rabbit in tales (see activity 1 above). John was a slave but spent most of his time tricking his master. Read several tales of John the Conqueror (see Sanfield, 1989 and Hamilton, 1985). Have each student create a one-page conversation between himself/herself and John, and bind these together into a book, *John and I.*

3. "Juneteenth" is the day on which descendants of slaves in the South remember the Emancipation, which gave them their freedom from slavery. Hold a Juneteenth day and have each student (or group of students) retell a favorite African-American tale.

4. Have students locate Africa on the map and involve students in learning about the history of slavery in the United States. Explain the underground railroad, the complex system through which many slaves escaped to freedom, by reading aloud such books as *Aunt Harriet's Underground Railroad in the Sky* by Faith Ringgold (Crown, 1992).

5. Ask students to locate a favorite illustration of a favorite African-American folktale. Have them recreate this picture and add a caption that either tells about the tale or about the event in the picture. Have students share their pictures and summarize the folktale from which it came.

## Tall Tales

Within our own country, tales have evolved that tell of the exploits of the lumberjacks, the railroad men, the cowboys, and others who have helped to make our country strong. Tales of these heroes matched the vastness of the country and their accomplishments were described in hyperbole. Paul Bunyan, Captain Stormalong, Mike Fink, Daniel Boone, Davy Crockett, Johnny Appleseed, Windwagon Smith, John Henry, and Pecos Bill embodied the American virtues of courage, fortitude, and ingenuity. Some of these heroes were real people; others, embodying a cornucopia of qualities, became real through the yarns spun about them. These tales, uniquely American, are often referred to as "tall tales."

### References:

Aliki. (1987). *The story of Johnny Appleseed.* New York: Prentice-Hall.
Dewey, A. (1984). *Febold Feboldson.* New York: Greenwillow.
Dewey, A. (1987). *Gib Morgan, oilman.* New York: Greenwillow.

Dewey, A. (1990). *The narrow escapes of Davy Crockett.* New York: Greenwillow.

Dewey, A. (1983). *Pecos Bill.* New York: Greenwillow.

Kellogg, S. (1988). *Johnny Appleseed.* New York: Morrow.

Kellogg, S. (1984). *Paul Bunyan.* New York: Morrow.

Kellogg, S. (1986). *Pecos Bill.* New York: Morrow.

Lindbergh, R. (1990). *Johnny Appleseed.* Illustrated by K. Jakobsen. Boston: Little, Brown.

McCloskey, R. (1963). *Burt Dow, deep-water man: A tale of the sea in the classic tradition.* New York: Viking.

Osborne, M. (1991). *American tall tales.* Wood engravings by M. McCurdy. New York: Knopf.

Purdy, C. (1985). *Iva Dunnit and the big wind.* Illustrated by S. Kellogg. New York: Dial.

Rounds, G. (1977), adapter. (1984). *The morning the sun refused to rise: An original Paul Bunyan tale.* New York: Holiday House.

Shapiro, I. (1962). *Heroes in American folklore.* Illustrated by D. McKay and J. Daugherty. New York: Messner.

Shephard, E. (1941). *Paul Bunyan.* Illustrated by R. Kent. San Diego: HBJ.

Stoutenburg, A. (1966). *American tall tales.* Illustrated by R. Powers. New York: Viking.

## Activities:

1. Read aloud several tall tales. To guide the students in gaining an appreciation for tall tales, ask them, "What do these stories have in common?" Ask each student to write his/her own definition of a tall tale and record the responses. Try to reach a group consensus.

2. Read several tall tales aloud and discuss the difference between fact and exaggeration. Have students read a tall tale with a partner and create a chart that lists actual facts from the story in the left-hand column and the exaggerations in the right-hand column. Have students illustrate the chart with a picture that represents their favorite exaggeration.

3. Ask students to imagine that they are visitors to the United States from another country. The only thing they know about the U.S.A. is what they got from reading the literature of the country — specifically its tall tales. In groups, have them write a newspaper article, with illustrations and captions, that tells the people in their country about Americans (for example, their clothing, climate, occupations, customs, geography, and the like).

4. Have students watch filmstrips of several tall tales. Have them select a favorite tall-tale character and create a caricature on TALL paper. Have them list several words and phrases that they believe best describe this character. Bind these together into a big book.

5. Have students create their own recipes for tall tales. Have them write it on poster paper and illustrate it with scenes from their favorite tall tales. (Example: Ingredients — one giant hero, three cups of exaggeration, five cups of imagination, four tablespoons of historical facts. Directions — Mix ingredients thoroughly and serve in large portions with a straight face. Serves thousands.)

6. Have students decide on an object(s) to represent each tall-tale character they have learned about. Have them place these objects on a map nearby the area where the character lived.

7. Discuss with students how the tall tales of the United States are thought to symbolize our country. Record their responses to the following: A tall tale is like America because _____ _____ .

# Primary Unit: Measurement and Sizes

**Theme:** MEASUREMENT AND SIZES

**Focus:** Students will become familiar with the various applications of measurement and how it relates to mathematics.

**Objectives:** On completion of this thematic unit, students will:

1. Recognize that measurement is important in their everyday life.

2. Be aware that measurement can be used in all aspects of life.

3. Learn about a variety of measurement tools (rulers, clocks, thermometers, scales, etc.) and how they are used.

**Initiating Activity:** Brainstorm, with the children, about vocabulary that relates to size — enormous, huge, tiny, etc. List these on the chalkboard. Then discuss different kinds of measurement that helps determine size, for example, weight, height, length, etc. Create a "Measurement Center" and provide the children with an opportunity to experiment with different types of measurement tools by providing a scale, tape measure/yard stick, etc.

## General Activities:

1. Divide the children into groups. Give each group the same size object (for example, a piece of paper, a chalkboard eraser, a pencil, etc.), or allow each group to select their own object. Then ask the group to find five objects that are larger than their selected object and five objects that are smaller. Make a display of each group's collection and discuss.

2. Using the objects collected in Activity 1, ask each group to put their objects in order from smallest to largest according to the same criteria. such as height, weight, thickness, etc.

3. Provide the children with large sheets of paper and then ask them to draw a picture of their families in the order of their sizes. Allow time to share.

4. Read books from the Supplemental Literature list such as *Big Gus and Little Gus* by Lee Lorenz, *The Little Girl and the Dragon* by Else Minarik, or *Revenge of the Small Small* by Jean Little. Then have the children discuss the advantages and disadvantages of being small and/or big.

5. Explain that people originally used their body parts to measure things. Have the children create their own measurement tools by tracing around their foot or hand and cutting out what they have traced. Tell the children to use their "body part" measuring tool to measure the width of their desk, height of a friend, length of an arm, etc. Prior to measuring, ask the children to estimate the height, width, length, or some other dimension of what they are measuring. You may want to have the children record their different measurements as follows:

| Object | Estimate | Actual Measurement |
|---|---|---|
|  |  |  |
|  |  |  |
|  |  |  |

6. Provide the children with a metric and non-metric ruler. Allow them to measure objects, using both rulers. Discuss the difference between the two rulers and the reason for having two measuring systems.

7. Provide the children with at least four containers of different sizes, (for example, tall and thin, short and fat). Ask them to hypothesize which container holds the most, which holds the least, and so on. After they have made their estimates, allow time for them to fill the container they think holds the most with water, rice, or sand, etc. Then tell them to test their other estimates by pouring the water, rice, sand into the other containers.

8. Using the vocabulary words related to size that were generated in the Initiating Activity, brainstorm about things that are enormous, huge, tiny, etc. Ask each student to select one size word and then complete the following statement and illustrate it, "(size word) is..." Their responses could be put together to make a class book. Have them give the book a clever title.

9. Provide a balance scale and then ask the children to put an object on one side of the scale, for example, a small rock. Tell the children to find another object they feel would weigh about the same as the small rock and then put it on the scale to check whether they were correct or not. Continue this activity, with children finding more balancing objects. Discuss the concept that size may not affect whether the scale balances or not (for example, a big ball of cotton or a big pile of feathers may weigh less than a smaller rock).

10. Provide a copy of the Guiness Book of World Records. Ask the children to find out such things as what is the heaviest and lightest animal, tallest building, shortest person, etc. Allow time to share their findings.

## Disucssion Questions:

1. What is the biggest object you have ever seen? Describe it.

2. What is the smallest object you have ever seen? Describe it.

3. Over the years, many tools have been developed to measure various things — time, weight, etc. What are some of these tools? Which of these tools is most important to you?

4. When you hear the word measure, what comes to mind?

| Title: | *Tiny for a Day* |
| --- | --- |
| Genre: | Picture Book |
| Author: | Dick Gackenbach |
| Bibliographic Information: | Clarion Books, New York, 1993 |
| Summary: | Stanley has a new invention that he uses to shrink things. He shrinks the dog, his sister, and finally himself. |
| Interest Level: | Grades K–3 |

1. **Pre-Reading Activity:**

   Read the title of the book and show the children the cover. Discuss the concept of tiny. Ask the children to name things that are tiny as you list them on the board. Remind them that tiny is a relative term and it depends on what an object is being compared to. For example, a fish may not be tiny, but when compared to a whale, it is truly tiny. Ask the children to fold a piece of paper in half and on each half draw something tiny (fish) and something large (whale).

2. **Learning Activities:**

   a. Sidney shrank his sister and his dog as well as himself. He came out of his machine being only three inches tall. Use a ruler to identify other things that are three inches tall and compare them to the height of Stanley.

   b. Discuss with the children the advantages and disadvantages of being tall and of being short. Make a list of these and then ask the children to write a story about either being short or being tall. Allow time to share stories.

   c. Stanley was only three inches tall after he shrank himself. Provide a yard stick and allow time to measure the height of all the children in the class. Record the children's height on a growth chart. Measure the children each month and compare heights from previous months.

   d. Help the children make a tiny book by cutting 3" x 3" pieces of paper for the pages. Ask the children to draw something tiny on their piece of paper and write the sentence, This is a tiny _____. Compile the pages into a class booklet titled "Our Tiny Book." Share the book with other classes.

3. **Discussion Questions:**

   a. What events in this story could really happen? Which events are make-believe?

   b. What are some things Stanley could do when he was short that he couldn't do when he was taller?

   c. What would your mother say if you did the things like Stanley did?

   d. Would you like to be Stanley's friend? Why or why not?

   e. Do you think Stanley liked being small?

| Title: | *Little Grunt and the Big Egg* |
| --- | --- |
| Genre: | Fairy Tale |
| Author: | Tomie de Paola |
| Bibliographic Information: | Holiday House, New York, 1990 |
| Summary: | Little Grunt, the smallest member of the Grunt Tribe, is sent out to gather eggs. He finds a very large egg and brings it home. Later that night, the egg hatches and out comes a dinosaur. Mama and Papa Grunt allow Little Grunt to keep the dinosaur as a pet until it grows too big for the cave. |
| Interest Level: | Grades K–3 |

1. **Pre-Reading Activity:**

   Read the title of the book, *Little Grunt and the Big Egg,* and show the children the cover of the book. Ask the children to predict what they think the book will be about. Write the predictions on the chalkboard and then compare the predictions with what actually happened in the story.

2. **Learning Activities:**

   a. At the beginning of the story there is a picture of all the members of the Grunt Tribe. Ask the children to draw a picture of the Grunt Tribe in which the tribe members are put in order from largest to smallest. Tell them to label the pictures, Unca Grunt, Ant Grunt, Granny Grunt, Mama Grunt, Papa Grunt, Chief Rockhead Grunt, and Little Grunt.

   b. In this story the Grunts called George a Tyrannosauros Rex, which was a huge dinosaur that lived during prehistoric times. Tell the children to look through a dinosaur book such as *Dinosaurs, Dinosaurs* by Byron Barton (New York: Crowell, 1989) to determine the size of some of the largest and smallest dinosaurs. Two dinosaur books, *The Smallest Dinosaurs* and *The Largest Dinosaurs,* both by Seymour Simon, are also listed in Supplemental Literature.

   c. There were many very large dinosaurs that lived during prehistoric times. Ask the children to name some animals that are living today that they consider to be large animals, (for example, elephants, hippopotamuses, giraffes, etc.). Next, categorize these animals by those that are the heaviest, tallest, biggest, and so forth.

   d. Little Grunt went hunting for eggs and found a large dinosaur egg. It was too big for him to carry so he wove a mat, put the egg on it, and pulled it home. As a group, brainstorm about some other ways in which Little Grunt could have gotten the egg home.

3. **Discussion Questions:**

   a. How do you think Little Grunt felt about being the smallest of the Grunt Tribe?

   b. The older Grunts kept saying that "a nice little cockroach" would make a good pet. Why did they say this?

   c. What would have happened to the Grunt Tribe if George, the dinosaur, hadn't rescued them from the volcano?

   d. What do you think the Grunts will do with all the baby dinosaurs?

| Title: | *Bigger and Smaller* |
|---|---|
| Genre: | Informational Book |
| Author: | Robert Froman |
| Illustrator: | Gioia Fiammenghi |
| Bibliographic Information: | Thomas Crowell, New York, 1971 |
| Summary: | The author introduces the reader to the relativity of size. The concept of big and bigger, of small and smaller, is introduced by using examples to show how these words make sense only when two or more objects are compared. |
| Interest Level: | Grades K–4 |

1. **Pre-Reading Activity:**

   Discuss the title, <u>Bigger and Smaller</u>. Ask the children to name some things that are big. List these on the chalkboard. Then ask them to name some things that are small. List these on the chalkboard. Ask them how they know that the things they said are big are big and the things they said are small are small. Read the book and then review this activity to see if they still agree with what they said.

2. **Learning Activities:**

   a. The author provides information on who the tallest and heaviest men in the world are. This book was written in 1971. Provide a copy of the *Guineas World Book of Records.* Help the children do research to find out whether the information about the tallest and heaviest men provided in *Bigger and Small* is accurate. Write the height and weight of these men on the chalkboard. Provide the same information for women.

   b. There are many activities to do in this book. For example, look on page 13. Divide the children into cooperative learning groups and assign each group a page and tell them to investigate and present the information they find related to the activity.

   c. There are advantages and disadvantages to being a tall person as well as being a short person. Put the statements, "I would like to be tall because…" and "I would like to be short because…" on the chalkboard. Tell the students to brainstorm as a group. Make lists of the responses to these two statements on the chalkboard

   d. Tell the children to fold a sheet of paper in half twotimes to make four boxes. Tell them to draw something that is tall and short in the first box, heavy and light in the second box, big and small in the third box, and huge and little in the fourth box. Allow time to share.

3. **Discussion Questions:**

   a. How can you tell if something is big? (by comparing it to something else)

      How can you tell if something is small? (by comparing it to something else)

   b. What is a pygmy? (a person who lives along the Congo River and is only a little over four feet tall when fully grown)

   c. What is the smallest living animal you have ever seen?

   d. What is the largest living animal you have ever seen?

Title:          *Paul Bunyan*

Genre:          Legend

Author:         Steven Kellogg

Bibliographic Information:          William Morrow & Co., New York, 1984

Summary:        This story tells about a lumberjack, Paul Bunyan, whose unusual size and strength equipped him for many fantastic adventures. He and his big, blue ox, Babe, did many extraordinary things. For example, they fought the wild Gumberoos in the Appalachians, dug out the Great Lakes and St. Lawrence River, and gouged a trench we call the Grand Canyon.

Interest Level:  Grades K–4

1.  Pre-Reading Activity:

    Read the first page and show the illustrations to the children. It says "Paul was the largest, smartest, and strongest baby ever born in the state of Maine." Brainstorm, with the children, about other vocabulary words that mean the same as large (for example, huge, big, giant, etc.). List these on the chalkboard. Ask the children to share one thing that they think is large.

2.  Learning Activities:

    a.  Paul Bunyan was very large and strong. Brainstorm with the children about other stories in which a character is very large and strong (for example, the giant in Jack and the Beanstalk). List all of these characters on the chalkboard. Then ask the children to select the one character that they liked best and to tell why they selected that character.

    b.  Tell the children to look closely at the signs that are posted throughout the illustrations. Have the children pretend that Paul Bunyan is coming to their community. Ask them to create a sign for his visit. Display the signs. Discuss what changes would need to be made to accommodate his size.

    c.  Paul Bunyan and his men traveled from Maine to California. Using a United States map, help the children trace a route Bunyan and his companions may have followed. Remember that they went through the Appalachian Mountains, the Great Plains, the Rocky Mountains, Texas, and Arizona. Once they have traced the imaginary route, discuss the different time zones Bunyan would have gone through. Discuss what forms of transportation would be available for someone the size of Paul Bunyan.

    d.  Ask the children to write a short story about all the things they would be able to do if they were large and strong like Paul Bunyan.

    e.  Duplicate and distribute a copy of Literature Log II (Chapter 2, pages 57-58) and ask the children to complete it. After they have completed the log, allow them to get together in pairs or small groups to discuss their logs.

3.  Discussion Questions:

    a.  Why did Paul's parents move to the backwoods? (Answers might include: Because too many people complained about Paul and life would be more peaceful.)

    b.  What were some of the problems Paul encountered on his trip west? (Answers might include: being ambushed by a gang of Gumberoos, being able to make enough flapjacks to feed his crew, being caught in a great blizzard, and so forth.)

c.  Would you have liked to travel with Paul? Why or why not?

d.  What is the most extraordinary or unusual thing Paul did?

**Culmination:**  Divide the children into groups of 4 or 5. Tell them they are going on a "Measuring Scavenger Hunt." Give them a copy of the following and allow two or three days for them to collect the information, as a team.  Allow time to share, compare, and defend their findings. The children with the most accurate answers are the winners.

1.  Height of the tallest building in your community _____.

2.  Height of the tallest building in the United States _____.

3.  Number of miles to the nearest grocery store from your school _____.

4.  Number of miles to the nearest beach from your school _____.

5.  The adult male who weighs the most in the United States _____.

6.  The adult male who weighs the least in the United States _____.

7.  The adult male who is the tallest in the United States _____.

8.  The adult male who is the shortest in the United States _____.

9.  The amount of time it takes for the earth to revolve around the sun _____.

10. The coldest temperature it has ever been in your community _____.

11. The hottest temperature it has ever been in your community _____.

12. The day of the week on which President Clinton was born _____.

13. The season that most people in your class like best _____.

14. The time of the day that the first space ship was launched _____.

15. The month when the most people in your class were born _____.

# Supplemental Literature

### Primary (Grades 1–3):

Baker, Alan. (1990). *Two tiny mice.* New York: Dial Books.
 Two small mice explore their environment, observing many different-sized animals before finally going home to sleep in their tiny nest.

Kellogg, Steven. (1976). *Much bigger than Martin.* New York: Dial Press.
 This is a humorous, but realistic presentation that will charm everyone who has ever suffered from being the smallest.

Kroll, Steven. (1982). *The big bunny and the Easter egg.* Illustrated by Janet Stevens. New York: Holiday House.
 Wilbur, who was very big and very tall, was an Easter Bunny that got so sick he almost missed his Easter deliveries.

Lionni, Leo. (1968). *The biggest house in the world.* New York: Pantheon Books.
 The advantages and disadvantages of a big house versus a little house, from a snail's point of view is simply described in this wondrous tale.

Little, Jean. (1992). *Revenge of the small small.* Illustrated by Janet Wilson. New York: Penguin Group.
 Patsy Small, the youngest in her family, tells about the perils of being the smallest in the family. At the end, however, the bigger Smalls apologize and repent.

Lord, John Vernon. (1982). *The giant jam sandwich.* Boston: Houghton Mifflin.
 In order to get rid of the millions of wasps, the town made a giant jam sandwich. The wasps dived into the jam and got stuck.

Lorenz, Lee. (1982). *Big Gus and little Gus*. Englewood Cliffs, NJ: Prentice-Hall, Inc.

    Two friends, one big and one little, go out to explore the world and to seek their fortunes. Big Gus is rewarded despite his foolishness.

Miles, Miska. (1977). *Small rabbit*. Illustrated by Jim Arnosky. Boston: Little, Brown and Co.

    After a long search, little rabbit finally finds someone to play with.

Minarik, Else Holmelund. (1991). *The little girl and the dragon*. Illustrated by Martine Gourbault. New York: Greenwillow Books.

    A big dragon jumps out of the little girl's storybook and proceeds to swallow up all her toys.

Muntean, Michaela. (1982). *Big and little stories*. Illustrated by Maggie Swanson. Racine, WI: Western Publishing Co.

    The concept of big and little are introduced through the Sesame Street characters.

Pienkowski, Jan. (1983). *Sizes*. New York: Puffin.

    Pairs of objects with similarities and differences are show, (for example, big whale, little fish; big lady, little boy). This concept book is usually regarded as a pre-school text; however, older children have also been challenged by it.

Srivastava, J.J. (1974). *Area*. New York: Thomas Y. Crowell.

    Explains in simple ways how areas are measured.

## Intermediate (Grades 4–6):

Andersen, Hans Christian. *Thumbelina*. Retold by Amy Ehrlich. New York: Dial Books.

    This is the story of a girl who is the size of your thumb.

Ardley, N. (1983). *Making metric measurement*. New York: Franklin Watts.

    Includes projects for constructing simple measuring instruments and understanding how to use metric units.

Branley, F.M. (1975). *Measure with metric*. New York: Thoams Y. Crowell.

    Through a variety of simple experiments, the principles of the metric system are introduced.

Dahl, Roald. (1982). *The BFG*. New York: Farrar, Straus, Giroux.

    BFG- the Big Friendly Giant — kidnaps Sophie and takes her to Giantland with him. There she meets nine other giants. The story continues with Sophie and BFG conspiring to end the loathsome activities of the other giants.

Kesey, Ken. (1990). *Little Tricker the squirrel meets Big Double the bear*. New York: Viking Penguin.

    This story portrays the squirrel, Little Tricker, and his encounters with Big Double, the bear, as he terrorizes the forest animals one by one. In the end, Little Tricker gets revenge.

Norton, Mary. (1990). *The borrowers*. New York: Harcourt Brace Javonovich.

    The borrowers are tiny people who live under the floorboards. They "borrow" all the things that are missing, such as pencils, pins, etc.

Simon, Seymour. (1986). *The largest dinosaur*. Illustrated by Pam Carroll. New York: Macmillan.

    Examples of the largest dinosaurs, along with their names, are provided in addition to where they lived.

Simon, Seymour. (1986). *The smallest dinosaur*. New York: Crown Publishers, Inc.

    Seven dinosaurs, all about the size of a chicken or dog, are introduced. These dinosaurs are believed to be the prehistoric cousin of the birds living today.

Swift, Jonathan. (1963). *Gulliver's travels*. New York: Amerton, Ltd.

    There are many expeditions but one of the most famous of Gulliver's adventures is his visit to Lilliput.

White, E.B. (1945). *Stuart Little*. New York: Dell.

    Stuart is about 2 inches tall, has a tail and a pointed nose. He looks like a mouse. Because of his size he is very helpful around the house and the Stuart family loves him. One day he set out to find his friend Margalo and encountered many adventures along the way.

Wild, Margaret. (1984). *Something absolutely enormous*. New York: Scholastic.

    Sally knits an enormous thing. When the circus comes to town and the big top burns down, Sally's thing is put to use and saves the day. The story ends with Sally getting ready to bake something absolutely enormous.

# MINI-THEMES

## Time

Time of occurrence and length of duration are two attributes of events that can be measured. To describe time of occurrence, you can give a time span such as, "it happened last night" or "it happened in September." For this, the children need to become familiar with the vocabulary and concept of days, months, and seasons, which are presented in two of the mini units in this section.

Length of duration can be described by discussing such things as, "how long did it take you to walk to school?" or "which is longer, the hours you sleep at night or the time you are in school?" This mini unit is intended to help children become more familiar with telling time, the concept of time which leads to being able to measure length of duration.

### References

Abisch, R. (1968). *Do you know what time it is?* Illustrations by Boche Kaplan. New York: Prentice-Hall.

Carle, E. (1977). *The grouchy lady bug*. New York: Thomas Crowell.

Fitzhugh, L. (1982). *I am five*. Illustrations by Susan Bonners. New York: Delacorte Press.

Fitzhugh, L. (1982). *I am three*. Illustrations by Susan Bonners. New York: Delacorte Press.

Fitzhugh, L. (1982). *I am four*. Illustrations by Susan Bonners. New York: Delacorte Press.

Fleischman, P. (1991). *Time train*. Illustrations by Claire Ewart. New York: Charlotte Zolotow Book.

Harper, A. (1987). *Just a minute!* Illustrations by Susan Hellard. New York: G.P. Putnam's Sons.

Hastings, S. (1988). *The man who wanted to live forever*. Illustrations by Reg Cartwright. New York: Henry Holt.

Hissey, J. (1986). *Old bear*. New York: Philomel Books.

Horowitz, R. (1991). *Bat time*. Illustrations by Susan Avishai. New York: Macmillan Publishing Co.

Jennings, T. (1988). *Junior science time*. New York: Gloucester Press.

Maestro, B. and G. (1984). *Around the clock with Harriet*. New York: Crown Publishing.

Paine, P.C. (1990). *Time for Horatio*. Santa Barbara, CA: Advocacy Press.

Taber, A. (1993). *The boy who stopped time*. New York: Macmillan Publishing.

Williams, J. (1992). *Projects with time*. Illustrations by Malcom Walker. Milwaukee, WI: Gareth Stevens Children's Books.

### Activities

1. Often people say, "I'll be ready in a minute" or "It will only take a minute." Tell the children to think about how long a minute is and what are some things they could do in a minute. Using a minute hand, time a minute. Then ask the children to tell you all the things they could *and* could not do in a minute. Make a list of these and then, as a class, write a story about "I could do _____ in a minute, but I couldn't do _____ in a minute." Illustrate the pages. This would be a good time to read the book, *Just a Minute!* by Anita Harper.

2. Read the book, *Bat Time* by Ruth Horowitz. In this book, Leila and her father like the night time because Leila likes to watch for the fluttering bats as they come to have their insect feast. Discuss with the children things they like to do at night time, morning time, and so forth.

3. Discuss the fact that as time goes by, people and things get older. Also, as time goes by people are able to do different things. Read books such as *I Am Three, I am Four, I Am Five*, by Louise Fitzhugh; *Old Bear* by Jane Hissey; or *The Man Who Wanted to Live Forever* by Selina Hastings. Decide on different age groups — 2 years old, 6 years old, 16 years old, for example — and then brainstorm things people of these ages can do and can't do. Finally, have the children identify a time in life that they would most like to be in and to explain why.

4. Read the book *Around the Clock with Harriet* by Betsy and Giulio Maestro, which tells what Harriet

does from the time she gets up (8:00 A.M.) until she does to bed (8:00 P.M.). Tell the children to draw a clock showing the time of day for each activity they do and describe what they do. For example:

Get out of bed,

brush my teeth,

get dressed,

and eat breakfast.

8:00 AM

5.  Directions for making a model clock can be found in *Projects with Time* by John Williams on page 5. Help children construct clocks and then do numerous activities with setting the clock at designated times.

# Months and Seasons

A month is a way of recording a specific number of days. Months also relate to seasons — fall, winter, spring, and summer. Children will enjoy learning more about the months of the year and the seasons through reading the recommended books and participating in the activities designed for this mini unit.

## References

Branley, F.M. (1985). *Sunshine makes the seasons*. Illustrations by Guilio Maestro. New York: Thomas Crowell.
Dragonwagon, C. (1993). *Alligators and others all year long: A book of months*. Illustrations by Jose Aruega and Ariana Dewey. New York: Macmillan Publishing.
Gerstein, M. (1993). *The story of May*. New York: HarperCollins Publishing.
Good, E.W. (1987). *That's what happens when it's spring*. Illustrations by Susie Shenk. Intercourse, PA: Good Books.
Hirschi, R. (1990). *Winter*. Illustrations by D. Mangelsen. New York: Cobblehill Books.
Hirschi, R. (1990). *Spring*. Illustrations by D. Mangelsen. New York: Cobblehill Books.
Hirschi, R. (1990). *Summer*. Illustrations by D. Mangelsen. New York: Cobblehill Books.
Knotts, H. (1981). *The summer cat*. New York: Harper and Row.
Knotts, H. (1972). *The winter cat*. New York: Harper and Row.
Maass, R. (1990). *When autumn comes*. New York: Henry Holt and Company.
Ockenga, S. (1990). *Then and now: A book of days*. Boston: Houghton Mifflin.
Provensen, A. and M. (1978). *The year at maple hill farm*. New York: Atheneum.
Richardson, J. (1992). *The seasons*. New York: Franklin Watts, Inc.
Schweninger, A. (1993). *Springtime*. New York: Viking.
Schweninger, A. (1990). *Wintertime*. New York: Viking.
Schweninger, A. (1992). *Summertime*. New York: Viking.
Sendak, M. (1962). *Chicken soup with rice*. New York: Harper.
Spohn, K. (1989). *Clementine's winter wardrobe*. New York: Orchard Books.
Steward, S. (1991). *The money tree*. Illustrations by David Small. New York: Farrar, Straus, Giroux.

## Activities

1.  Read some of the recommended books for this unit to the children. Then ask the children to select their favorite season of the year, estimate the time and length of the season, and write a brief story

explaining what they like about the season they selected. Tell the children to make an illustration to accompany their story. Compile stories into a class book.

2. Read *Clementine's Winter Wardrobe* by Kate Spohn. Discuss the different types of clothes Clementine selected for her winter wardrobe. Then divide the children into three groups — a spring group, a summer group, and a fall group. Then tell each group to create a Clementine's _____ wardrobe story for the assigned season. Allow time to share.

3. Introduce the book, *Then and Now* by Stan Ockenga. This book puts together an array of real and literary characters and events for each month. As a group, create a similar type of book about members of your class and community, as well as popular people, objects, and events the children want to include. Share the completed book with other classes and the community.

4. Help the children write a rhyming verse for the month you are currently in. To motivate them for this activity, read *Alligator and Others All Year Long* by Crescent Dragonwagon. The author of this book writes a rhyme for each month. After the children have written the rhyme for the current month, divide them into eleven groups and assign each group a remaining month for which to write a rhyme. Allow time to share.

5. Make a birthday chart by charting the children's birthdays for each month of the year.

6. Ask the children to select their favorite month and explain why it is their favorite.

# Days of the Week

It is important that children learn the days of the week and the sequence in which they occur, because much of what they do is measured in days of the week. Specific days of the week are significant in planning the frequency with which activities and classes happen. For example, children may say they have art once a week, on Monday, or P.E. twice a week on Tuesday and Thursday. Children can learn more about the days of the week by reading some of the selected books and doing the activities suggested for this mini unit.

## References

Carle, E. (1993). *Today is Monday*. New York: Scholastic.
Carle, E. (1987). *The very hungry caterpillar*. New York: Philomel Books.
Domanska, J. (1985). *Busy Monday morning*. New York: Greenwillow Books.
Holabrid, K. (1989). *Angelina's birthday surprise*. New York: Clarkson N. Potter.
Lyon, G.E. (1985). *Father time and the day boxes*. New York: Bradbury Press.
Martin, B., Jr. (1970). *Monday, Monday, I like Monday*. New York: Holt, Rinehart and Winston.
Sharmat, M. (1983). *The seven sloppy days of Phineas pig*. San Diego, CA: Harcourt Brace Jovanovich.

## Activities

1. Read the book, *Father Time and the Day Boxes* by George Ella Lyon. Ask each child to bring in a small box (jello or pudding box could work). Cut 365 small pieces of paper per child. Help the children write the numerals 1 to 365 on the papers. Put the papers in the box and then tell the children to take one paper out each day and when all papers are gone, one year will have passed. Ideally, this activity of taking papers out of the box should begin on January 1; however, demonstrating the concept of a year passing can begin at any time.

2. Read the book *Today is Monday* by Eric Carle. In this book a different food is introduced for each day of the week. For example, Monday it is string beans, Tuesday it is spaghetti, Wednesday it is zoooop, and so forth. Each day the food from the previous day is repeated. As a group, create a new version of *Today is Monday* by introducing new foods for each day. Illustrate each day and compile the work into a book. Share with other classes.

3.  Tell the children to select their favorite day of the week and then write a brief paragraph telling why the day they selected is their favorite day. Allow time to share. This would be a good time to read the book, *Monday, Monday, I Like Monday* by Bill Martin, Jr.

4.  Read *The Very Hungry Caterpillar* by Eric Carle. In the book, the caterpillar eats through different foods each day. For example, "On Monday he ate through one apple but he was still hungry," "On Tuesday he ate through two pears but he was still hungry." Help the children create new foods for the caterpillar to eat through for each day of the week.

# Temperature

Prior to initiating this mini unit with the children, introduce and discuss vocabulary related to temperature, such as, hot, cold, thermometer, centigrade, celsius, fahrenheit, weather reports, etc. Point out that other than for hot and cold, there are few other measurements and comparisons that can be made without the help of an instrument, usually a thermometer.

## References

Ardley, N. (1983). *Hot and cold*. New York: Franklin Watts.

Balestino, P. (1971). *Hot as an ice cube*. Illustrations by Tomie de Paola. New York: Thomas Y. Crowell.

Good, E.W. (1987). *That's what happens when it's spring*. Illustrations by Susie Shenk. Intercourse, PA: Good Books.

Harshman, M. (1990). *Snow company*. Illustrations by Leslie W. Bowman. New York: Cobblehill Books.

Keats, E.J. (1962). *The snowy day*. New York: Viking.

Maestro, B. and Maestro, G. (1990). *Temperature and you*. New York: Lodestar Books.

Munsch, R. and Martchenko, M. (1987). *50 below zero*. Toronto: Annick Press.

Simon, S. (1972). *Hot and cold*. New York: McGraw-Hill.

## Activities

1.  Read the book, *Snow Company* by Marc Harshman or *The Snowy Day* by E.J. Keats and have the children discuss things they like to do when it is cold outside (for example, eat hot soup, play in the snow, etc.). Then read *That's What Happens When It's Spring* by Elaine Good and discuss things the children like to do in the spring. Discuss what makes doing these things possible — mainly the weather and temperature.

2.  Provide the children with a thermometer and allow them time to experiment with reading how temperature changes depending on where the thermometer is placed. For example, tell the children to put the thermometer in the sun for about 20 minutes and to record the temperature. Then after placing the thermometer in a shaded or cool spot, read and record the temperature. What is the difference in the temperatures? Depending on the grade level of the children, discuss centigrade vs. fahrenheit readings of the thermometer.

3.  Place a thermometer outside the classroom in an area that is readily accessible. Assign a child to read and record the temperature readings twice a day (morning and afternoon) for a period of one month. Discuss the changes in temperature from morning to afternoon and also from day to day.

4.  Bring in the weather report section of the newspaper on a daily basis for a week. Help the children locate some of the major cities listed on the report and read the high and low temperatures recorded for that day. Discuss reasons for the differences in temperatures — the effect of being near or far from the equator, at high or low altitudes, and so forth. Read the daily weather reports for your area.

5.  Introduce books such as *Hot and Cold* by Seymour Simon or *Hot as an Ice Cube* by Philip Balestino. Provide time and materials for the children to try some of the suggested experiments.

# INTERMEDIATE UNITS

---

## Intermediate Unit: Space: The Final Frontier

**Theme:** SPACE: THE FINAL FRONTIER

**Focus:** Students will journey through our Solar System and share in many important discoveries that are the result of the human quest for knowledge of our world and our universe.

**Objectives:** Upon completion of this unit, students will:

1. uncover information about the uniqueness of the planets and other heavenly bodies that comprise our Solar System.

2. explore the only world in outer space ever visited by humans — the moon.

3. trace the various explorations of the Solar System and examine the most important expeditions to *the final frontier*.

4. assess the impact and future of the space program.

**Initiating Activity:** Many of the general activities in this unit will involve exploration of the sun and the planets of our solar system (other than Earth). Therefore, to arouse their curiosity about our solar system, involve students in a **Solar System Scavenger Hunt**. Create index cards — each should include an intriguing fact about each planet/sun without identifying the heavenly body (see examples below). There should be enough index cards so that each student gets one and there should be an equal number of cards for each planet/sun. Make many of the books listed in the reference section available and allow time for students to skim the books to locate the heavenly body that fits the fact on his/her index card. Based upon the heavenly body described on his/her index card, each student should then get into the appropriate planet/sun group and share the information on the index card.

Below are some of the facts you might wish to include on the index cards:

1. The Sun:
   1.3 million times the size of the Earth
   Uses four million tons of hydrogen every second
   Temperature is as high as 27 million degrees (F)
   The inner atmosphere is the chromosphere, the outer atmosphere is the corona

2. Mercury:
   One day on this planet is almost as long as a year
   Almost airless planet
   During the day the temperature is hot enough to melt lead and at night the temperature is -300 degrees (F)
   Covered with craters from meteoroid collisions

3. Venus:
   Called the Evening Star or Morning Star
   Rotates from east to west, the opposite of most other planets
   Sometimes called Earth's sister planet but is very different
   The hottest planet of the Solar System

4. Mars:      Named for the Roman god of war
              Doesn't have canals as once believed
              Scientists are still debating whether life forms exist there
              Soil contains iron oxide

5. Jupiter:   Has giant windstorm called the Great Red Spot
              The Great Red Spot, the planet's giant windstorm, is three times the size of Earth
              Four of its moons are big enough to be seen from Earth through binoculars or a small
                  telescope and are called the Galean moons
              One of its moons has exploding volcanoes

6. Saturn:    Its rings are made of thousands of smaller rings within rings
              Has the most moons of any planet in our Solar System
              One of its moons is the only moon in the Solar System to have an atmosphere
              It takes 30 years to orbit the sun

7. Uranus:    The planet is lying on its side in space
              Right now the south pole is in the midst of 42 years of constant sunlight
              Discovered by William Herschel in 1781
              Shines with a greenish-blue color

8. Neptune:   Has the strongest winds ever measured on a planet
              Its moon is colder than any other object in our Solar System
              The planet farthest from the Sun until 1999.
              Was discovered because of its gravitational pull on Uranus

9. Pluto:     Has an odd, stretched, tilted orbit
              Smallest, coldest planet in the Solar System
              Could have been a moon knocked out of a planet's orbit long ago or an asteroid
              One of its moons is Charon, named after the boatman on the river Styx in the
                  underworld

## General Activities

1.  Involve students in an in-depth exploration of their groups' planet/sun. Before beginning the research, suggest that each group become involved in the K-W-L strategy to access their knowledge of the planet/sun and aid them in determining what they would like to learn about the topic (see Chapter 2, pages 37-39). Since our knowledge of our Solar System has expanded greatly in recent years, encourage each group to gather information from recently published books (see references listed). The information gathered should include: size; location in the Solar System; atmosphere; unique land features; rotation; the possibility of life forms; explorations of the planet; discovery (when and by whom); legends and myths regarding the planet/sun; origin and appropriateness of its name; natural resources; and so forth. Have students create a bulletin board display for the planet assigned.

2.  Based on the information gathered in activity 1, have students create a visual representation of the planet that reflects some of its most significant features (for example, the rings of Saturn, the reddish color of Mars, the volcanoes of Jupiter, etc.).

3.  Based on the information gathered in activity 1, have students create a skit. This skit is based on the premise that the students have been involved in a ten-year mission to the planet and, as returning astronauts, they are ready to tell the world of their findings. The skit should be a mixture of fact and fiction. For example, students returning from Neptune might report on the underground homes of

the "Neptunians" because the strong winds and freezing temperatures on the planet make life on the surface impossible. Students can also discuss some of the hardships of their visit and technological innovations that were needed to deal with the realities of the planet/sun. It is possible that not all missions were successful. For example, imagine that the Sun Mission had to be aborted due to the fact that their specially made space suits absorbed too much heat. However, students would still be responsible for sharing information about the sun and about their mission there. Remind students to use the visual (activity 2) as part of their skit.

4. Involve students in experiments that will help them better understand the Solar System and space travel. Books such as Gustafson's *Planets, Moons and Meteors* (1992), Schatz's *The Astronomy Activity Book* (1991), and Van Cleaves's *Astronomy for Every Kid* contain exciting experiments for budding astronomers.

5. Play many of the popular songs that deal with the theme of space, such as "Aquarius" from the show *Hair,* or the themes from *Star Wars, Star Trek,* or *2001…A Space Odyssey.* Discuss how the music captures the mood of space. Have students either create their own modern dance, inspired by one of the pieces of music, or capture the mood through some type of artistic endeavor.

6. Have students create a "Space…The Final Frontier" time line. As students read about the advances in space exploration, have them add events, such as the various manned spaced programs (Mercury, Gemini, Apollo, Apollo-Soyuz, Sky Lab), space shuttles (Columbia, Challenger, Discovery, Atlantis, Endeavor) and unmanned NASA Planetary Exploration Missions (Mariner, Magellan, Pioneer, Viking, Voyager) to the time line. For each event, have students include the name of the mission, the dates, the astronauts/cosmonauts (if appropriate), the main purpose(s) of the mission, and its most significant contributions. You may wish to have poster paper cut into the desired size for the time line. Ask students to illustrate each of the events they highlight.

7. Have students select and research one of the world's space pioneers to learn about his/her background, contributions, successes, failures, motivations, and any other relevant and interesting information. Following the research, tell each student that they are now members of the SEA (Space Explorers Association) panel of experts. Have each student take on the persona of the space pioneer researched and take part in a panel discussion in which each first relates his/her contributions and then shares his/her views on the importance of the space program and its future. These pioneers include (but are certainly not limited to):

| | |
|---|---|
| Edward E. (Buzz) Aldrin, Jr. | Virgil Grissom |
| William A. Anders | Johannes Kepler |
| Neil A. Armstrong | James A. Lovell, Jr. |
| Guton S. Bluford, Jr. | Sharon (Christa) MacAuliffe |
| Frank Borman | Sir Isaac Newton |
| Scott M. Carpenter | Sally K. Ride |
| Michael Collins | Alan B. Shepard |
| Gordon Cooper | Wally Schirra |
| Robert L. Crippen | Valentina Tereshkova |
| Yuri Gagarin | Edward J. White |
| John H. Glenn, Jr. | Wernher von Braun |
| Robert H. Goddard | James W. Young |

8. Invite a local college astronomy professor to class to discuss space exploration. In advance, brainstorm possible questions.

9.  Create a bulletin board with the following quote: "Man must rise above the Earth…to the top of the atmosphere and beyond, for only thus will he understand the world in which he lives" (Socrates). Discuss this quote with students and have them react in essay form. As an alternative ask them to create their own quotes about one of the planets or the sun.

10. Ask students whether they agree that space is the "final frontier." Have students create a mural entitled "New Frontiers," on which they draw pictures to represent other frontiers that await exploration. Ask each to write a brief essay to explain the frontier they have pictured and display the essays on the mural.

## Discussion Questions:

1.  Of all the planets in the Solar System, which holds the greatest possibility for supporting some type of life form? Explain. (Mars — from soil samples picked up by Viking landers, many scientists think there is a possibility that the planet may be capable of supporting some type of life. Although none has been discovered there yet, some speculate that it may still exist on some unexplored parts of the planet.)

2.  What are the most significant contributions of the manned space missions? (An understanding of the challenges of living in space; carrying out many scientific experiments that will, in turn, improve life on Earth, and so forth.)

3.  What are some of the most significant contributions of the unmanned missions into space? (They have given us a close look at the planets of our Solar System and have helped us better understand the origins of our universe.)

4.  What, in your opinion, is the biggest challenge/danger associated with space exploration?

5.  What qualities do you think are most important for an astronaut to possess? Explain.

6.  Why is space referred to as "The Final Frontier"? Do you agree with this label?

    Why or why not?

# Literature Related Activities

| | |
|---|---|
| Title: | *Our Solar System* |
| Genre: | Non-fiction |
| Author: | Seymour Simon |
| Illustrator: | Photographs from manned and unmanned missions into space |
| Bibliographic Information: | Morrow Junior Books, New York, 1992 |
| Summary: | This volume contains up-to-date information about the sun and the planets, moons, asteroids, meteoroids, and comets that travel around our sun. The text is accompanied by photographs taken from manned and unmanned space missions. |
| Interest Level: | Grades 3+ |

1.  Pre-Reading Activity

    Have students identify each of the heavenly bodies on the cover of the book. In groups, have them select one (not the planet they have been assigned during the general activities) and create a small replica (from paper). Involve the entire class in a brainstorming session to discover what they know about each planet and the sun. Attach a list of responses to the appropriate replica.

2.  Learning Activities:

    a.  The front of the book contains a chart with all types of information regarding the planets/sun. Duplicate the chart and have each student create five questions that involve a comparison of the planets/sun.

    b.  Have students come up with statistical puzzles regarding the planets and the sun. For example: "The sun is ____ times bigger than all the planets put together." (Answer — 600 times bigger.) The chart in the book will help students create and solve these puzzles.

    c.  Involve students in a "Brain Bowl" in which they use the chart to answer the questions created in learning activities a and b (above). You may wish to divide students into teams for this competition.

    d.  Evenly assign each student one of the planets (except Earth) or the sun. Have students come up with a new name for the planet/sun. This name should be significant and be based on the information uncovered about this body. Have students prepare a short persuasive argument for changing the name and present the new names planet by planet. They might also launch a mini-campaign with advertisements outlining the reasons for the name change. After all speeches for one planet have been presented, allow students to vote for one of the names or for keeping the name as it is.

    e.  Based on the photographs of the planets, involve students in selecting one of the planets/sun and creating a map of its surface. Have students label unique features on the planet.

3.  Discussion Questions

    a.  Which of the planets did you find most interesting? Why?

    b.  How have the unmanned missions aided in our understanding of the planets of our Solar System? (We've learned about the surfaces of the planets and their moons, about the possibility of life existing, about the weather and temperature conditions, and we've been able to hypothesize about the origins of the planets.)

    c.  Of all the information uncovered by the unmanned missions, which do you think is the most relevant/important?

    d.  Of the planets in our Solar System, why does it appear that Earth and Earth alone can sustain any type of advanced living forms? (The extreme temperatures and atmospheric gases of the other planets make the existence of life forms there extremely unlikely.)

---

| | |
|---|---|
| Title: | *The Moon and You* |
| Genre: | Non-fiction |
| Author: | E.C. Krupp |
| Illustrator: | Robin Rector Krupp |

Bibliographic Information: Macmillan, New York, 1993

Summary:              Fascinating information on the moon and man's exploration of it is included along with
                      stories and folklore about the moon from all over the world

Interest Level:       Grades 3+

1.  Pre-Reading Activity:

    Have students brainstorm a list of songs, sayings, and phrases about the moon that have been handed
    down (for example: The man in the moon; the moon is made of cheese; once in a blue moon; harvest
    moon). Involve them in the Reflective Sharing Technique, in which they share and discuss ideas they
    have related to the topic of the moon (see Chapter 2, pages 45-46).

2.  Learning Activities:

    a.  Discuss the moon's phases and reasons for it. With students, recreate the demonstration on pages
        16-17 to explain the moon's phases.

    b.  Encourage students to keep a pictorial diary of the phases of the moon. Every three or four days,
        for a month, have them take pictures of the moon and keep track of the date and time the picture
        was taken. Have them create a booklet on the moon and accompany each picture with a
        descriptive simile or metaphor (for example: the full moon lights up the sky like a giant firefly).

    c.  Have students locate, copy, illustrate, and share a favorite poem on the subject of the moon.

    d.  Have students select a favorite myth/legend concerning the moon and have them create a short
        skit so that they can retell it to the class.

    e.  Discuss the first landing on the moon and the famous words of Neil Armstrong as he set foot on
        the surface, "That's one small step for a man, one giant leap for mankind." Have students imagine
        that they are the first humans to set foot on the moon. Have them create a diary entry to describe
        their feelings and what they would say.

    f.   The first men to set foot on the moon, Neil Armstrong and Buzz Aldrin left a plaque on the moon
        that said,

                              HERE MEN FROM THE PLANET EARTH

                              FIRST SET FOOT UPON THE MOON

                              JULY, 1969, A.D.

                              WE CAME IN PEACE FOR ALL MANKIND

    Have students design a plaque they would leave if they were the first to visit another world in our
    Solar System.

3.  Discussion Questions

    a.  Why is a calendar month close to 29- 1/2 days? (That is the length of time from one new moon
        to the next.)

    b.  How does the moon's gravity affect the Earth? (It affects ocean tides.)

    c.  Describe the moon, its atmosphere, its surface, size, etc. (There is no air; the temperature is
        freezing during the night and boiling during the day; the moon's sky always looks black; the
        moon is 2,000 miles across and 6,800 miles around; gravity is much weaker than on Earth; filled

with craters caused by meteorites; the moon's core is all rock; there is no water on the moon; and so forth.)

    d.   Describe the first landing of man on the moon.

    e.   Considering the fact that there are various theories to explain the origin of our moon, which do you believe? Why?

| | |
|---|---|
| Title: | *The Magic School Bus: Lost in the Solar System* |
| Genre: | Non-fiction/Fantasy |
| Author: | Joanna Cole |
| Illustrator: | Bruce Degen |

Bibliographic Information: Scholastic, New York, 1990

| | |
|---|---|
| Summary: | This adventure in the "Magic School Bus" takes the reader through the Solar System. A fantasy adventure is accompanied by many facts related to space and space travel. |
| Interest Level: | Grades 3+ |

1.  Pre-Reading Activity:

Discuss other books in the "Magic School Bus" series that students have read. Have them make predictions as to where the Magic School Bus will take them in this book. As an alternative, involve the students in using prediction cards to tap into their background knowledge of space (see Chapter 2, pages 36-37).

2.  Learning Activities:

    a.   After reading the book, have students compile a *Book of Facts: The Solar System.* Have students illustrate their pages and bind them together in book form. As an alternative, students may wish to create an A,B,C book based on the Solar System.

    b.   Throughout the book, the children on the bus have written short papers describing some aspect of space. Have each student select one of the papers and elaborate on it by researching the subject more fully.

    c.   Create a travel brochure and map of our Solar System to help those who are visiting — or lost!

    d.   On the last page of the book, the author gives reasons why the reader should not attempt this trip on their own school bus. Ask children to make up their own *Top 10* list of reasons why they **should or should not** try this same trip. Have students list these reasons on poster board and illustrate. (*Remember*: Humor counts.)

3.  Discussion Questions

    a.   Of all the information the students in Mrs. Frizzle's class uncovered, what surprised you the most?

    b.   What are some of the problems astronauts have to overcome in order to explore space? (gravity, or lack of it, lack of oxygen, extreme temperatures, distance from earth, etc.)

    c.   What career related to space exploration interests you most? Explain.

    d.   Would you consider this book to be more a book of fiction or of non-fiction? Explain.

Title:              *Sweetwater*

Genre:              Science fiction

Author:             Lawrence Yep

Illustrator:        Julia Noonan

Bibliographic Information:   Harper and Row, New York, 1973

Summary:            The story of Tyree, whose ancestors came from Earth, and his life in a star colony on the planet Harmony.

Interest Level:     Grade 4+

1.  Pre-Reading Activity:

    Have students look at the cover carefully and discuss the types of life forms in the picture. Explain to students that the story is set on a planet called Harmony. In groups, have them create a scenario of what might happen between the two life forms on a planet called Harmony and present it to the rest of the class.

2.  Learning Activities:

    a.  Many unusual life forms existed on Harmony. Ask students to create another life form which may have existed in Old Sion. Using clay, or other materials, have them make a model of this life form and tell the class about it and how it affected the lives of the people in the star colony. Use enough detail so that Tyree's sister would be able to "see" the creature.

    b.  Using the Bill of Rights and the Preamble to the Constitution, create a new Preamble and Bill of Rights to help govern Harmony.

    c.  The colonists in Old Sion split into two groups. In our country, people have split into many groups. Ask students to describe the groups that exist in their community. Involve them in a problem-solving exercise to see how they can bring the various groups together. They may wish to write up the best solutions and send them to the local newspaper in the form of editorials.

    d.  Discuss the ways in which the colonists who settled on the planet Harmony were similar to the pioneers of the American West. Have students select a favorite song of the Old West to use as a model for a new song that tells about life in a star colony.

3.  Discussion Questions

    a.  Compare life on Earth with life in the star colony.

    b.  What did Amadeus mean when he told Tyree that, "The only thing that matters in the changing universe is the song, the eternal song that waits for you"?

    c.  What can we learn about conflict and resolving conflicts from the different groups living on Harmony?

    d.  Why were star colonies important to Earth? (They shipped back materials that Earth needed, such as metal and soil.) What do you think of the possibility of this happening in the future? Explain.

    e.  Why is this book considered science fiction?

# Culminating Activity:

Have students hold a mini-debate in which they discuss the following issue: Should funding for space exploration and colonization be continued when money is so badly needed to solve social problems such as hunger, crime, and disease on Earth?

# Supplemental Literature

(*Note*: Unless otherwise noted, all books included are informational except books of science fiction which are indicated by an *.)

## Primary (Grades 1–3)

Arnold, C. (1990). *Ladybird first facts about space.* Illustrated by A. Accardo. Auburn, Maine: Ladybird Books.
  Includes an assortment of facts concerning our Solar System.
Branley, F. (1986). *Journey into a black hole.* Illustrated by M. Simont. New York: Harper and Row.
  Introduces the reader to this astronomical phenomena.
Branley, F. (1987). *The planets in our Solar System.* Illustrated by D. Madden. New York: HarperColllins.
  Includes interesting facts about the planets.
Branley, F. (1986). *What the moon is like.* Illustrated by T. Kelley. New York: Harper and Row.
  Introduces the reader to the moon — Earth's closest neighbor.
*Cameron, E. (1954). *The wonderful flight to the mushroom planet.* Illustrated by R. Henneberger. New York: Little.
  Two boys and a muschroom grower collaborate on plans to make a space ship and take off for adventure.
Coffelt, N. (1993). *Dogs in space.* San Diego: HBJ.
  [Picture Book] Take a tour of the Solar System with some of the craziest dogs in the universe.
Fowler, Allan. (1992). *The sun's family of planets.* New York: Children's Press.
  An introduction to our Solar System.
Hansen, R., and Bell, R. (1985). *My first book of space.* New York: Simon and Schuster.
  Developed in conjunction with NASA, this book on the Solar System is filled with color photos from NASA's archives.
*Harding, L. (1980). *The fallen spaceman.* New York: Harper and Row.
  A computerized spacesuit with a tiny spaceman is accidently hurled to Earth.
Krulik, N. (1991). *My picture book of the planets.* New York: Scholastic.
  [Picture book] Introduces young children to the wonders of our Solar System.
Mitton, J. (1991). *Discovering the planets.* New York: Troll.
  Recent information on astronomical and space exploration. Answers many commonly asked questions.
Moche, D.L. (1990). *The Golden Book of space exploration.* Paintings by T. LaPadula. Racine, Wisconsin: Western Pub.
  Includes all types of information about space and space exploration.
Nelson, N. (1993). *Space.* Illustrated by R. Archer. New York: Thomson Learning.
  Take a trip through outer space through the pages of this book.
*Slote, A. (1978). *My trip to Alpha I.* Illustrated by H. Berson. New York: Harper and Row.
  Jack travels to Alpha I, only to find his aunt acting very strangely.

## Intermediate (Grades 4-6)

Beasant, P. (1992). *1000 facts about space.* Ill. by P. Bull, G. Smith, and M. Steward. New York: Kingfish Books.
  Amazing facts about stars, astronomy, and space discovery.
Berger, M. (1992). *Discovering Mars.* Illustrated by J. Holub. New York: Scholastic.

An exciting look at the red planet.

*Danziger, P. (1986). *This planet has no atmosphere.* New York: Delacorte.
    The story of a lunar colony.

*Engdahl, S. (1970). *Journey between worlds.* New York: Atheneum.
    Explores the prejudice of Terrans against Maritian colonists.

George, M. (1992). *The moon.* Mankato, Minnesota: Creative Education.
    An aid to understanding the moon.

Gustafson, J. (1992). *Planets, moons and meteors.* New York: Julian Messner.
    Tips and activities for stargazing and using a telescope to explore the planets. Also introduces the reader to the planets and their unique features.

Moore, P. (1990). *The universe for beginners.* New York: Press Syndicate of the University of Cambridge.
    Takes reader on a journey into the infinite future and back to the beginning of time. Explores theories such as the big bang.

Nicolson, I. (1991). *The illustrated world of space.* New York: Simon and Schuster.
    Over 200 full-color illustrations, 40 maps, diagrams and charts concerning the universe.

Rathbun, E. (1989). *Exploring your Solar System.* Washington, D.C.: National Geographic Society.
    Travel to the sun and the nine planets. Includes outstanding photos and original artwork.

Schatz, D. (1991). *Astronomy activity book.* Illustrated by R. Doty. New York: Simon and Schuster.
    All kinds of activities introduce children to the wonders of our Solar System.

Simon, S. (1985). *Jupiter.* New York: Mulberry Books.
    Introduces the reader to this fascinating planet. The text accompanies photos taken on the Voyager Missions.

Simon, S. (1985). *Saturn.* New York: William Morrow.
    An intriguing look at the ringed planet.

Simon, S. (1986). *The sun.* New York: Mulberry Books.
    Explores the wonders of the sun, from nuclear explosions at its core to its sea of boiling gases at the surface. Contains over 20 full-color photos.

Simon, S. (1987). *Uranus.* New York: Mulberry Books.
    Contains photos and text to help us learn about this planet that is two billion miles from the sun.

Simon, S. (1992). *Venus.* New York: Morrow Jr. Books.
    Explores Earth's "sister planet." Full-color photos taken by NASA's Magellan and the Pioneer Venus Orbiter help us learn about Venus.

Van Cleaves, J. (1991) *Astronomy for every kid.* New York: John Wiley and Sons.
    Contains 101 easy experiments dealing with astronomy.

…(1993). *The visual dictionary of the universe.* London: Dorling Kindersley.
    Gives information on vocabulary associated with astronomy.

*Walsh, J. (1982). *The green book.* Illustrated by L. Bloom. New York: Farrar, Straus.
    A group of Britons leave a dying Earth for a new home on another planet.

*Wrightson, P. (1965). *Down to Earth.* Illustrated by M. Horder. San Diego: HBJ.
    A humorous story of a visitor from Mars.

# MINI-THEMES

## Men and Women in Space: Astronauts and Their Contributions

Space travel has come a long way from the crude-looking spherical object large enough to hold only one human passenger to today's space shuttles that carry entire teams of astronauts into space for weeks at a time. Beginning with the first man in space, Cosmonaut Yuri Gagarin, students can trace the journey of the men and women who have risked their lives to cross the boundaries of earth's atmosphere and take part in a new age of discovery.

### References

Allen, J. P. (1984). *Entering space: An astronaut's odyssey.* New York: Workman.

Barton, B. (1988). *I want to be an astronaut.* New York: Crowell.

Bean, Alan. (1988). *My life as an astronaut.* New York: Minstrel.

Bondar, B. with Bondar, R. (1993). *On the shuttle: 8 days in space.* Ontario: Greey de Pencier Books.

Fraser, M. *One giant leap.* New York: Holt.

Kennedy, G. (1991). *The first men in space.* New York: Chelsea House.

Pogue, W. (1991). *How do you go to the bathroom in space?* Cartoons by S. Harris. New York: Tom Doherty Associates.

Ride, S. with Okie, S. (1986). *To space and back.* New York: Beach Tree.

Sullivan, G. (1990). *The day we walked on the moon: A photo history of space exploration.* New York: Scholastic.

### Activities

a.  Have students create a cartoon to describe some aspect of living/traveling in space. For example, the cartoon may illustrate how an astronaut would eat in space, keep the page of a book open, etc. A wonderful resource to share with students before they begin this activity is Pogue's (1991) *How Do You Go to the Bathroom in Space?* It is filled with humorous cartoons depicting life in space and the problems that have to be overcome.

b.  Share several books dealing with manned exploration of space, such as *One Giant Leap* (Fraser, 1993), Kennedy's (1991) *The First Men in Space,* and *To Space and Back* (Ride and Okie, 1986). Ask students to select an astronaut/cosmonaut and write a newspaper article as this person to reflect his/her feelings about exploring space, concerns, highlights, frustrations, etc. Encourage students to give their articles creative headlines.

c.  Discuss with students the various problems that astronauts would have while living in space, such as weightlessness, sleeping, exercise, food, etc. Divide students into groups, one per problem and have them create a skit to demonstrate the problem and a way in which NASA solved the problem, along with their own solutions. Encourage students to bring in any visuals possible. For example, they may bring in dried food, pictures and photos of space suits, etc. Skits can be humorous or serious in nature.

d.  Have students create a SPACE AGE award to be given to the space pioneer they believe made the most important contribution(s) to the space program. Each student should nominate a space pioneer and deliver a one- to three-minute speech outlining this person's contributions. After all speeches have been made, allow students to vote. If the space pioneer is alive today, students can send the award — with a letter explaining the reasons for it — to the person, c/o NASA, Washington, D.C. 20546.

e.  Have students research various careers related to space travel. Have them divide into groups, one group per career. Have them create questions they would ask people in that field and research the questions through reading related books and talking to (or writing letters to) people in the field.

(Often university professors can suggest people to contact.) Have students compile their information into a booklet called "Careers for the New Space Age." When possible, invite speakers who have careers related to space travel.

## Space Technology: Satellites, Shuttles, Space Stations, and Colonization

Since the beginning of the Space Age on October 4, 1957, when the Soviet Union successfully launched Sputnik I, tremendous advances have been made in space technology. Satellites, such as weather and communication provide all types of services, from helping us predict the weather to bringing us our favorite television programs. Space stations are being developed to serve as a laboratory to conduct research, an observatory, a manufacturing plant, an assembly plant where structures can be put together, a storehouse to keep spare parts, and a garage where other spacecraft can be repaired. The technology of the space age has improved by leaps and bounds and, with continued funding, the sky is no longer the limit.

## References

Asimov, I. (1990). *Colonizing the planets and stars.* New York: Careth Stevens.

Bendick, J. (1982). *Space travel.* New York: Franklin Watts.

Branley, F. (1986). *From sputnik to space shuttles: Into the new space age.* New York: Crowell.

Butterfield, M. (1985). *Satellites and space stations.* New York: Usborne.

Dwiggings, D. (1985). *Flying the space shuttles.* New York: Dodd, Mead.

Herbst, Judith. (1993). *Star crossing: How to get around the universe.* New York: Atheneum.

Maurer, R. (1989). *Junk in space.* New York: Simon and Schuster.

Rickard, G. (1989). *Homes in space.* Lerner Publications.

Ridpath, I. and Muirden, J. (1992). *The world around us — space.* Illustrated by R. Jobson. New York: Kingfisher Books.

Smith, H.E. (1987). *Daring the unknown: A history of NASA.* San Diego: HBJ.

Weiss, M. (1984). *Far out factories: Manufacturing in space.* New York: Lodestar Books.

## Activities

a.  Have students select and create a model of one of the space satellites in use today. Have them share the satellite by developing a commercial describing its benefits. (You may also wish to have one group concentrate their efforts on the Hubble Telescope.)

b.  Have students read about several experiments conducted in the space shuttles. Have them design their own experiments that could be conducted in space and send their ideas to NASA.

c.  Have students create their own space shuttles. (For example, they can split open large plastic jugs so that one side is still attached. Cut out cardboard semicircles and glue them inside the jugs to make decks. Cut holes for hatches and make toothpick ladders to go through the hatches. Label the various decks — flight, living, storage, etc.)

d.  As of this writing, plans are being made to assemble *Freedom,* a space station that will provide living space for eight people. In June, 1993, the U.S. House of Representatives approved the NASA bill for $1.9 billion for continued space station development. The project is expected to cost $16 billion to complete. Have students research the amount of spending that is allocated for space exploration, the amount of jobs generated, and other pertinent information. They can get this information by writing to their congressional representative or to NASA, Washington, D.C. 20546. Have students research the many ways space exploration has enhanced our own lives. For example, satellites give us the ability to beam television live all over our planet. Have students list their findings on one large classroom chart that includes two columns — one "pro" and one "con" continued space spending. Discuss findings.

e.  Encourage students to research the effects of the comet which slammed into Jupiter in July, 1994. Ask the class to imagine that a huge comet will destroy three-quarters of the earth. They must find a way to colonize another planet. In groups, have them choose a planet from our Solar System best suited for colonization, and using what they know about the planet, have them make drawings of what they think a space colony on this planet would look like.

f.  Space has become littered with rockets and other "space junk" over the past 30 years. In November, 1993, the space shuttle *Endeavor* had to change its plans or it would have come within six-tenths of a mile of a spent Russian rocket launched in 1965. On Earth we have many ways for eliminating our trash. Read *Junk in Space* (Maurer, 1989). Have students brainstorm ways of eliminating space trash. Have them display their ideas on poster board and illustrate them.

## The Night Sky: The Constellations

From the beginning of time, early humans have studied the night sky. To these early watchers of the sky, the stars seemed to form patterns that looked like the shapes of familiar animals and the heroes of their myths and legends. To these figures, or constellations, they gave names. Today, with our scientific advancements, we are still fascinated with the myths and legends surrounding the stars, yet we are constantly trying to add to our scientific knowledge of the night sky. This mini-unit explores both the facts and legends regarding the constellations.

## References

### *Legends:*

Birdseye, T. (1990). *A song of stars: An Asian legend.* Illustrated by J. Chen. New York: Holiday.
Gallant, R. (1979). *The constellations: How they came to be.* New York: Four Winds.
Goble, P. (1993). *The lost children: The boys who were neglected.* New York: Bradbury.
Mayo, G. (1987). *Star tales: North American Indian stories about the stars.* New York: Walker.
Vautier, G. (1980). *The shining stars.* Illustrated by J. Bezencon. Cambridge: Cambridge University Press.
Vautier, G. (1982). *The way of the stars: Greek legends of the constellations.* Illustrated by J. Bezencon. Cambridge: Cambridge University Press.

### *Informational Books:*

Apfel, N. (1988). *Nebulae: The birth and death of stars.* New York: Lothrop.
Branley, F. (1987). *Star guide.* New York: Crowell.
Branley, F. (1990). *Superstar.* Illustrated by T. Kelley. New York: HarperCollins.
Gallant, R. (1986). *The private lives of the stars.* New York: Macmillan.
Gustafson, J. (1992). *Stars, clusters, and galaxies.* New York: Messner.
Krupps, E.C. (1989). *The Big Dipper and you.* New York: Morrow.
Lampton, C. (1988). *Stars and planets.* New York: Doubleday.
Reigot, B.P. (1988). *A book about planets and stars.* New York: Scholastic.
Simon, S. (1986). *Stars.* New York: Morrow.
Stott, C. (1993). *Night sky.* London: Dorling Kindersley.

## Activities

a.  Using any artistic or dramatic form, have students retell a myth explaining one of the constellations.

b.  On a clear night, encourage students to observe the night sky and draw what they see. Have them look through books of constellations and try to identify the stars and constellations they have drawn.

c.  Have students create a new constellation using the steps below:

1.  Read a myth dealing with the origin of one of the constellations.

2.  Summarize the myth.

3.  Read factual information about the constellation and list three facts.

4.  Divide a piece of paper in half. On the left side, draw the picture of the constellation, name the constellation, and label its stars. On the right, place the stars of the constellation in the correct place but connect them differently to form a new constellation. Label the stars and give the constellation a new name.

5.  Create a myth to explain the origin of the new constellation. Use actual mythological characters and at least three facts about the constellation (see step 3 above.)

d.  Divide the class into four groups corresponding to the seasons. Have each group diagram the sky for its season and include the constellations that may be seen during this time period.

e.  Have students create a book of "Star Facts," in which they include interesting facts about the stars and constellations (for example, How is a star made? What is a star composed of? What happens when a star dies?) Have them illustrate each fact included.

## Third Planet from the Sun: The Earth

A study of space and our Solar System would not be complete without a look at our own planet, Earth. Our planet is unique in the Solar System; it is the only one supporting any type of life form, as we know it. And yet, with all the technological advancements, with our ability to explore the depths of outer space, we tend to forget the fragility of our own world. This mini-unit explores planet Earth, its unique resources, natural land formations, and the need for each of us to protect and live in harmony with our environment.

## References

Bain, I. (1984). *Mountains and earth movements.* New York: Franklin Watts.

Brownstone, D.M. and Franck, I.M. (1989). *Natural wonders of America.* New York: Atheneum.

Cole, J. (1987). *The magic school bus inside the Earth.* Illustrated by B. Degen. New York: Scholastic.

Durell, Al, et al. (Eds.) (1993). *The big book for our planet.* New York: Dutton.

The Earthwords Group. (1990). *50 simple things kids can do to save the Earth.* Illustrated by M. Montez. Kansas City: University Press.

Ferndon, J. (1992). *How the Earth works: 100 ways parents and kids can share the secrets of the Earth.* Photos by M. Dunning. New York: Readers' Digest Association.

Ganeri, A. (1991). *Explore the world of forces of nature.* illustrated by M. Saunders. Racine, Wisconsin: Western Publishing.

George, J.C. (1984). *One day in the alpine tundra.* New York: Harper and Row.

George, J.C. (1993). *One day in the desert.* New York: Harper and Row.

George, J.C. (1986). *One day in the prairie.* New York: Harper and Row.

George, J.C. (1988). *One day in the woods.* New York: Harper and Row.

Lauber, P. (1986). *Volcano.* New York: Bradbury Press.

Pringle, L. (1987). *Restoring our earth.* Hillside, NJ: Enslow.

Radlauer, E. and Radlauer, R. (1987). *Earthquakes.* New York: Children's Press.

Robin, G. (1984). *Glaciers and ice sheets.* San Diego: HBJ.

Rutland, J. (1980). *Exploring the violent Earth.* New York: Warwick Press.

Simon, E. (1991). *Earthquakes.* New York: Morrow.

Simon, S. (1988). *Volcanoes.* New York: Morrow.

Williams, B. (1992). *The living world.* New York: Kingfisher Books.

Williams, B., and Williams, B. (1993). *The Random House book of 1001 questions and answers about planet Earth.* New York: Random House.

## Activities

a.  In *The Big Book for Our Planet* (Durell, et al., 1993), many well-known authors and illustrators of children's books have pooled their talents to honor the Earth. Read to the children the "Earth Game" by author Pam Conrad who describes a special game in which you can involve your students. Gather students into a circle and tie the end of a ball of twine to your finger. Toss the ball in the air to one of the students, who in turn wraps the string around his/her thumb and tosses it to another student. Have students do this until all are joined in the circle with the twine. Have students imagine that they are the Earth. Each student becomes a different part of the Earth (for example, the Arctic Ocean, the jungles in Africa, a rain forest in Brazil) and tells one way that this area is being ruined by polluters, hunters, etc. As each student speaks, he/she tugs on the twine so that all students feel the effects. Once all the students have spoken, repeat the process, but have each student tell one thing that can be done to improve his/her part of the Earth. After the game, have students react to what has been said and to the significance of the twine that connected them all.

b.  Our Earth has been shaped by various natural phenomena. Group students by such phenomena as earthquakes, rivers and glaciers, erosion, volcanoes, and so forth. Have each group research its phenomenon to create a demonstration that illustrates the ways this phenomenon has shaped the land. Books such as *Land Masses* (Arnold, 1985), *Volcanoes* (Simon, 1988), and *Earthquakes* (Simon, 1991) can help with this.

c.  Have students create a large floor map of one of the continents (select a continent that reflects your social studies curriculum). Group students and assign each a different physical feature (mountain, desert, glacier, river, etc.) of the continent. Have each group research its feature, select a specific example of the feature (for example, the Painted Desert, the Sierra Nevada Mountains, Carlsbad Caverns, etc.) and learn its location and how it was created. Have them create a symbol to represent the physical feature. Ask each group to present a skit that teaches the class about the feature, its location, and its effect on the land and people around it. Students should place the symbols they created in the correct locations on the class map.

d.  Read aloud portions of books about various geographical regions. For example, Jean Craighead George has a series of books that deals with various regions, such as *One Day in the Desert* (1983), *One Day in the Alpine Tundra* (1984), *One Day in the Prairie* (1986), and *One Day in the Woods* (1988). Assign groups of students their own regions and have them create their own *One Day in the* _____ books.

e.  Have students create collages that reflect the variety of geographical features on our planet. Using the song "America the Beautiful" as a model, create a song to honor planet Earth.

f.  Contact a local environmentalist and ask him/her to speak to the class on the subject of environmental protection. Have students compose several interview questions before the guest arrives.

g.  Read various poems and stories from *The Big Book for Our Planet* (Durell, et al., 1993) and discuss students' reactions to each. Many of the entries can be used as models for the students' own work. For example, based on Tana Hoban's contribution, have students create a picture book that will arose environmental awareness. Ask each student to submit at least one photo that reflects the beauty of our world (for example, a butterfly, a tree, the ocean tide, a seashell, a mountain peak, a green plant). As a class, create a text for the book that encourages readers to protect the Earth and all its natural wonders.

# Intermediate Unit: The Wild, Wild West

**Theme:** THE WILD, WILD WEST

**Focus:** The Wild West comes alive as students travel through time to one of the most colorful and romanticized periods of American history.

**Objective:** Upon completion of this unit, students will:

1. relate significant historical events that reflect how the West was won — and lost.

2. describe the reasons for moving west and relate the dangers the pioneers faced.

3. compare the reality of life in the Wild West with the way it was depicted through legend and lore.

4. become familiar with the art and music of the Wild West — pictures and songs that capture the courage and spirit of the Wild West.

**Initiating Activity:** The opening of the American West and the growth of photography took place during the same time. By the 1850s, frontier photographers were traveling throughout the West, capturing and preserving for posterity the life and times of the pioneers who journeyed to and settled the West. Photocopy many of the photographs that appear in such book as *Children of the Wild West* (Freedman, 1983) and *Cowboys of the Wild West* (Freedman, 1985), and distribute them to students. Group students and ask them to make predictions about all the aspects of life during the time, based solely on what they can hypothesize from the pictures. Have students share their photographs and predictions. At the end of the unit have students re-evaluate their interpretations based on the knowledge and understandings they have gained.

## General Activities:

1. Have students create their own Wild West character. To do this, divide students into groups and have each group trace one of its members on butcher paper. Students can then staple the front and back of the traced pattern, leaving a temporary opening so that the figure can be stuffed with rolled up pieces of newspaper. Using the information and photographs in the many reference books on life in the West, have students recreate a Wild West character (for example, cowboy, Native American, teacher, store clerk, etc.) they find especially interesting. Have students use various clothing and objects to make their figure look authentic and life-like. Allow time for students to share their character and tell the class something about his/her life during the time of the Wild, Wild West.

2. After reading about the Wild West, have students create a large mural in which they depict one aspect of life in the Wild West (for example, a cowboy roping cattle; branding cattle; a schoolhouse; a general store; panning for gold; hunting for food and fur; keeping law and order; building the railroad to the West; and so forth). The characters created in general activity 1 can then be placed in an area with the appropriate background scenery.

3. The West inspired its own music. Many of the songs were sung by cowboys around the campfire during the long trail drives. Have each group of students select and learn a favorite song about life in the Wild West and have them teach their song to other groups of students. Many of these songs can be found in books such as *America Sings* by Carl Carner (1942) and in *From Sea to Shining Sea* (Cohn, ed., 1993).

4. Read *The Quilt* by Ann Jonas (Greenwillow, 1984) to students. Explain that quilting was a popular craft in the days of the Old West and remains a popular art form today. Since many communities have people involved in quilting, try to locate a local quilt-maker willing to demonstrate the craft. (Ask

people in local craft stores or fabric stores to help you locate quilters.) Provide each student with a 12" by 12" piece of fabric. Have students illustrate a scene from the Wild West on their piece of fabric. Combine squares to form a quilt.

5.   Group students and have them become one of the states of the West. *As the state* have each group present a brief skit telling about its life during the days of the Wild West, why it became a popular location for settlement, how/when it became a state, as well as containing any anecdotes and stories about famous people associated with the area.

6.   Horace Greeley, editor of the New York *Tribune* during the mid 1800s, once penned the words, "Go west, young man, go west and grow up with the country." Ask students to create a poster, using these famous words as a caption to entice people to travel West. Their posters should capture one or more of the compelling reasons (for example, fur trade, gold rush, opportunity for religious freedom, etc.) that would cause people to uproot themselves and face the dangers associated with travel to the West.

7.   The West was settled by many men and women of courage and perseverance. Have students research one of the following men/women who have had a part in how the West was won — and lost. (Other names can be added.) After their research is completed, have them share their findings with the class in a creative way. For example, they might create a ballad about the person, set to the tune of a song of the Old West, or they might create a monologue that that person would use to describe his/her exploits, and so forth.

Stephen Austin and the Texas Rangers

William Becknell

James Butler (Wild Bill Hickok)

Brigham Young

Martha Jane Cannary (Calamity Jane)

Kit Carson

Butch Cassidy

George Catlin

John Chisholm

Buffalo Bill Cody

Wyatt Earp

John Fremont

James Gadson

Zane Grey

Horace Greeley

James Harte

Doc Holiday

President Andrew Jackson

Frank and Jesse James

William Clark and Meriwether Lewis

Henry McCarty (Billy the Kid)

Annie Oakley

Frederic Remington

Charles Russell

Susanna Salter

Levi Strauss

John Sutter

Henry Wells and William Fargo

8.   Read *The Cowboy and the Black-Eyed Pea* (Johnson, 1993), a parody of *The Princess and the Pea*, with language and details of the Wild West. As a class, create a story frame (see Chapter 2, page 60) based on this book to help students organize their thoughts about the story and its elements. Have students create and illustrate their own folktales of the Wild West based on their favorite childhood folktale. Bind each story and have students share them with younger children.

9.   After reading about actual life in the Wild West, allow students to watch a video of a well-known movie that depicts the West, such as *Dances with Wolves*. Involve students in a discussion of the stereotypes fostered by the movie, the inaccuracies, and so forth.

10.  Many artists have captured the spirit of the Wild West. Encourage students to look at pictures of sculptures and other artistic media by such people as Frederic Remington, Charles Lewis, and Ansel

Adams. *Wild West*, a bimonthly publication of Empire Press, Inc. ( 602 S. King Street, Suite 300, Leesburg, VA, 22075), features photos of many such works. Have students select a favorite sculpture, painting, and the like and try to recreate it. Have them accompany their artwork with a brief essay on how the original work captured the feelings of the Wild West.

11. Historian Cathi Luchetti wrote, "Women experienced an autonomy never before dreamed of… and 'women's work' soon came to mean whatever had to be done." Locate specific information/photos to support her views. Have students create a "Go west, young woman go west" collage.

12. Create a "Wild West" time capsule that might have been left by one of the settlers of the Wild West. To do this, divide students into groups based on various disciplines of social studies and science (for example, anthropology, sociology, politics, economics, geography, history, biology). After explaining each discipline, have the groups bring in and/or make replicas of items that reflect the Wild West from the perspective of the discipline assigned (for example, clothing, pictures, crafts, copies of songs and poetry, books). As they place these items in the box, have students describe the item's significance. You may wish to keep this time capsule and use it to introduce the unit on the Wild West next year.

## Discussion Questions:

1. Life in the Wild West was often quite different from the legends and lore that surround it. What do you believe is the most important difference between fact and fiction regarding the Wild West?

2. Why do you think the time/place was referred to as "The Wild West"? Do you agree or disagree with this term? What term do you think would be more appropriate?

3. Many people risked their lives to travel to the West. Do you think the advantages outweighed the disadvantages? Explain.

4. Imagine that you lived during the mid-1800s in New York. What would entice you to travel to and settle in the Wild West?

5. Many people have various reasons to explain the end of the era of the Wild West. How would you explain it?

6. What if the first immigrants to this country had settled on the west coast instead of the east coast?

## Literature Related Activities

| | |
|---|---|
| Title: | *Cowboys of the Wild West* |
| Genre: | Informational |
| Author: | Russell Freedman |
| Illustrator: | Photographs from the days of the Wild West |
| Bibliographic Information: | Clarion, New York, 1985 |
| Summary: | Newbery Medalist Russell Freedman provides insight into life in the Wild West of the 1800s. Through text and photographs , the reader can feel the spirit and courage of those who inspired the legends of the old-time, trail-driving cowboy. |

Interest Level: Grade 4+

1.  Pre-Reading Activity:

    Ask students to close their eyes and picture a "cowboy" in their minds. Involve students in a semantic webbing (see Chapter 2, pages 34-35) of the word "cowboy" based on the images they "see." Share the cover of *Cowboys of the Wild West*. Involve them in a discussion of the ways in which the cowboys pictured differed from the way they imagined they would look.

2.  Learning Activities:

    a.  Have students create a journal entry written by a cowboy at the end of a long day on the trail.

    b.  Have students create a chart that pictures the different clothing and equipment worn/used by the cowboys. Next to each have them explain how the item was developed to solve a specific problem. Ask students to think of life today and what we could do to make our clothing more functional.

    c.  Have students select a favorite picture from the book. Ask them to write a descriptive paragraph in such a way that others will see it, feel the emotion, mood, and so forth that the picture evokes.

    d.  Reprint the map on page 15. Have the students create questions about distances between various cities and routes between cities. Involve them in further research to learn about the terrain that had to be crossed as cowboys moved cattle from one area to another.

    e.  Have students compile the poems and songs referenced in this book, along with other favorites, to create a *Cowboy Anthology — Poems and Songs of the Wild West*.

3.  Discussion Questions

    a.  Why was the cowboy's job so important during the days of the Wild West? (As the demand for beef grew, the cattle-raising industry spread from Texas. Cattle had to be moved from Texas to railroad towns to be shipped to meat-packing plants.)

    b.  Who were the original cowboys? (Cowboys originated over four hundred years ago in Mexico when Spanish settlers brought the first domesticated horses and cattle to North America. Ranchers who looked after the herds were called vaqueros — from "vaca," the Spanish word for cow.)

    c.  According to the book, only a few cowboys stayed on the job for more than ten years. What do you think was the most difficult thing about being a cowboy — the lifestyle or the physical work? Cite specific references from the book to support your answer.

    d.  In what ways did this book change your perceptions about cowboys and cowboy life?

    e.  Discuss the lines on page 79 that are from a Texas song. What do they tell you about the reasons for the end of the cowboy era? (Cattle ranchers were putting up barbed-wire fences that kept livestock from straying. The network of railroad tracks was spreading and by the 1890s reached into central Texas, making long trail drives unnecessary.)

---

Title:                          *The Righteous Revenge of Artemis Bonner*

Genre:                         Fiction

Author:                        Walter Dean Myers

Bibliographic Information:   HarperCollins, New York, 1992

Summary: Fifteen-year-old Artemis Bonner leaves New York City in 1880 to find his uncle's murderer and to find the gold mine his uncle sketched on a map from memory. The story traces Artemis's journey and adventures through the Old West.

Interest Level: Grade 5+

1. Pre-Reading Activity:

   Ask students to discuss the following questions: "What do you think the term *righteous revenge* in the title means?" "How is the term *righteous revenge* an oxymoron?" "Do you believe that there should be such a thing as *righteous revenge* — why or why not?"

2. Learning Activities:

   a. Artemis traveled throughout the Wild West. During his journey he said, "If a town could be a bird or an animal, Seattle would be a seagull. It did not as much mind what it was doing as take wings and fly. And just like a sea gull it took its own sweet time about doing anything." Based on the students' knowledge of the Wild West and based on the descriptions Artemis gave, have students create a metaphor similar to the one above for each of the following cities Artemis visited, comparing it to a bird or an animal, and explain the comparison: Tombstone, Arizona; Lincoln, Nebraska; Juarez City, Mexico; Seattle, Washington; and Anchorage, Alaska. Ask each student to select their favorite metaphor, then illustrate and display it.

   b. Tall tales grew out of America's dream for freedom and the vastness of the wide-open spaces of the Wild West. Many feats told through tall tales were based on fact but were exaggerated into legendary proportions, as was the story told to Artemis by O'Hara, the prospector who told how he had found the biggest hunk of gold ever found, "It was so big, it took two horses just to drag it around town." Involve students in reading tall tales of the Wild West, such as those about Pecos Bill and Paul Bunyan. Have students discuss what factual information was included about the Wild West and what was exaggerated.

   c. The gold rush of 1849 brought many men and women west. Have the students research this era. Research can include the methods used for finding gold; the dangers involved; the numbers of people the gold rush attracted; how the gold rush affected life in the Wild West; and so on. Have students present their findings in a creative way (for example, become a prospector and tell about your life; become a piece of gold nugget and tell how you were found).

   d. In groups, have students create a sequel to the story and present it in some form of creative dramatics. Remind students that details in the sequel should be accurate in terms of time and place.

3. Discussion Questions

   a. How did the book portray the Wild West? Based on your knowledge of the Wild West, how accurate was this portrayal?

   b. What other ways might Artemis and Cat Fish have solved their differences other than resorting to violence?

   c. Explain the irony of the statement, "Moby might have been honorable in the killing department, but I did not know that much about him, or even if he had come from a decent home." (page 81)

   d. Artemis believed that the Wild West was settled by cutthroats, heathens, and foreigners. Agree or disagree with him, citing specific references from this book and others.

| Title: | *Across America on an Emigrant Train* |
| Genre: | Informational |
| Author: | Jim Murphy |
| Illustrator: | Illustrated with Photographs and Prints |
| Bibliographic Information: | Clarion, New York, 1993 |
| Summary: | Follow the journey made in 1879 by writer Robert Louis Stevenson, when he set out from Scotland headed for California. He and his fellow travelers crossed the Atlantic and then undertook a three-thousand-mile train ride to settle in the American West. Through Stevenson's eyes, we meet the people and visit what has been referred to as the Wild West. |
| Interest Level: | Grade 5+ |

1. **Pre-Reading Activity:**

    Ask students if they know who Robert Louis Stevenson was. See which of his writings they are familiar with (for example, *Treasure Island*, *A Child's Garden of Verses*, *The Strange Case of Dr. Jekyll and Mr. Hyde*, *Kidnapped*). Also, discuss the difference between immigration and emigration. Ask them, "Why do you think the book was called *Across America on an Emigrant Train* rather than on an *Immigrant Train?*" (Generally, to emigrate is to leave from a country or place. To immigrate is to enter or arrive in a country or place. As the book explains, Stevenson's traveling companions, though they were in America, had not yet arrived at their final destinations. Stevenson believed, therefore, that they were still in the process of emigrating.)

2. **Learning Activities:**

    a.  Read aloud Jacqueline Geis's book *Where the Buffalo Roam* (1992), in which she expands a popular song of the West to describe the vegetation of America's Southwest. Based on Stevenson's descriptions of the West, have students create their own verses to add to the song. Have them illustrate their verses and compile them into *A Song Book of the West*.

    b.  Based on the information related in the book, have students create the "Top Ten Reasons to Immigrate to America's West." The list can be humorous but it should be based on fact.

    c.  States competed with one another for immigrants. To lure people west and especially to their state, advertisements and pamphlets were written and distributed. Have students form groups (one per state west of the Mississippi) and have them create an advertisement similar to those pictured in the book (page 3). Their advertisement should include factual information about the territory and what it offers the immigrant.

    d.  Many settlers to the Wild West wrote to their relatives telling them about their lives and asking them to journey west. Write a letter to a relative describing your life in the Wild West and explaining why he/she should join you.

    e.  Brainstorm a list of countries from which a large number of people immigrated to the Wild West. Divide students into groups based on the list of countries and involve them in research to learn why so many decided to leave their homes, the type of work they did in the West, and where in the West they mainly settled. Have students create a poster to display their findings, along with a graph to indicate appropriate information.

3. Discussion Questions

   a. Why were the government, individual states, and the railroad so eager to attract immigrants? (The government needed people to work the land and harvest the natural resources of the West. The states wanted the money immigrants brought with them, the railroads needed people to lay tracks, and so forth.)

   b. List five things that surprised you most about Stevenson's journey across America.

   c. The Sioux chief, White Cloud, said, "Wherever the whites are established the red hunter must die of hunger." To what was he referring? (The white settlers were killing all the bison and other game that the Indians relied on for survival. Much of the time the killing was for sport.)

   d. Discuss Stevenson's feelings about the treatment of the Native Americans. How do his beliefs coincide/disagree with yours?

   e. Looking at life in the West as it is depicted in the photographs, would you have liked living during the days of the Wild West? Why or why not?

| | |
|---|---|
| Title: | *Calamity Jane — Her Life and Her Legend* |
| Genre: | Biography |
| Author: | Doris Faber |
| Illustrator: | Illustrated with photographs |
| Bibliographic Information: | Houghton Mifflin, Boston, 1992 |
| Summary: | Who was Calamity Jane? Was she really a sharp-shooter as legend claims? Was she married to Wild Bill Hickok? Was she a scout for General Custer? This biography attempts to separate fact from fiction as it explores the life of Martha Jane Cannary — Calamity Jane. |

Interest Level: Grade 5+

1. Pre-Reading Activity:

   Discuss the fact that often actual people were transformed into legendary figures. Some of these include Johnny Appleseed, Buffalo Bill Cody, and Calamity Jane. Have students study the picture of Calamity Jane on the cover. Ask them why they think Calamity might have become a legend. Does the picture offer any clues?

2. Learning Activities:

   a. Calamity Jane seemed to create much of the legend that surrounded her. Have students select one of Calamity Jane's adventures and use it as a basis for a tall tale. Have them present it in storytelling form.

   b. Have students create a picture postcard depicting one of Calamity Jane's feats. On the other side of the card have them write a brief message describing Calamity Jane to a friend.

   c. From the photographs in the books have students create a diorama to depict a scene common to the Wild West.

   d. Create a monument to Calamity Jane or to any other person who immigrated to the West. (See the monument built to honor Wild Bill Hickok on p. 30.)

e.   Many legendary heroes/heroines of the Wild West had nicknames, such as Wild Bill, Buffalo Bill, Calamity Jane. Ask students to give themselves a nickname and create a story about themselves as a hero of the Wild West. Have students write their stories in the style of those written by Ned Wheeler for the dime novels (see pages 37 and 39) and remind them to keep the details authentic in terms of character, setting, and the like. Compile class stories into a Wild West paper.

3.   Discussion Questions

a.   How was Calamity Jane's life like the Wild West? (untamed, free, larger than life, daring, and so forth.) How did Calamity Jane differ from "The Spirit of the Frontier" pictured on page 3? (Women were supposed to inspire men, not seek out adventures of their own.)

b.   How was Calamity Jane different from most of the women of her time? (She dressed like a man, spent all her time with men, drank whiskey, pretended to be a boy to get more exciting jobs, and so forth.)

c.   The legend of Calamity Jane seems to be an inter-weaving of fact and fiction. How do you account for this phenomena?

d.   Of Calamity Jane, one western historian wrote, "She was most certainly somebody." Defend this statement.

**Culminating Activity:**   Hold a Wild West Extravaganza with Buffalo Bill Cody as host! Have students dress up in the costumes of the time, share their songs, art, and stories of the Wild West around a simulated campfire! Have students prepare foods associated with the Wild West. Group students and involve them in a role-playing activity in which they act out one of the following situations as if they lived during the mid and late 1800s:

1.   You and your family are recent immigrants to America. You've been living on the East Coast but see little hope for business opportunities. Some members of your family do not want to venture West, others do.

2.   You are on a wagon train heading West during the last weeks of Fall. There are two routes to follow — a shorter, more dangerous one by water; a much longer but safer one by land. Your supplies are running low and your oxen are near exhaustion. The members of your wagon train are divided as to what to do.

3.   You and your companions have found a gold deposit but are afraid that one of your group will stake the claim before the rest of you have the opportunity.

4.   You live in a small western town. A young Indian has been accused of shooting and killing one of the town's citizens. The youth admits to the killing but says it was in self-defense. The crowd wants him hung and the judge isn't expected for several months.

5.   You are members of the Texas Rangers. You learn that a very prominent citizen has been rustling cattle and branding it as his own.

6.   Create and act out a problem situation that was common in the days of the Wild West.

# Supplemental Literature

(*Note*: Unless otherwise noted, the books listed are informational.)

## Primary (Grades 1–3)

Courtault, M. (1989). *Going West: Cowboys and Pioneers*. Illustrated by D. Grant. New York: Young Discovery Library.
Traces travel to and life in the West.

Freeman, R. (1983). *Children of the wild west*. Illustrated with photographs. New York: Clarion.
A history, in words and photographs, of the lives of the children who traveled west in wagon trains and settled on the frontier.

Geis, J. (1992). *Where the buffalo roam*. Nashville, TN: Ideals.
Pictures depicting the West accompany Geis's own adaptation of the song "Home on the Range."

Johnson, T. (1993). *The cowboy and the black-eyed pea*. Illustred by W. Ludwig. New York: G.P. Putnam's Sons.
[Picture Book ] A parody of *The Princess and the Pea*, rich with the language and details of the Wild West.

Johnston, T., and DePaola, T. (1985). *The quilt story*. New York: G.P. Putnam's Sons.
[Fiction] The story of a quilt made during the pioneer days and the children it comforted.

Levine, E. (1986). *If you traveled west in a covered wagon*. Illustrated by C. Shaw. New York: Scholastic.
Takes children on a trip to the American West in a covered wagon and explains every aspect of life in a covered wagon and the dangers the travelers faced.

Stevens, C. (1979). *Trouble for Lucy*. Illustrated by R. Himler. New York: Clarion.
[Historical Fiction] Using information from first-person accounts of life on the Oregon Trail, the book focuses on the adventures of a young girl heading west.

Williams, D. (1993). *Grandma Essie's covered wagon*. Illustrated by W. Sadowski New York: Knopf
A recording of an oral history of a turn-of-the-century American childhood. The book captures the experience of traveling west in a covered wagon.

## Intermediate (Grades 4–6)

Brink, C. (1936). *Caddie Woodlawn*. New York: Macmillan.
[Historical Fiction] An account of the life of Caddie Woodlawn and her family as they live and survive the many dangers of life in the West.

Carmer, C. (1942). *America sings*. New York: Knopf.
Includes poems that celebrate every aspect of American history.

Cohn, A.L. (1993). *From sea to shining sea*. Illustrated by 15 Caldecott Medal/Honor Book Artists. New York: Scholastic.
This volume contains over 140 American folktales, folk songs, poems, and essays, with a large section devoted to the pioneers who settled the American West.

Freeman, R. (1983). *Children of the wild west*. Illustrated with photographs. New York: Clarion.
A history, in words and photographs, of the lives of the children who traveled west in wagon trains and settled on the frontier.

Freeman, R. (1985). *Cowboys of the wild west*. Illustrated with photographs. New York: Clarion.
A history, in words and photographs, of the lives of the cowboys who inspired the legends of the Wild West.

Geis, J. (1992). *Where the buffalo roam*. Nashville, TN: Ideals.
Pictures depicting the West accompany Geis's own adaptation of the song "Home on the Range."

Hammer, T. (1986). *The advancing frontier*. New York: Franklin Watts.
Emphasizes the settlement of the West and the role of women and blacks. Also discusses the "dark side" of western expansion — the descrimination against minorities and the treatment of Native Americans.

Ingoglia, G. (1991). *The big Golden Book of the Wild West.* Illustrated by G. Biggs. New York: Western Publishing.
    Traces the settlement of the West from the first setttlers to the Old West as it is today.
Lomax, J. A. and Lomax, A., compilers. (1938). *Cowboy songs and other frontier ballads.* New York: Macmillan.
    Includes many songs sung by the cowboys.
Metropolitan Museum of Art. (1991). *Songs of the Wild West.* New York: Simon and Schuster.
    A collection of tunes created by the cowboys and settlers of the Old West.
Meyer, C. (1992). *Where the broken heart still beats.* San Diego: Harcourt Brace Jovanovich.
    [Historical Fiction] The story of a 12-year-old girl who is kidnapped and raised by the Comanches for 25
    years before being "rescued" by Texas Rangers.
Moeri, L. (1981). *Save Queen of Sheba.* New York: Dutton.
    [Historical Fiction] The story of two children who survive an Indian attack while traveling in a wagon
    train.
Place, M. (1967). *American cattle trails: East and West.* New York: Holt Rinehart & Winston.
    Describes the trails traveled by the cowboys as they herded the cattle across the land.
Wilder, L.I. *The little house series.* New York: Harper and Row.
    [Historical Fiction] The life of Laura Ingalls Wilder and her family as they settle in different areas of the
    American West and face the dangers and triumphs of pioneer life.

# MINI-THEMES

## Legends of the Wild West

The men and women who tamed the Wild West were courageous, ambitious, and determined to build a home in a new frontier. Some of these men and women became legendary. Some were famous, while others were infamous. Yet their names have become synonymous with the term "Wild West" and remind us of an unparalleled chapter in American history.

### References:

Alderman, C. L. (1979). *Annie Oakley.* New York: Macmillan.
Baldwin, M. and O'Brien, P. (1981). *Wanted: Frank and Jesse James.* New York: Julian Messner.
Collier, E. (1952). *The story of Buffalo Bill.* New York: Grosset and Dunlap.
Holbrook, S.H. (1956). *Wyatt Earp: U.S. Marshall.* Illustrated by E. Richardson. New York: Random House.
May, R. (1986). *Daniel Boone and the American West.* Illustrated by G. Wood. New York: Bookwright Press.
Moody, R. (1955). *Kit Carson and the wild frontier.* New York: Random House.
Pelz, R. (1990). *Black heroes of the Wild West.* Illustrated by D. Piana. Seattle, Washington: Open Hand
    Publishing.
Quackenbush, R. (1988). *Who's that girl with the gun: A story of Annie Oakley.* New York: Simon and Schuster.
Surge, F. (1970). *Western outlaws.* Minneapolis: Lerner Publications.

### Activities:

1. Have students select a famous legendary figure of the Wild West and create a "Wanted Poster" for the person that outlines the reasons for his/her fame — or infamy — and includes a description and picture of the person, along with other relevant information. (Legends of the Wild West include, but are not limited to: Buffalo Bill; Calamity Jane; Wild Bill Hickok; George Washington Bush; Wyatt Earp; Jesse and Frank James; Billy the Kid; Belle Starr; Black Bart; and the Dalton Gang.)

2. The United States Postal Service brought out a series of stamps honoring legendary figures representing all areas of endeavor. Annie Oakley, a well-known figure of the Wild West, was one of those so honored. Ask each student to select another legendary character of the Wild West and create

a stamp that honors his/her contributions. You might involve the class in a contest to select several stamps and send them to the Postal Service suggesting that a series of stamps honoring the men and women of the Wild West be issued.

3.  Have students select a favorite Wild West legendary character and create a comic book dedicated to his/her exploits. Remind students that the details in the comic book should be authentic in terms of the time and place. The story can be factual or told in hyperbole (as a tall tale).

4.  Ask each student to select a favorite legend of the Wild West, take on the persona of that person, and tell about his/her life. Cassette tapes or videotapes can be made to create a library of "oral histories."

5.  Ask students to imagine who might emerge from the present time to become legendary heroes/ heroines of tomorrow and list responses on the board. Ask students to select one hero/heroine and write a futuristic newspaper article describing the person and his/her exploits. Remind students that the article should be a combination of fact and exaggeration.

## Native Americans of the Wild West

The area known to us as the Wild West belonged to Native Americans. As more and more settlers moved west and the states extended westward, the Native Americans were either forced to accept the government's offers to resettle elsewhere or be driven away by force. As their land was stolen, so too was their way of life.

### References:

Brandt, K. (1985). *Indian crafts.* Illustrated by G. Guzzi. New York: Troll .

Brandt, K. (1985). *Indian homes.* Illustrated by G. Guzzi. New York: Troll.

Collier, P. (1973). *When shall they rest: The Cherokee's long struggle with America.* New York: Holt, Rinehart, and Winston.

Doherty, C.A., and Doherty, K.M. (1991). *The Apaches and Navajos.* New York: Franklin Watts. (Part of a series on Native American tribes)

Driving Hawk Sneve, V., compiler. (1989). *Dancing teepees: Poems of American Indian youth.* Illusrated by S. Gammell. New York: Holiday House.

Force, R., and Force, M. (1991). *The American Indians.* New York: Chelsea House.

Gobel, P., and Goble, D. (1969). *Red Hawk's account of Custer's last stand.* New York: Pantheon.

Hook, J. (1989). *Indian warrior chiefs.* Dorset, England: Firebird Books.

Lowre, R. H. (1954). *Indians of the Plains.* New York: McGraw Hill.

Marrin, A. (1984). *War clouds in the West: Indians and cavalrymen 1860-1890.* New York: Atheneum.

Porter, F. III (General Ed.). *Indians of North America.* New York: Chelsea House. (a series of books)

Ruoff, A. (1991). *Literature of the American Indians.* New York: Chelsea House.

Stein, R.C. (1983). *The story of Wounded Knee.* Illustrated by D. J. Catrow III. Chicago: Children's Press.

Wyatt, E. (1953). *Cochise.* Illustrated by A. Houser. New York: McGraw-Hill.

Wyatt, E. (1952). *Geronimo.* Illustrated by A. Houser. New York: McGraw-Hill.

### Activities:

1.  Have students simulate a "Meeting of Chiefs" in which various leaders of Native American tribes discuss whether to agree to the government's conditions or fight. Before the simulation, students need to be involved in research on the various Indian leaders, take on the persona of one, and determine what that chief's position would be and why.

2.  Discuss with students the Indian Removal Act of 1830. (Between 1830 and 1840, 50,000 Indians were forced to leave their homes and were moved to Indian Territory, which is now the state of Oklahoma. During this time, over 4,000 Cherokees lost their lives. The journey is now referred to as The Trail of Tears.) Have students create a television documentary recreating this time.

3. Involve students in creating a Native American Museum in which they recreate objects that were of special significance to the various tribes living in the West (for example, the sacred pipe, Indian headdress, the sacred hoop, beads). Have students label each item and briefly explain its importance. If possible, take students on a field trip to a museum to see actual Native American artifacts.

4. Read aloud many of the poems included in *Dancing Teepees*, compiled by Virginia Driving Hawk Sneve (1989). The poems included were generally passed from generation to generation of Indian youths and offer insights into their lives. Ask each student to select a favorite poem and use it as a model for an original poem that reflects an aspect of the life of Native American youth that each finds especially intriguing. Have them create their own illustrations to accompany their poetry.

5. Have students imagine that they are Native Americans living in the West during the mid-1800s. Have them write a journal entry (either as an Indian maiden, a warrior, the tribe's medicine man, etc.) describing their feelings as the settlers move into their territories and the way this immigration is affecting their lives.

## Wagons Ho: The Trail West

One hundred and fifty years ago the only way to go west by land was to travel across the country on a horse or as part of a wagon train. The journey west was filled with dangers and, at best, living conditions were extremely difficult — one out of every 17 pioneers never reached his or her destination. However, despite the risks, thousands and thousands of people made the journey, traveling along such immortal trails as the Santa Fe, Oregon, Chisholm, and Mormon.

### References:

Fisher, L.E. (1990). *The Oregon Trail*. New York: Holiday House.

Grant, B. (1971). *Famous American trails*. Illustrated by L. Bjorklund. Chicago: Rand McNaly.

Lavender, D. (1963). *Westward vision: The story of the Oregon Trail*. New York: McGraw-Hill. (One of a series of books published by McGraw-Hill describing various American Trails.)

Laycock, G., and Laycock, E. (1980). *How the settlers lived*. New York: David McKay.

Levine, E. (1986). *If you traveled west in a covered wagon*. Illustrated by C. Shaw. New York: Scholastic.

William, D. (1993). *Grandma Essie's covered wagon*. Illustrated by W. Sadowski. New York: Knopf.

### Activities:

1. Have students imagine that they are leaving on a wagon train heading West on one of the famous trails. Have them list 10 personal items they would like to take. Next, have them limit the list to three items and ask them to explain the significance of each item.

2. Have students research the actual items that the settlers took with them on their journey. In groups, have students create a model of a covered wagon complete with miniature items to represent the food, tools, and so forth that the settlers took with them.

3. Have students research one of the trails that took settlers west in the 1800s (for example, Chisholm Trail, Santa Fe Trail, Oregon Trail, Mormon Trail, Donner Pass). Have them identify the trail on a large map, using yarn or other material. In groups, have students plan and present an oral talk describing any interesting stories connected with the trail and place the summaries next to the map.

4. Involve students in a problem-solving exercise based on the difficulties encountered during a wagon train trip on one of the trails to the West. For example, students might wish to focus on the problem of leadership, and one of their solution ideas might center on the need for rules for the wagon train.

5. Have students consider the problems of journeying west on a wagon train and, as a class, create a "Survival Guide" to help those considering the journey. Have students brainstorm the types of chapters the guide should contain. Each group of students can then work on a different chapter (for

example, "Outfitting your Wagon"; "The Best Time of Year to Travel"; "Dangers "; "Crossing Different Terrain — Mountains, Rivers, Forests"; "Types of Clothing to Take"; "Tricks of the Trail").

## Today's Cowboy

By the 1890s, the open range roundups and the trail drives faded into history and the life of the cowboy changed forever. But, as long as there is a West, there will be cowboys, still singing of their home on the range, still doing many of the same jobs that the cowboys of the past did. But, with some changes...

## References:

Haney, L. (1975). *Ride 'em cowgirl*. New York: G.P. Putnam's Sons.

Johnson, N. (1992). *Jack Creek cowboy*. New York: Dial.

Lomax, J. A. and Lomax, A., compilers. (1938). *Cowboy songs and other frontier ballads*. New York. Macmillan.

Murdock, D. (1993). *Cowboy*. Photographs by G. Brightling. New York: Knopf.

Rounds, G. (1972). *The cowboy trade*. New York: Holiday House.

Scott, A. H. (1993). *A brand is forever*. Illustrated by R. Rimler. New York: Clarion.

Sullivan. (1993) *Cowboys*. New York: Rizzoli.

Taylor, L. and Maar, I. (1983). *The American cowboy*. Washington, D.C.: Library of Congress.

Tyler, R. (1975). *The cowboy*. New York: William Morrow.

## Activities:

1.  With the help of a travel agent, try to get the names and addresses of various working ranches in the West. Brainstorm a list of questions students might ask about life on a ranch and have students write letters to the cowboys/cowgirls who work at the ranches to discover the answers.

2.  Share the poetry and art included in Charles Sullivan's *Cowboys* (1993). Have students select one of the types of media in the book (photograph, sculpture, painting, poem and so forth) and use this form to create a tribute to today's cowboy. For example, students may wish to create a life-size sculpture using a variety of materials or write an original ballad.

3.  Teach students "The Texas Song" (Lomax and Lomax, 1938), which describes the end of the cowboy era of the Wild West. Ask each student to use the song as a model and write an original verse for a song honoring today's cowboy/cowgirl and the work he/she does. Put the verses together and make copies so that the class can learn the entire new version.

4.  Involve students in a game of mime by asking each student to select one of the many jobs undertaken by today's cowboys/cowgirls and mime it for the rest of the class.

5.  Divide students into pairs. One student in each pair should represent the cowboy of the Wild West and one should represent the cowboy of today. Have students plan and present (in costume ) a factually based skit in which each tries to better the other by making his/her life sound more exciting, more fulfilling, and so forth.

# Intermediate Unit: Poetry: The Words and the Music

**Theme:**   POETRY: THE WORDS AND THE MUSIC

**Focus:**   To create in children a delight for poetry and an understanding of the elements that make poetry so appealing to the senses.

**Objectives:**   Upon completion of this unit, students will:

1.  gain an appreciation for and enjoyment of poetry.

2.  become familiar with traditional and contemporary poets and their poems.

3.  become familiar with a variety of poetic forms.

4.  recognize and experiment with the various devices used in poetry.

5.  use quality poetry as models for their own verses.

## Initiating Activity:

Create a cluster or semantic map (see Chapter 2, pages 34-35) of poetry on the chalkboard by having students generate as many words as they can to describe poetry. Using the cluster/map as a guide, ask students to write their own definitions of poetry by completing the phrase, "Poetry is _____." Next, group students, asking each group to come up with one single definition by combining the ideas of the individuals in the group. Finally, after each group shares its definition, create a class definition. Copy the definition onto a large piece of butcher paper and display it in the room as a mural. Throughout the unit, encourage students to add to the mural, including verses from favorite poems, their responses to and feelings about poetry, and original illustrations. When appropriate, share the quotes below and discuss them with the children, along with the responses they have added to the mural. At the end of the unit, have students revisit their class definition and discuss what changes they would make.

> Poetry is not a rose, but the scent of the rose…
> Not the sea, but the sound of the sea.
> —*Eleanor Farjeon*

> Poetry is a meteor.
> — *Wallace Stevens*

> Prose =words in their best order
> Poetry =the best words in their best order.
> — *Samuel Taylor Coleridge*

> A poem… begins as a lump in the throat, a sense of
> wrong, a homesickness, a love sickness…It finds
> the thought and the thought finds the words…
> — *Robert Frost*

> But at the core of every good poem, every poem that
> touches me, is the language… Language that
> surprises the reader. Language that lets a good poem sing.
> — *Paul Janeczko*

## General Activities

1.  Introduce children, through reading aloud and choral reading, to the poetry of some of the most popular contemporary poets. (See page 196.) Have the students select the class's favorite poet and plan a special week dedicated to the poet and his/her work. During the week, you may decorate the bulletin board and door with copies of poems and student-made illustrations; have students create their own poems modeled after various poems written by the poet; involve students in choral readings of favorite poems as well as group and individual readings; involve students in researching the life of the poet and collectively write a brief biographical sketch; create an anthology of favorite poems by the poet. Once students have become hooked on contemporary poets, repeat this activity based on the work of some of the more traditional poets.

2.  Encourage students to keep poetry journals (similar to literature logs discussed in Chapter 2, pages 56-58) in which they write reactions to poems they have listened to and read. Allow time for students to discuss specific poems with their classmates through small group (literary circles) and class discussions. Discussion may focus on their responses to the poems, interpretations, poetic devices and techniques that affect the poem and affect their feelings about the poem, and so forth.

3.  Encourage each student to skim through books of poetry to find a poem that says something special to him/her. Many of the more contemporary poems contain verses that children can readily identify with, poems that reflect their experiences, their hopes, their fears, and their dreams. Some of these include poems from Eloise Greenfield's *Honey, I Love*, Langston Hughes' *The Dream Keeper*, Nancy Larrick's *Bring Me All of Your Dreams*, and Judith Viorst's *If I Were in Charge of the World*. Have students research the life of the author of the poem. Have them create original presentations to introduce these poets to the class. Each presentation should also include a reading of the poem that initiated the project. Combine the poems selected into an illustrated anthology of *Poetry that Speaks to Us: Our Classroom Favorites*. Students who have selected the work of the same poet might be encouraged to combine their efforts into a group presentation.

4.  Introduce students to the very original style of poetry written by Paul Fleischman in his Newbery Award-winning book, *Joyful Noise: Poems for Two Voices*. To get students accustomed to this type of poetry, divide the class into two groups and have each group choral read one of the two columns in the poem. Once students are comfortable with this type of reading, divide them into groups, giving each group a different poem. Have them practice reading the poem and choreographing movements as suggested by the music of the poetry . You may also wish to follow a similar strategy with Fleischman's *I Am Phoenix: Poems for Two Voices*.

5.  Every culture has its own poetry. Read examples of poems from different cultures to the students and discuss how they depict life. For example, the following collections reflect African-American poetry: *The Dream Keeper* by Langston Hughes; *The Poetry of Black America: Anthology of the 20th Century*, edited by Arnold Adoff; *Honey I Love* and *Night on Neighborhood Street* by Eloise Greenfield; and *Sing to the Sun* by Ashley Bryan.

6.  Discuss the question, "For what reasons are poems written?" Possible responses include: to tell a story; to offer insight; to create a feeling; to capture a mood or a moment; to entertain. Divide students into groups, one group per purpose. Ask each group to select one favorite contemporary and one favorite traditional poem that seem to be written for the purpose they were assigned. For example, Alfred Noyes' "The Highwayman" tells an incredible story of a highwayman and lost love, whereas Eloise Greenfield's poem, "By Myself" (from *Honey I Love*) offers insights into liking and accepting oneself. Have each group choral read the poem and lead a class discussion of the poem's purpose.

7.  An understanding of the devices poets use — such as rhythm, alliteration, blank or free verse, rhyme, figurative language [simile, metaphor, personification], repetition, and onomatopoeia, to name a few — helps students better understand, appreciate, and write their own poetry. Periodically, select and

real aloud/choral read poems that use one or more of these devices. For example, a study of alliteration might include "Sea Fever" by John Masefield, and "Fireflies" by Paul Fleischman (from *Joyful Noises*). A study of personification might include "Silver" by Walter De la Mare, or "The Cherries' Garden Gala" (from *The New Kid on the Block*) by Jack Prelutsky. A study of free verse might include many of the poems found in the two collections by Arnold Adoff, *Eats Poems* and *Chocolate Dreams*.

8. After reading several poems that reflect one or more poetic devices (see activity 7), have students use the poem as a model and write their own poems, experimenting with using the same poetic device(s).

9. Poetry is an ideal form of literature for dramatic activity. Encourage students to add physical movement to rhythmical poems. Story poems are perfect for dramatic interpretation as well. Students can become involved in such activities as story theater.

10. A favorite type of poetry, the haiku, originated in Japan hundreds of years ago. Have students explore this poetic form through the following activities:

   a. Divide students into groups and give each group a book of haiku poetry, such as *The Moment of Wonder* (Lewis, 1964); *Cricket Songs* (Behn, 1964); and *In a Spring Garden* (Lewis, 1964).

   b. Ask each group to list five characteristics of the haiku. The list might include the following: a haiku is often based on nature; it has three lines; usually the first line has five syllables, the second has seven and the third has five (this may vary in some poems because of the difficulty of translating Japanese into English); it evokes an image or emotion; every words counts. Make a class list of the characteristics of the haiku.

   c. Show a picture of some aspect of nature — a waterfall, a lagoon, a mountain, an animal. As a class, select one of the pictures. Create a cluster or map based on the picture to generate a quantity of words that could be used in a haiku.

   d. Divide students into groups, and tell each group to write a haiku based on the picture and cluster. Share poems.

   e. Give students magazines and allow each student to select a picture related to nature. (*Natural Geographic* has incredible photographs.) Have them create a haiku based on the picture.

   f. Have students affix their poems and pictures to paper and bind the poems into book form.

## Discussion Questions

1. What is poetry?

2. How does poetry differ from prose? (Poetry invites the reader to go beyond literal interpretation. Poetry helps us see life from different perspectives. Poetry appeals to the senses, to thoughts and feelings. Poetry evokes strong images and emotional responses, and so forth.)

3. Who are your favorite poets (both traditional and contemporary)? What is there about their poetry that appeals to you?

4. What are some of the elements or devices of poetry? (rhythm, rhyme, blank verse, alliteration, figurative language [simile, metaphor, personification], repetition, onomatopoeia, etc.)

5. How does the use of figurative language appeal to our senses?

6. It has been said that good poetry draws the reader back again and again. Explain this phenomena.

## Poets of the Past and Present

*Traditional Poets*
(Body of Work Written Prior to 1960s)

Rosemary and Stephen Binet
Lewis Carroll
Elizabeth Coatsworth
Samuel Taylor Coleridge
e.e. cummings
Walter De la Mare
Emily Dickinson
T.S. Eliot
Ralph Waldo Emerson
Eleanor Farjeon
Eugene Field
Robert Frost
Oliver Wendell Holmes
Langston Hughes
Rudyard Kipling
Emma Lazarus
Edward Lear
Vachel Lindsay
Henry Wadsworth Longfellow
John Masefield
Edna St. Vincent Millay
A.A. Milne
Ogden Nash
Alfred Noyes
Edgar Allan Poe
James Whitcomb. Riley
Christina Rossetti
Carl Sandburg
Robert Louis Stevenson
Sara Teasdale
Alfred Lord Tennyson
Ernest L. Thayer
Walt Whitman

*Contemporary Poets*
(Body of Work Written 1960 to the Present)

Arnold Adoff
N. M. Bodecker
Beatrice Schenck De Regniers
Barbara Juster Esbensen
Norma Farber
Aileen Fisher
Paul Fleischman
Eloise Greenfield
Lee Bennett Hopkins
Denise Lee
Myra Cohn Livingston
David McCord
Eve Merriam
Lillian Moore
Lillian Morrison
Jack Prelutsky
Joanne Ryder
Cynthia Rylant
Diane Siebert
Shel Silverstein
Judith Viorst
Nancy Willard
Valerie Worth
Jane Yolen

# Literature Related Activities:

(*Note to teachers:* The four story poems included here were selected to provide a balance between traditional and contemporary poetry, between poems that are nonsensical and those that are more serious in nature. They were selected to provide children with poetry written for a variety of purposes, poetry that uses a variety of devices, poetry that is imaginative and offers insights into meaningful ideas. And, they were selected to involve students in poetry that draws the reader back again and again.

| | |
|---|---|
| Title: | *Jabberwocky* |
| Genre: | Poetry |
| Author: | Louis Carroll |
| Illustrator: | Graeme Base |
| Bibliographic Information: | Harry N. Abrams, Inc., New York, 1989 |
| Summary: | Carroll's poem, *The Jabberwocky*, is imaginatively illustrated by Graeme Base, creator of *Animalia, The Eleventh Hour,* and *The Sign of the Seahorse.* The poem, written with nonsense words, tells of a boy who ignores his father's warning about the dangers of encountering the vicious Jabberwocky. |
| Interest Level: | Grade 5+ |

1. Pre-Reading Activity:

   Ask students, "What would a Jabberwocky look like"? Have students create their own artistic renderings of this creature and then compare them with Graeme Base's image. Involve them in discussing other divergent questions that require a diversity of responses, as outlined in Chapter 2, page 47.

2. Learning Activities:

   a. Read the poem, "Jabberwocky," several times. Involve students in a choral reading.
      You might wish to rewrite the verses on a large chart or on a transparency for use with an overhead projector.

   b "Jabberwocky" is made up of nonsense verses composed of portmanteau words, that is, words that combine the meaning and parts of two other words to create a new one. For example "Brillig" could be a combination of the words brilliant and light. Discuss what words were possibly combined to create the word Jabberwocky. Have each student select four portmanteau words from the poem and experiment with finding the words that might have been combined to create them. Ask students to come up with their own definition for these words and combine them into a *Jabberwocky Dictionary.* Multiple definitions can be included in case more than one student selected the same word.

   c. Assign each group of students a different verse of the poem. Ask students to rewrite their verse by substituting known words for the nonsense words. Encourage them to use a thesaurus to select words that sound right and that create a special image. Have students illustrate their verses to create a new version of "Jabberwocky."

   d.   Compare this version of *Jabberwocky* with others such as that illustrated with pictures from the Disney Archives (Disney Press, New York, 1992) or with the original illustrations by John Tenniel (Macmillan, 1963). Engage students in a discussion focusing on which version they prefer and why.

   e.   Involve students in research into the life of Charles Lutwidge Dodgson (Lewis Carroll), whose work, even thought it is over 100 years old, still appeals to children and adults alike.

3.   Discussion Questions

   a.   What do you believe accounts for the incredible popularity of "Jabberwocky"? What do you find most remarkable about the poem?

   b.   In what ways do the illustrations in the book affect the poem and its impact on the reader?

   c.   What do you think is going through the young boy's mind as he stands at the top of the castle and leans against the "tumtum tree"?

   d.   What type of threat do you think the beast posed to the village and its people?

   e.   Look closely at the last illustration in the book, in which the king is congratulating his son. What item(s) seem out of place? (The telephone doesn't seem to fit the mood or setting.) Why do you think Graeme Base drew the picture this way? Can you find any other such examples elsewhere in the book? (For example, an alarm clock is sitting on the grass in the forest, a crushed can of Coke is under a tree, various automobile symbols are affixed to the son's horse, and so on.)

─────────────────────────────

| | |
|---|---|
| Title: | *Casey at the Bat* |
| Genre: | Poetry |
| Author: | Ernest Lawrence Thayer |
| Illustrator: | Jim Hull |

Bibliographic Information:   Dover Publishers, New York, 1977

Summary:          One of American's best-loved poems, the classic baseball saga tells of mighty Casey who is expected to save the day for his team and instead strikes out.

Interest Level: Grade 3+

─────────────────────────────

1.   Pre-Reading Activity:

   Discuss sports that students are involved with. Have them relate some of their triumphs and (if they will) defeats.

2.   Learning Activities:

   a.   After reading the poem, "Casey at the Bat," several times, involve students in a story theater. While one or several students read the narrative, others dramatize the action.

   b.   "Casey at the Bat" has been the stimulus for a song, two silent movies, two animated cartoons, and an opera. Involve students in selecting an art form to retell the story. For example, students could create a sight-and-sound show by making slides from photographs of the book's illustrations (or their own original renditions) and create a cassette version on which the poem is read to accompany the slides.

c. Many poems have been dedicated to the sport of baseball, such as those that appear in *Extra Innings* (Hopkins, 1993). They capture the hope, drama, and joy of America's favorite pastime. Share several poems that reflect the theme of baseball and have students compare these poems with their reactions to "Casey at the Bat."

d. Many have tried to explain the popularity of "Casey at the Bat." In his introduction to the book, Martin Gardner (p. viii) wrote, "It is precisely the blend of the absurd and the tragic that lies at the heart of Thayer's remarkable poem." Hold a discussion with students in which they discuss this quote. What about the poem seems absurd? What is tragic? Is Casey, as Gardner suggests, both a pathetic and a comic figure?

e. Have students look at various baseball cards. What type of information is included? As a class, list the members of Casey's team (students will have to make up several names to accompany Flynn, Blake, Cooney, Burrows, and Casey). Divide students into groups and have each create a baseball card for one of the members of the Mudville team. When the cards are completed, compare statistics and other relevant data, and display the cards.

3. Discussion Questions

a. How would you describe Casey?

b. What did Thayer mean when he said, "…The rest clung to the hope which springs eternal in the human breast…" Tell about a time during a sporting event when you clung to hope despite the odds.

c. When you first heard the last lines of the poem, what was your reaction?

d. What lessons for life does "Casey at the Bat" suggest?

---

Title: *Stopping by Woods on a Snowy Evening*

Genre: Poetry

Author: Robert Frost

Illustrator: Susan Jeffers

Bibliographic Information: Dutton, New York, 1978,

Summary: The poem gives the reader a memorable picture of the delights of winter and of a person with "promises to keep."

Interest Level: Grade 4+

---

1. Pre-Reading Activity:

Involve students in a discussion of snow. What does it look like, feel like, taste like, smell like? Have them *become snow* and imagine how they would move during a blizzard, during a light snow-fall, and so forth.

2. Learning Activities:

a. Read the poem to the class several times and encourage students to join in. Allow the mood of the poetry to permeate the room. Ask students to share the mood the poem evoked — in one word, in one phrase or sentence. Have them create large snowflakes and affix their word or phrase/sentence to it. Display these on a "Snowy Evening" bulletin board.

b. Robert Frost once explained that, "Every poem is a new metaphor inside or it is nothing." Poetry helps develop new insights and new ways of seeing the world. Involve students in a literary circle in which they discuss insights gained from the poem and how the poem offered new perspectives.

c. Ask students to tell about a time when they had to put off doing something they really wanted to do because of certain responsibilities. Using the poem as a model, ask students to write an original poem that describes their experience, with the title "Stopping by _____ on a _____ Day."

d. Robert Frost's poetry speaks to children in a special way. Read Frost's poem, "The Road Not Taken." Discuss with children the metaphor inside, by asking "What might the two roads represent?" Have students write and deliver a brief talk that tells about a time whenthey had to make an important choice.

3. Discussion Questions

a. Of all your senses, which one does the poem most heighten? Explain.

b. Why do you think Frost repeated the last line? How does this add to the mysterious element of the poem?

c. Why do you think the illustrator, Susan Jeffers, choose to create most of the images in black and white, using color very sparingly? What effects did this have?

d. Imagine that you were the person in this poem, telling about your experiences in the woods. Describe your feelings as you spend time in the woods and how you feel about having to leave.

═══════════════════════════

| | |
|---|---|
| Title: | *Life Doesn't Frighten Me* |
| Genre: | Poetry |
| Author: | Maya Angelou |
| Illustrator: | Jean-Michel Basquiat |

Bibliographic Information: Stewart, Tabori and Chang, New York, 1993

Summary: The poem speaks of those things in our lives that frighten us and celebrates the courage to face whatever we fear.

Interest Level: Grade 3+

═══════════════════════════

1. Pre-Reading Activity:

Share the title and cover with students. Have each of them create a picture that represents something in their lives that frightens them. Ask them to share their pictures. Collect the pictures and hold them for Learning Activity C.

2. Learning Activities:

a. After reading the poem aloud and sharing the pictures, discuss the words and images that they contained. What mood does the poem create? How is this mood achieved?

b.  Together, compile a list of things that seem to frighten the author and things that seem to frighten the illustrator. Discuss how each of these fears affect students in the class.

c.  Write several of the verses on a chart board or on a transparency for use with an overhead projector. Using these verses as a model, group the children, and have them combine the ideas represented by their own illustrations (pre-reading activity) into new verses for the poem. Encourage them to refine their drawings and then put the verses and drawings of each group together to form a sequel — *Life Doesn't Frighten Me, Part II.*

d.  From the verses in the book alone, how would you describe Maya Angelou's life? How would you describe Jean-Michel Basquiat's life? Compare your analysis with the biographies of these creative individuals that is found at the end of the book.

e.  Encourage the students to react to the information in the poem/illustrations/biographies in their poetry or writing journals. Allow time for the students to share their entries.

f.  Invite a counselor or local psychologist to discuss fears and ways of overcoming those fears that negatively affect our lives. Prior to the talk, encourage each student to write several questions on the topic of "fear" that he/she would like to have discussed.

3.  Discussion Questions

a.  If you could meet Maya Angelou, what would you like to ask her regarding *Life Doesn't Frighten Me?* What is one thing you'd like to tell her about the book and how it affected you? (You may wish to send these questions and comments to Ms. Angelou, c/o the publisher.)

b.  When is it healthy to fear?

c.  When can fears be considered unhealthy or even dangerous?

d.  What is something you especially fear? Is it a healthy fear? If not, what might be one effective way of overcoming this fear?

e.  Did the poem in anyway change the way certain fears affect you? Explain.

## Culminating Activity

Plan and hold a **Poetry Festival** in which students are involved in the following:

1.  Create invitations (written in rhyme or free verse) and send them to school staff, the children's families and the local media (newspapers, television, radio).

2.  Poetry Readings — of published poems and students' original poetry.

3.  Dramatic and Artistic Interpretations — of specific poems, traditional and contemporary.

4.  Poetry Picnic: Students and their families enjoy a picnic lunch together and read favorite poems to one another.

5.  Featured Speakers: Invite local poets to discuss and read their work as well as discuss the creative process.

6.  Storytelling: Invite a local storyteller to retell several narrative poems.

7.  Decorate the area with many of the displays and products students created during the unit.

8.  Involve the audience in choral readings of specially selected favorites.

Many of the activities can involve the whole group, while others can be run concurrently to allow guests to make choices as to what they would like to take part in.

# Supplemental Literature

Each of the single-story poems are superbly illustrated versions of classic poems that will delight students.

## Primary (Grades 1–3)

Lear, E. (1991). *The Owl and the Pussy Cat.* Illustrated by J. Brett. New York: Putnam.
Lear, E., and Nash, O.. (1968). *The Scroobious pop.* Ill. by N. E. Burkett. New York: Harper.
Longfellow, H.W. (1993). *The Children's hour.* Illustrated by G. Lang. Boston: David R. Godine.
Nash, O. (1991). *The Adventures of Isabel.* Illustrated by James Marshall. New York: Little, Brown.
Riley, James Whitcomb. (1991). *Frost is on the punkin.* Illustrated by G. Lang.Boston: David R. Godine.
Sandburg, Carl. (1993). *Arithmetic.* Illustrated by Ted Rand. San Diego: Harcourt.
Stevenson, R.L. (1990). *My shadow.* Illustrated by T. Rand. New York: Putnam.

## Intermediate (Grades 4–6)

Blake, William. (1993). *The tyger.* Illustrated by N. Waldman. San Diego: Harcourt.
Frost, R. (1988). *Birches.* Illustrated by E. Young. New York: Henry Holt.
Longfellow, H.W. (1983). *Hiawatha.* Illustrated by J. Jerrers. New York: Dial.
Noyes, A. (1983). *The highwayman.* Illustrated C. Mikolaycak. New York: Lothrop, Lee & Shepard.
Siebert, D. (1989). *Heartland.* Paintings by W. Minor. New York: HarperCollins.
Willard, N. (1981). *A visit to William Blake's inn.* Illustrated by Alice and Martin Provensen. San Diego: Harcourt.

## Collections (Grades 1–6)

[*Note:* Each of these collections contain poems generally appropriate to a wide variety of ages.]

Adoff, A., ed. (1973). *The poetry of black America: Anthology of the 20th Century.* New York: HarperCollins.
Adoff, A. (1989). *Chocolate dreams.* New York: Lothrop.
  A collection of poems that reflects the author's love for sweets.
Adoff, A. (1979). *Eats poems.* New York: Lothrop.
  An entertaining collection of poems for children that celebrates food.
Behn, H. Ed. (1964). *Cricket songs.* New York: Harcourt, Brace, and World.
  A collection of haikus.
Blishen, E., compiler. (1963). *Oxford book of poetry for children.* Illustrated by B. Wildsmith. New York: Watts.
  Comprehensive anthology with a rich collection of work by traditional poets.
Bryan, A. (1992). *Sing to the sun.* New York: HarperCollins.
  First collection of poetry for children to be written by an African-American male. Contains 23 poems that deal with life as seen through the poet's eyes.
Cole, J., ed. (1984). *A new treasury of children's poetry: Old favorites and new discoveries.* Garden City, NY: Doubleday.
  Comprehensive collection of over 200 poems that range from nonsensical to serious.
de Paola, T., ed. ( 1988 ). *Tomie de Paola's book of poems.* New York: Putnam.
  An anthology of eighty-six poems including classical and contemporary poems. Some of the poems are in Spanish.
de Regniers, B.S., et al., eds. (1988).*Sing a song of popcorn.* New York: Scholastic.
  Illustrated by nine Caldecott Medal artists in full color, the book contains over 125 poems, arranged thematically, that will captivate children. The work of both classical and contemporary poets is included.
Fleischman, P. (1985). *I am phoenix: Poems for two voices.* New York: Harper and Row.
  A collection of poems for two readers (or two groups of readers) that capture the world of birds.

Fleischman, P. (1988). *Joyful noise: Poems for two voices:* New York: Harper and Row.
  A collection of poems for two readers (or two groups of readers ) that capture the music of the insect world.

Frost, Robert. (1949). *Complete poems of Robert Frost.* New York: Holt.
  A collection of poems written by Frost.

Frost, Robert. (1959). *You come too.* Illustrated by T. W. Nason. New York: Holt.
  A collection of Frost's poems especially appropriate for younger readers.

Greenfield, E. (1978). *Honey I love and other love poems.* Illustrated by Diane and Leo Dillon. New York: HarperCollins.
  The sixteen poems included elicit a new appreciation of everyday life, offering new insights and accompanied by beautiful drawings.

Greenfield, E. (1991). *Night on neighborhood street.* New York: Dial.
  Poems depicting contemporary children and their world.

Hopkins, L.B., ed. (1993). *Extra innings.* Illustrated by S. Medlock. San Diego: Harcourt, Brace Jovanovich.
  A collection of poems that capture the excitement, hope, drama, and joy of America's favorite pastime — baseball.

Hopkins, L.B., ed. (1988). *Voyages: Poems by Walt Whitman.* San Diego: HBJ.
  A collection of the poetry of Walt Whitman.

Hughes, L. (1932). *The dream keeper and other poems.* New York: Knopf.
  Poems depicting the African-American experience.

Janeczko, P.B., compiler. (1990). *The place my words are looking for.* New York: Bradbury Press.
  Includes the poems of approximately 40 poets as well as photographs of the poets and brief commentaries they've written concerning the writing of poetry and the creative process.

Larrick, N., ed. (1980). *Bring me all of your dreams.* New York: M. Evans.
  Contains poems by well-known contemporary poets that help children discover who they are and address many of the concerns of childhood.

Larrick, N., ed. (1968 ). *Piping down the valleys wild.* Illustrated by E. Raskin. New York: Delacorte.
  A collection of over 250 poems ranging from poems from the traditional to the contemporary.

Lear, Edward. (1946). *The complete nonsense book.* New York: Dodd, Mead.
  A collection of poems that could only have been written by Lear!

Lewis, R., ed. (1964). *In a spring garden.* Illustrated by E. Keats. New York: Dial.
  Collection of haikus poetry.

Lewis, R., ed. (1964). *The moment of wonder.* New York: Dial.
  Collection of haikus.

Prelutsky, Jack. (1984). *The new kid on the block.* Illustrated by J. Stevenson. New York: Scholastic.
  106 poems that take a humorous look at life.

Prelutsky, Jack., ed. (1983). *The Random House book of poetry for children.* New York: Random House.
  Contains over 500 poems by contemporary and traditional poets.

Silverstein, S. (1981). *A light in the attic.* New York: Harper and Row.
  A collection of poems that continue in the tradition of those included in *Where the Sidewalk Ends.* The poems are often humorous, often tender, always entertaining and wonderous.

Silverstein, S. (1974). *Where the sidewalk ends.* New York: Harper and Row.
  A collection of poems that are both funny and profound.

Slier, D., ed. (1991). *Make a joyful sound: Poems for children by African-American poets.* New York: Checkerboard Press.
  A collection of poems written by some of the best-loved African-American poets.

Sneve, V.D. H., ed. (1989). *Dancing teepees: Poems of American Indian youth.* New York: Holiday House.
  A weaving of poems that have been handed down from generation to generation of American Indians and poems written by Indian youths today. The poems describe the traditions and life of this great culture.

Viorst. Judith. (1981). *If I were in charge of the world and other worries.* Illustrated by L. Cherry. New York: Macmillan.
The poems in this collection capture the dreams, hopes, and fears of childhood.

# MINI-THEMES

## Curricular Connections

Poetry touches children in a very special way and offers them insights not generally found in prose. It is important, therefore, to include poetry whenever possible to augment a theme or topic under study, giving students the opportunity to gain additional perspectives. Many poems, both contemporary and classic, can be found to supplement the topics being taught throughout the curriculum. Many anthologies have been published in which the selection of poems is based on a specific subject, such as the seasons, weather, Indian life, nature, animals, insects, and so forth. Other anthologies are based on the work of a specific poet, while still others are a collection of poetry that the compiler found meaningful and appealing. Single-story poems are also available to supplement a specific theme or topic. The poetry below is just a sampling of the myriad of choices available and the activities that follow will help you integrate poetry into your curricular plans.

## References:

Brewton, S., and Brewton, J., compilers. (1976). *American forever new.* New York: Crowell. (Americana)

Eliot, T.S. (1991). *Mr. Mistoffelees with Mugojerrie and Rumpelteazer.* Illustrated by E. LeCain. San Diego: Harcourt. (Cats)

Fleischman, P. (1985). *I am phoenix: Poems for two voices.* New York: Harper and Row. (Birds)

Fleischman, P. (1988). *Joyful noise: Poems for two voices.* New York: Harper and Row. (Insects)

Hopkins, L.B., ed. (1986). *The sea is calling me.* Illustrated By W. Gaffney-Kessell. San Diego: Harcourt. (Ocean life)

Hopkins, L.B., ed. (1987). *Dinosaurs.* Illustrated by M. Tinkelman. San Diego: Harcourt. (Dinosaurs)

Larrick, N., ed. (1991). *To the moon and back.* Illustrated by C. O'Neill. New York: Delacorte. (Contains many poems on Native-Americans and Eskimos.)

Lewis, J.P. (1991). *Earth verse and water rhymes.* Illustrated by R. Sabuda. New York: Atheneum. (Nature)

Livingston, M.C. (1988). *Space songs.* Illustrated by L. E. Fisher. New York: Holiday. (Space)

Longfellow, H.W. (1983). *Hiawatha.* Illustrated by J. Jerrers. New York: Dial.(Native Americans)

Longfellow, H.W. (1990). *Paul Revere's ride.* Illustrated by T. Rand. New York: Dutton. (Revolutionary War)

Siebert, D. (1989). *Heartland.* Illustrated by W. Minor. New York: Crowell. (Environment)

Siebert, D. (1991). *Sierra.* Illustrated by W. Minor. New York: HarperCollins. (Environment)

Sneve, V.D. H., ed. (1989). *Dancing teepees: Poems of American Indian youth.* New York: Holiday House. (Native Americans)

Sullivan, C. (1993). *Cowboys.* New York: Rizzoli. (The West)

Volavkova, H., ed. (1978). *I never saw another butterfly: Children's drawings and poems from Terezin Concentration Camp, 1942-1944.* New York: Schocken. (The Holocaust)

Yolen, J. (1990). *Birdwatch.* Illustrated by T. Lewin. New York: Philomel. (Nature/Birds)

## Activities:

1.  With the tremendous scope of poetry available, both traditional and contemporary, poems can be found on virtually every topic. Allow students to help compile poetry anthologies for the various units or topics you are studying. Criteria for the anthologies need to be established by the entire class, for example, it is meaningful, relates to subject; entertaining; gives new perspectives; reflects contemporary and traditional poetry; and so forth. For example, an anthology on the Revolutionary

War can include "The Midnight Ride of Paul Revere" (Longfellow), one on the Civil War might include "O Captain! My Captain!" (Whitman), and one on immigration might include " The New Colossus" by Emma Lazarus. For each anthology, a different student or pair of students can act as editor(s). Each student in the class should submit a poem related to the subject. Once the poem has been approved by the editors, the person who has submitted it can type it and either illustrate it or find photographs to accompany the poem. Anthologies can be then be duplicated for each class member. During the unit, poems from the anthology can be used to introduce or supplement the lesson and other literature. Poems can be read chorally, dramatized, used to model original poetry, and discussed.

2.  Many poems add new dimensions to the way we see things. Some poems, especially those that are more narrative, lend themselves well to creative dramatics and story theater. Others lend themselves to artistic responses.  As they do with various works of literature, students should have the opportunity to respond to poetry in a variety of ways (speaking, writing, drama, art, music, etc.) and activities can be developed to tie the poem to a specific content area being taught. During a study of insects, for example, you may wish to use Paul Fleischman's *Joyful Noise: Poems for Two Voices*. Divide students into different groups, giving each a different insect poem. Have students read the poem (in two voices) and put it together with interpretive movement. After the presentation of one of the poems, involve students in a discussion of the way the words captured the sound of the insect and its movements.

    To connect the poem with a science lesson, have students determine what other insect(s) they would like to learn more about. If possible, have them collect several specimens of the insect (in jars with ventilation, food, and water). Have students observe the insect and after several days have them create a cluster of words that recreate the way the insect sounds and moves. Aid students in using these words to create their own poem for two voices. Be sure students return the insects to their original environment.

3.  Involve students in creating a poetry calendar based on a specific topic, such as the seasons, environment, animals, or friendship. Students can all work on the same topic or you may wish to allow them to select other topics that have been, or will be, studied that appeal to them most. Have students select 12 poems, one for each month of the year. Have students affix each poem to a piece of paper and illustrate it, attaching pictures and poems that correspond to each month on facing pages. (You may wish to make up a generic calendar form on which students insert the months and days.)

4.  Depending upon the topic being studied, match poetry with trade books to enhance the lesson and provide additional insights. For example, if students have been studying about Christopher Columbus in such books as I *Discover Columbus* by Robert Lawson (1941, Little, Brown), or *Where do you think you're going, Christopher Columbus?* by Jean Fritz (1980, G. P. Putnam's Sons), have them read "Columbus" from *America Forever New* (Brewton and Brewton, 1968). Allow students to discuss such questions as "What ideas did the poem present that seemed unique?" " What images of Columbus did the poem introduce that the books did not?"

5.  Depending upon the topic being studied, have students create a poetry bulletin board that contains various poems related to the subject. Different students can be in charge of the poetry board each month. In addition to poems, pictures and biographies of the poets and accompanying illustrations can be displayed. Instead of a bulletin board, students can create three-dimensional objects related to what is being studied and display the poems on these objects. For example, during a study of the environment, students can create a poetry tree.

6.  Have students create recordings of favorite poems that extend specific lessons. Have them select music (orchestration only — no lyrics) that fits the subject to accompany the recording of the poem.

## Poems of Everyday Life

Poetry reflects life, both the good and bad aspects of it. It reflects our hopes, our dreams, our ideas. It reflects our fears, our doubts, our concerns. Poetry helps us see the remarkable in the unremarkable, the "beauty in a grain of sand." Poetry has been written on subjects ranging from the most common human experiences to the most profound social issues. Poetry intensifies our experiences, heightens our senses, and provides new ways in which to view our world. The poetry listed in this mini-lesson varies in scope, yet each provides us with a look at life through images that are fresh and thought provoking.

### References:

Bryan, A. (1992). *Sing to the sun*. New York: HarperCollins.

Dakos, K. (1990) *If you're not here, please raise your hand*. New York: Four Winds.

Esbensen, B. (1992). *Who shrank my grandmother's house? Poems of discovery*. Ilustrated by E. Bellows. New York: HarperCollins.

Greenfield, E. (1978). *Honey I love and other love poems*. Illustrated by Diane and Leo Dillon. New York: HarperCollins.

Greenfield, E. (1991). *Night on Neighborhood Street*. Illustrated by J. Spivey Gilchrist. New York: Dial.

Hopkins, L.B. (1992). *Through our eyes: Poems and pictures about growing up*. Photogrpahy by J. Dunn. New York: Little, Brown.

Hughes, L. (1932). *The dream keeper and other poems*. New York: Knopf.

Larrick, N., ed. (1980). *Bring me all of your dreams*. New York: M. Evans.

Livingston, M., ed. (1987). *I like you if you like me: Poems of friendship*. New York: McElderry.

Prelutsky, J. (1984). *The new kid on the block*. Illustrated by J. Stevenson. New York: Scholastic.

Rylant, C. (1984). *Waiting to waltz: A childhood*. Illustrated by S. Gammell. New York: Bradbury.

Silverstein, S. (1974). *Where the sidewalk ends*. New York: Harper and Row.

Viorst, J. (1981). *If I were in charge of the world and other worries*. Illustrated by L. Cherry. New York: Macmillan.

### Activities:

1. Have the class create a mural that depicts various experiences from their childhood. Scenes might include: snowball fights; playing with a pet; moving to a new city; eating spinach; playing baseball; facing a bully; peer pressure; and so forth. (Students may wish to use some of their own photographs as well.) Involve students in finding several poems that speak to the same experiences that they created on the mural. Have them copy their favorite poem and place it next to the appropriate scene. Allow time for students to talk about the experience, share the poem, and discuss how the poem reflected their childhood experience and how it made them see it differently.

2. Read the title poem from Judith Viorst's *If I Were in Charge of the World*. Have students brainstorm all the things they would do if they were in charge of the world. Ask each to create a verse for the poem, using the original as a model. Have them create a book of their verses and illustrations.

3. Share many verses of poetry that deal with things children love, (for example, "Honey, I Love," Greenfield, 1978); things they dislike ("Sarah Cynthia Sylvia Stout Would Not Take the Garbage Out," Silverstein, 1974); things that worry them ("Fifteen, Maybe Sixteen, Things to Worry About," Viorst, 1981); and things that make them laugh ("The New Kid on the Block," Prelutsky, 1984). Involve students in a survey to find out what things cause other students to love, hate, fear, and laugh (or any other emotion they choose). Divide students into groups—one per emotion—and have them create an anthology of poems that speak to that emotion. Create a classroom environment reminiscent of the 1950s during which poets sat on stools in dimly lit coffee houses and read to their audience. Ask each group to put together a poetry reading in which they read several of the poems they collected in their anthologies.

4. Many poems address social issues, problems with which our society and we as individuals ,must

deal. Have students research both traditional and contemporary poetry to discover what social issues were addressed. Divide students into groups and have them research one of these social issues. Encourage them to read newspaper and magazine articles that deal with the subject. After each group has completed its research, have it present a creative oral report on the social issue and include a reading of several of the poems that deal with the subject. Allow time for class discussion of the issue, how it affects them, how the poems changed or enhanced their understanding of the problem, and ways that the issue can be resolved.

5. Poems are often set to music. For example, Shel Silverstein's "The Unicorn" (1974) was also a very popular musical recording. Have students select a favorite poem. It can be one that reminds them of a childhood experience, one that reflects their attitude toward life or one that speaks to them in a very personal way. Have them put this poem to music, using either an original piece or using the music of another song that seems to fit the poem. Have students teach a group of students the new version and allow them to share it with the rest of the class.

## Humorous Poems

The humor of poetry has long been one of childhood's special treats. In fact, studies of children's poetic preferences have discovered that narrative rhyme and humorous verse are their favorites. The popularity of humorous poetry is evident in children's reactions to the limericks of Lear, the puns of Nash , and the verses of such contemporary poets as Silverstein and Prelutsky . Often, humorous poems deal with many of the life experiences children find difficult and even painful to face. Moreover, humorous poetry can help children deal with their own realities. Often it is humor that allows us to wake up to a new day with courage and conviction.

### References:

Adoff, A. (1989). *Chocolate dreams.* New York: Lothrop.

Adoff, A. (1979). *Eats poems.* New York: Lothrop.

Brewton, S., et al., eds. (1977). *Of quarks, quasars and other quirks: Quizzical poems for the supersonic age.* Illustrated by Q. Blake. New York: Harper.

Cole, W., compiler. (1970), *Oh, how silly!* Illustrated by T. Ungerer. New York: Viking.

Cole W., compiler. (1972). *Oh, that's ridiculous!* Illustrated by T. Ungerer. New York: Viking.

Cole, W., compiler. (1966). *Oh, what nonsense!* Illustrated by T. Ungerer. New York: Viking.

Kennedy, X.J. (1990). *Fresh brats.* New York: McElderry.

Kennedy, X.J. and Kennedy, D., compilers. (1982). *Knock at a star: A child's introduction to poetry.* Illustrated by K.A. Weinhaus. New York: Little, Brown.

Lear, Edward. (1946). *The complete nonsense book.* New York: Dodd, Mead.

Nash, O. (1980). *Custard and company.* Selected and Illustrated by Q. Blake. New York: Little, Brown.

Prelutsky, J., ed. (1991). *For laughing out loud: Poems to tickle your funnybone.* New York: Knopf.

Prelutsky, J. (1984). *The new kid on the block.* Illustrated by J. Stevenson. New York: Scholastic.

Prelutsky, J. (1990). *Something big has been here.* Illustrated by J. Stevenson. New York: Greenwillow.

Silverstein, S. (1981). *A light in the attic.* New York: Harper and Row.

Silverstein, S. (1974). *Where the sidewalk ends.* New York: Harper and Row.

### Activities:

1. Read several limericks to students, such as those by Edward Lear. Have students list the characteristics of limericks and then read several more to see if they fit the form students suggested. (Limericks have five lines. Lines 1, 2, and 5 rhyme and have a similar rhythm, while lines 3 and 4 are shorter, have a similar rhythm pattern, and rhyme with each other. ) As a class, select a favorite limerick and

together use it as a model for a new one. Discuss whether the new limerick fits the pattern established for a limerick. Have students individually create their own limericks. Encourage students to use famous characters from science, history, and current events as the subject of their limericks. Have them find pictures of the people and use them to illustrate their limericks. They may also include brief biographical sketches of the subject.

2.  Introduce the class to a variety of humorous poems written by a variety of poets, both traditional and contemporary. Allow time for students to read through the poetry collections to become familiar with additional humorous poems. Create a class chart of the students' favorite humorous poets and hold a mini-debate in which students defend their selections.

3.  Many authors of humorous poetry have created imaginary characters, such as the "Yipiyuk "(Silverstein, 1974) or "The Wumpaloon, Which Never Were" (Prelutsky, 1990). Read several of these poems to children and have them draw their own version of one of the characters. Pictures can be affixed to "wanted posters" or "missing creature posters" that contains relevant information about the creature.

4.  Have students create a newspaper based on favorite humorous poems. The newspaper can contain factual stories, editorials, advertisements, an advice column, and so forth. For example, one headline might read, "Boy Mysteriously Turns into Television Set" based on Silverstein's (1974) poem, "Jimmy Jet and His TV Set. " Based on the same poem, an editorial can be written about the dangers of watching too much television, an advice column can focus on suggestions to Jimmy's parents to help him break his TV habit, and so forth.

5.  Many poets have tried to capture the rhythm or subject of their poems by the shapes of the words on the page. This is known as concrete poetry. For example, in "Rope Rhyme" by Eloise Greenfield (1978), the last three lines are each indented, separating them from the rest of the poem, just as a person jumps away from the rope at the end of his/her turn. Eve Merriam's poem "Windshield Wiper" (in Kennedy and Kennedy's *Knock at a Star*, 1982), is written in two columns to resemble windshield wipers. Share many of these concrete poems with students and encourage them to create their own.

6.  Have students select a nonsense poem and try to convert it to a more serious type of poetry. Alternatively, students may select a more serious type of poem and change it into one with a more humorous tone.

## Mother Goose for Older Children

The rhymes of Mother Goose are often a child's first introduction to poetry. Its rhythm, rhyme, and repetition captivate children. They move to the words, and create rhythmic sounds to accompany the verse. However, the rhymes of Mother Goose are perfect for older children as well. They are an excellent source for teaching various poetic devices, analyzing meaning and purpose, and for learning to enjoy poetry for the sheer magic of its sound.

## References:

De Angeli, M. (1954). *Marguerite de Angeli's book of nursery and Mother Goose rhymes*. New York: Doubleday.

DePaola, T. (1988). *Hey diddle diddle and other Mother Goose rhymes*. New York: Putnam's Sons.

Lobel, A., compiler. (1986). *The Random House book of Mother Goose*. New York: Random House.

Marcus, L.S. and Schwartz, A. eds. (1990). *Mother Goose's little misfortunes*. New York: Bradbury.

Opie, I., and Opie, P., compilers. (1955). *Oxford nursery rhyme book*. Illustrated from old chapbooks, and by J. Hassal Walck. New York: Oxford University Press.

Sendak, M. (1993). *We are all in the dumps with Jack and Guy*. New York: HarperCollins.

Spier, P. (1967). *London Bridge is falling down!* New York: Doubleday.

Sutherland, Z., Ed. (1990). *The Orchard book of nursery rhymes.* Illustrated by Faith Jacques. New York: Orchard.
Wyndham, R. (1968). *Chinese Mother Goose rhymes.* Illustrated by ed Young. New York: Philomel.

### Activities:

1.  Involve students in reading a variety of Mother Goose rhymes. They provide a perfect vehicle for teaching poetic devices, such as alliteration ("Sing a Song of Sixpence"); rhyme ("Hickory, Dickory, Dock"); onomatopoeia ("Pat-a-Cake-Pat-a Cake"); repetition ("Polly Put the Kettle On"), and so on. Introduce students to these devices, and give them the opportunity to find examples of them in books of Mother Goose rhymes. Have students create an "encyclopedia" of poetic devices with examples from the rhymes. Pages can be illustrated and bound together.

2.  Many of the Mother Goose rhymes were originally written as a commentary on life and society at the time, revealing bits of history, customs, and culture. Involve students in researching the origin of one or two various rhymes. They can even use some ingenuity and come up with their own histories of the rhymes!

3.  Recently, Maurice Sendak illustrated two traditional rhymes from Mother Goose and joined them together in one creative book, *We Are All in the Dumps with Jack and Guy.* Involve students in a discussion of the fact that even though the rhymes are centuries old, they are still relevant today; along with the Sendak illustrations, they provide a social commentary on life. Discuss the social problems depicted by the rhymes and pictures.

4.  Encourage students to select a favorite Mother Goose rhyme and illustrate it in such a way that the words and pictures give their opinion about a significant happening or problem in our world today. (See activity 3 above.)

5.  Have student make up new Mother Goose rhymes by replacing characters and actions. For example, "Old King Cole" could become "Perky Princess Di." Have students illustrate their rhymes and create Mini-books. To create a mini-book, each student needs only one piece of typing paper, 8 1/2" by 11":

    Step 1: Fold the paper in half.

    Step 2: Fold the paper in half again.

    Step 3: Fold the paper in half, sideways.

    Step 4: Open the paper to half sheet (step 2) and cut from the center of the fold to the middle.

    Step 5: Open the sheet to its original size.

    Step 6: Fold the paper lengthwise.

    Step 7: Push the outer edges together to form the book.

# Intermediate Unit: Geometry

**Theme:** GEOMETRY

**Focus:** Students will develop an understanding of the usefulness of geometry in their daily lives.

**Objectives:** On completion of this thematic unit, students will:

1. Understand various geometric forms and shapes.

2. Be able to use geometry in everyday pursuits.

3. Understand the role of geometry in selected occupations.

4. Describe and use various shapes.

**Initiating Activity:** Invite students to bring in photographs from home — particularly photographs of rooms and spaces in and outside their homes. Divide the class into several ad hoc groups and invite each group to list the various types of geometric shapes (circles, squares, rectangles, etc.) found within each of the photographs. Invite each group to compose a graph of the number of squares, rectangles, and the like found in each photograph as well as the entire assembly of photos. (Students may wish to make predictions as to which geometric shapes will "show up" most often in the collection of photos and then compare their final results with their predictions). Post these around the room.

## General Activities:

1. Provide students with one or more copies of David Macauley's architectural books (see the bibliographies on page 219). Invite students to note the various geometric shapes displayed within each of the books. Ask students to take their own "personal field trips" throughout their neighborhood or community to note similar structures and shapes. What comparisons can they make?

2. Invite students to look for geometric shapes that occur naturally in nature. For example, how many circles can be found in a single flower? Are there any squares or rectangles represented in the trees and bushes around the school? Do animals exhibit any geometric shapes (for example, diamondback rattlesnake)? Invite students to construct books illustrating the shapes found.

3. Provide students with several examples of Tana Hoban's "shape" books (see the bibliographies). Invite students to work together in small groups to construct their own original shape books for younger students in another grade. If possible, provide students with a camera and ask them to photograph items around the school or community that could be combined into a shape book for a grade lower than yours.

4. Provide students with light wire coat hangers and invite them to create some of the more familiar geometric shapes. Ask students to create some new shapes and assign various names to those shapes. Do the names have anything to do with the actual shape? Should the name be functional?

5. Invite a mathematician from a local college or university to visit your class. Ask the invited speaker to discuss some of the geometric shapes represented in the "outside world." Ask the speaker to discuss the importance of geometry in everyday life.

6. Invite students to brainstorm for songs or song titles that contain the names of various geometric shapes. Do they know any songs that use the words "circle," "square," or "rectangle," for example? Which geometric word seems to be used most often?

7. Provide each student group with a box of sugar cubes and some white glue. Invite each group to construct a variety of 3-dimensional geometric models (for example, cubes, pyramids, etc.) for

display in the classroom. Ask students to discuss any difficulties they have in constructing the shapes and whether there is any relationship between the frequency of that shape in the "outside world" and the difficulty people might have in building the shape.

## Discussion Questions

1.  Why would it be important for architects to have a knowledge of geometry? (structural weight and size are related to geometry)

2.  Can you think of any other occupations that need to have a knowledge of geometry? (billiards player, race car driver)

3.  How will geometry be useful in your own life?

4.  How do your parents or relatives use geometric shapes in their jobs or at home?

5.  What are some of the largest geometric figures you can think of? (sphere: planet; pyramid: pyramid) What is the smallest geometric figure you can think of?

# Literature Related Activities

Title:                  *The Boy with Square Eyes*

Genre:                  Picture Book

Author:                 Juliet Snape and Charles Snape

Bibliographic Information:   Prentice-Hall, New York, 1987

Summary:                Charlie likes to watch lots of television. As a result his eyes eventually become square, just like his TV set. Everything he sees is square-shaped until he figures out how to return his eyes to normal.

Interest Level:         Grades 3–6

1.  Pre-Reading Activity:

    Discuss with the class the effects of having everything in the world in a square shape. In other words, what if curves did not exist? What would be some of the most significant changes? What accommodations would students have to make in their lives? What would be some of the most unusual changes (for example, square cars, square basketballs, etc.)? How would their neighborhood or community look if everything was constructed in square shapes?

2.  Learning Activities:

    a.  Ask students to retrieve a picture or illustration each of them has drawn for any other previous activity. Invite students to redraw the picture using nothing but squares. What difficulties do they encounter? What allowances do they have to make?

    b.  Work with the school's art teacher and share some cubist art with students. The work of artists such as Pablo Picasso or Georges Braque would be appropriate. Discuss with students some of the modifications those artists used to create their paintings. Invite students to draw in the cubist style.

    c.   Invite students to measure the TV sets they have at home. What are the dimensions? Is there a relationship between the height and width of a TV set? Can students determine any patterns?

    d.   How would the world look if everything was in the shape of a circle? Discuss with students the changes that would occur in Charlie's life (or their lives) if everything was round (as opposed to square).

3.  Discussion Questions:

    a.   What made Charlie such an interesting character?

    b.   How do you think Charlie felt at the end of the story?

    c.   What do you think would have happened if Charlie's eyes were triangular?

    d.   What part of the story did you like least? What part of the story did you like most?

---

| | |
|---|---|
| Title: | *Shape: The Purpose of Forms* |
| Genre: | Nonfiction |
| Author: | Eric Laithwaite |

Bibliographic Information:   Franklin Watts, New York, 1986

Summary:   This book illustrates the various shapes students encounter in their daily lives. It also looks at the function of shapes, how they are made, and some of their uses.

Interest Level:   Grades 4–6

---

1.  Pre-Reading Activity:

Invite students to brainstorm for a list of human-made items in (a) the classroom, (b) at home, and/ or (c) their parents place of employment. Ask students to create lists of the various shapes represented in each of those sites. What two-dimensional shapes seem to predominate? What three-dimensional shapes seem to dominate? Invite students to graph or chart their results.

2.  Learning Activities:

    a.   Ask each student to select a manmade item in the classroom and list all the various shapes it contains. Are there shapes represented in that item for which there is no name?

    b.   Ask students to work together in two-person teams. Invite each team to determine the reasons why certain manmade items are shaped as they are. Ask students to discuss the implications if a particular item was in a different shape. How would the new shape affect the function of that item? (For example, if a clock were rectangular instead of circular, how would it function?)

    c.   Students may wish to create their own spheres (soap bubbles). Invite them to create a series of bubbles or bubble-like objects. What observations can they make about the size and shape of those bubbles? Why are bubbles round?

    d.   The book contains illustrations of "netts." Invite students to create their own cubes as illustrated in the book. Ask them to list all the items in the classroom or their house that have that same shape. Why is that a functional shape?

3.  Discussion Questions:

    a.  What do you think is the most prevalent three-dimensional shape in nature?

    b.  What is the least frequent two-dimensional shape in nature?

    c.  What are some examples of symmetry that occur naturally in the environment around our school?

    d.  How would a knowledge of shapes help someone become a better architect? (structure, relationships)

---

Title:                  *Grandfather Tang's Story*

Genre:                  Fiction

Author:                 Ann Tompert

Bibliographic Information:   Crown, New York, 1990

Summary:                A boy and his grandfather spend an afternoon making various shapes with their tangrams. The shapes evolve into a story about two fox fairies and the shapes they can assume.

Interest Level:         Grades 2–5

---

1.  Pre-Reading Activity:

    Invite students to cut various shapes from construction paper (for example, squares, rectangles, parallelograms, and so forth). Ask each student to select two or three shapes, place them on his or her desk, and create a make-believe story about the shapes. The shapes can also be used as body parts for different characters, props within the setting of the story, or as specific objects. Students may wish to draw faces or other illustrations on the pieces to complete their stories. This activity can be done in small groups or teams.

2.  Learning Activities:

    a.  Provide each child with the "t" shape illustrated below. Ask each child to cut out the shape and then to cut along the dotted lines (thus forming five separate pieces). Have children mix the pieces and challenge a friend to put the "t" back together again.

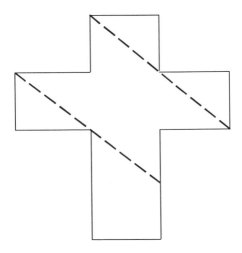

b. Invite students to cut out a series of squares, triangles, and rectangles from pieces of construction paper. Invite students to assemble a collection of those geometric shapes into various letters of the alphabet. (Can the letter "A" be assembled using nothing but triangles? What is the least number of squares and rectangles necessary to put together the letter "M"?)

c. Invite children to select a folk tale or fairy tale with which they are familiar. Challenge them to retell the story using a variety of tans to stand for characters or special items within the story.

d. Students may want to retell the story of Wu Ling and Chou to a lower grade using their own self-created tans. These renditions may be videotaped and shared with several classes.

3. Discussion Questions:

a. What was the most distinctive element of this particular story?

b. What made this story significantly different from or similar to other folk tales or fairy tales with which you are familiar?

c. What did you enjoy most about Grandfather Tang? How is he similar to or different from your own grandfather?

d. Do you like this type of story/book?

---

| Title: | *What Can She Be? An Architect* |
|---|---|
| Genre: | Nonfiction |
| Author: | Gloria and Esther Goldreich |
| Bibliographic Information: | Lothrop, Lee & Shepard, New York, 1974 |
| Summary: | This book takes the reader through some of the projects one architect does during her career. It also looks at some of the skills necessary to become an accomplished architect. |
| Interest Level: | Grades 3–6 |

---

1. Pre-Reading Activity:

   Ask students to brainstorm a list of occupations their parents hold. Invite them to divide the list into two groups — those occupations traditionally thought of as male-dominated and those occupations traditionally thought of as female-dominated. What similarities or differences do they note? Afterward, have students select those occupations in which shapes play a major role. In what occupations, other than as architects and teachers, do people need to know a lot about shapes?

2. Learning Activities:

   a. If possible, borrow some building blocks from a kindergarten teacher in your school. Invite students to experiment with the blocks to create various structures and buildings. Based on their "experiments," which types of buildings seem to be the most stable, the least stable, constructed the fastest, the one able to support the greatest weight, and so forth?

   b. Invite a local architect to address your class. Ask the individual to discuss how he or she uses shapes in the design of various buildings. If possible, have the person bring a set of building blueprints and illustrate for students the different shapes used in the plans for a building.

   c. Invite students to illustrate selected buildings in their town or neighborhood according to scale.

Have students measure the height, length, and width of each building and draw the building according to a predetermined scale (for example, 1" = 10'). Provide students with graph paper for their drawings.

3. Discussion Questions:

   a. Why is it important for architects to know geometric shapes? (structure, function, support)

   b. Can you list at least five other occupations in which a knowledge of geometry is essential?

   c. What other math skills, besides geometry, are used in the construction of a building?

   d. What geometric skills do you use around your house on a regular basis?

**Culmination:**   Invite students to assemble a "Geometry Notebook" — a collection of shapes and forms naturally occurring in nature and a collection of shapes that can be found in human-made items. For each two-dimensional or three-dimensional shape, a page in the notebook can be devoted to (a) a list of various items that exhibit that shape, (b) photographs of different examples of that shape in the community or in nature, (c) surveys of parents and other adults on how they use or see that shape in their daily lives, (d) pop-up cardboard models illustrating the shape, or (e) other examples of the shape. Students may wish to create a special book to be shared with students in grades lower than yours. A permanent display for one of the school's display cases could also be developed.

# Supplemental Literature

**Primary (Grades 1–3):**

Anno, M. (1991). *Anno's math games III.* New York: Philomel Books.
   Two characters, Kris and Kross, get themselves into all sorts of geometric adventures in this delightful and engrossing text.

Brown, J. (1964). *Flat Stanley.* New York: Harper and Row.
   Stanley is flattened by a falling bulletin board. His adventures in his new dimension and his brother's attempts to return him to normal make an interesting introduction to plane geometry.

Hoban, T. (1970). *Shapes and things.* New York: Macmillan.
   This book provides readers with several opportunities to observe the shapes of things in their natural state. Students will be amazed at some things they take for granted!

Hoban, T. (1986). *Shapes, shapes, shapes.* New York: Greenwillow.
   This book, another in Hoban's delightful series, illustrates shapes in combination with each other. Again, there is much to see and much to discover!

Rahn, J. (1984). *Holes.* Boston: Houghton Mifflin.
   Students will never take holes for granted after reading this book which looks at all the different kinds of holes we have in our everyday world.

Rogers, P. (1989). *The shapes game.* New York: Henry Holt.
   Nine basic geometric shapes are illustrated in this delightful introduction to geometry. Colorful drawings highlight the text.

Seuss, Dr. (1988). *The shape of me and other stuff.* New York: Random House.
   Readers are encouraged to use their imaginations to think about the shape of many items — those that are real as well as those that are imaginary.

Sitomer, M., and Sitomer, H. (1970). *What is symmetry?* New York: Crowell.
   Various types of symmetry are presented to readers, including those that occur in nature as well as those represented in manmade items.

### Intermediate (Grades 4–6):

Charosh, M. (1970). *Straight lines, parallel lines, perpendicular lines.* New York: Crowell.
This is a "hands-on" book in which readers are able to use lengths of string to create various patterns and shapes.

Froman, R. (1975). *Angles are easy as pie.* New York: Harper and Row.
This book describes how angles are formed when two lines meet and how readers can create their own angles.

Froman, R. (1972). *Rubber bands, baseballs, and doughnuts.* New York: Crowell.
This book is a wonderful introduction to the science of topology. It provides readers with a diversity of projects and experiments that will sharpen their powers of observation and increase their awareness of this fascinating topic.

Isaacson, P. (1988). *Round buildings, square buildings, and buildings that wiggle like a fish.* New York: Knopf.
This book looks at the different shapes buildings have and the reasons why they are designed the way they are.

Macauley, D. (1973). *City.* Boston: Houghton Mifflin.
Students will never again look at their town or city in the same way after reading this book. The author takes the reader for a true "inside look" at the structure and construction of a city.

Read, R. (1965). *Tangrams, 330 puzzles.* New York: Dover.
Hours of fun and hundreds of discoveries about shapes can be found within the pages of this book.

Sitomer, M., and Sitomer, H. (1974). *Spirals.* New York: Crowell.
Readers will be amazed to discover that there are so many different types of spirals that occur in nature. Also included is a discussion of the difference between spirals and circles.

Small, D. (1987). *Paper John.* New York: Farrar, Straus & Giroux.
A delightful and colorful story about a strange character who encounters an even stranger demon. A bright and creative addition to the math library.

Van Note, P. (1968). *Sam Loyd's book of tangram puzzles.* New York: Dover.
A delightful compliment to the classroom library, this book offers numerous tangram puzzles appropriate for a study of geometry.

# MINI-THEMES

## Architecture

Children often wonder about the utility of geometry in their daily lives. A mini-unit on architecture can help them understand the various ways in which shapes are used in everyone's daily life — particularly as they relate to the buildings in which we live. The study of shapes becomes much more understandable for youngsters when they see its application in the world outside the classroom.

## References

Clinton, S. (1986). *I can be an architect.* Chicago: Children's Press.
Devlin, H. (1969). *What kind of house is that?* New York: Parents Magazine Press.
Lobel, A. (1965). *Sven's bridge.* New York: Harper and Row.
Macauley, D. (1975). *Pyramid.* Boston: Houghton Mifflin, 1975.
Macauley, D. (1973). *Cathedral.* Boston: Houghton Mifflin.
Macauley, D. (1977). *Castle.* Boston: Houghton Mifflin.
Macauley, D. (1980). *Unbuilding.* Boston: Houghton Mifflin.
Munroe, R. (1985). *The inside-outside book of New York City.* New York: Dodd, Mead.
Robbins, K. (1984). *Building a house.* New York: Four Winds.
Wilson, F. (1968). *Architecture: A book of projects for young adults.* New York: Reinhold.

## Activities

1.  Provide each of several student groups with a camera and a roll of film. Invite each team to take a selected number of photographs of various buildings in their town or community. Have students assemble the developed photographs into one or more selected categories, such as buildings of the same architectural style, buildings with squares and rectangles, and/or buildings which do not use a selected geometric shape in their design.

2.  Invite each student to select a building in their town and to write a story about the construction of that building as though it might be told by the building itself — "My life while growing up."

3.  Obtain the blueprints for the school (these can be obtained through the central office or superintendent's office). Invite students to discuss the various geometric shapes represented in the drawings.

4.  Invite each student to design his/her ideal house. What shapes or designs would they use in order to complete their diagrams? Does the location of the house (for example, at the beach, in the mountains, etc.) dictate the shapes that might be used?

## Paper Folding

Paper folding activities are a wonderful way of demonstrating the "hands-on" aspects of geometry. Children are always fascinated by the shapes, figures, and designs they can create with paper and are amazed at the variety of objects that can result from a single sheet of paper. The stories associated with paper folding can become a magical part of the language arts program, too.

## References

Churchill, E. (1989). *Fast and funny paper toys you can make*. New York: Sterling Publishing.
Coerr, E. (1977). *Sadako and the thousand paper cranes*. New York: Putnam.
Corwin, J. (1988). *Papercrafts*. New York: Franklin Watts.
Harbin, R. (1960). *Paper folding fun*. Newton Centre, MA: Charles T. Branford.
Massaglio, E. (1959). *Fun time paper folding*. Chicago: Children's Press.
Nakano, D. (1985). *Easy origami*. New York: Viking.
Phillips, J. (1975). *Exploring triangles: Paper folding geometry*. New York: Crowell.
Phillips, J. (1972). *Right angles: Paper folding geometry*. New York: Crowell.
Sarasas, Claude. (1964). *The ABC's of origami*. Rutland, VT: Charles E. Tuttle.
Temko, F. (1978). *Paper cutting*. Garden City, NY: Doubleday.
Tofts, H. (1989). *The 3-D paper book*. New York: Simon and Schuster.

## Activities

1.  Using one or more of the books above, invite students to create paper folded characters for one or more of their favorite stories. Which story characters lend themselves to a paper folded figure? How should that figure be folded or represented?

2.  Invite the class to create one thousand paper cranes as represented in Sadako and the Thousand Paper Cranes. What geometric figures are represented in the cranes? Invite students to display the cranes throughout the classroom.

3.  Invite students to create three-dimensional paper models of some geometric figures. What techniques, learned from the reference books suggested, can be used to design those shapes?

4.  Provide students with random geometric shapes and invite them to create an original story using that shape as the central figure. What types of adventures or discoveries will that shape make?

## Lines and Angles

Lines and angles are everywhere! Our world is filled with them and when children realize the enormous variety of lines and angles in their everyday lives, then they begin to appreciate this all-important concept. In fact, geometric principles presented in class in a two-dimensional shape achieve relevancy when demonstrated outside of the classroom in the three-dimensional world.

### References

Charosh, M. (1970). *Straight lines, parallel lines, perpendicular lines.* New York: Crowell.

Fisher, L.E. (1987). *Look around! A book about shapes.* New York: Puffin Books.

Gundersheimer, K. (1986). *Shapes to show.* New York: Harper and Row.

Hoban, T. (1974). *Circles, triangles, and squares.* New York: Macmillan.

Juster, N. (1963). *The dot and the line.* New York: Random House.

Kessler, E., and Kessler, L. (1966). *Are you square?* Garden City, NY: Doubleday.

Podendorf, I. (1970). *Shapes, sides, curves, and corners.* Chicago: Children's Press.

Russell, S. (1965). *Lines and shapes.* New York: Henry Z. Walck.

Sitomer, M., and Sitomer, H. (1972). *Lines, segments, polygons.* New York: Crowell.

Yenawine, P. (1991). *Lines.* New York: Delacorte Press.

### Activities

1. Ask each child to select one object from inside the classroom. Invite each person to add up the total number of lines in each three-dimensional object as well as the total number of angles. Students may wish to chart or graph their results.

2. Ask students to predict the number of lines necessary to draw a selected three-dimensional figure (for example, a pyramid). Provide students with straws and modeling clay (to attach the ends of the straws together) and invite them to create replicas of selected objects using only straight lines.

3. Challenge students to disprove the famous maxim — "A line is the shortest distance between two points." Can students figure out a situation in which that statement would not be true? Ask them to prove their ideas.

4. Invite a math teacher from the local high school to visit your class and explain the use of lines and angles in various occupations such as architect, land surveyor, draftsman, and so forth.

## Non-Geometric Shapes

An understanding of shapes is not only an important mathematical concept, but a valuable science concept as well. Why certain items take on the shape(s) they do, how the size and shape of objects can be determined by what is inside them, and the shapes which naturally occur in nature (and the effects of the environment on those shapes) are all important concepts for students to understand.

### References

Brown, M. (1979). *Listen to a shape.* New York: Franklin Watts.

Charlip, R., and Joyner, J. (1975). *Thirteen.* New York: Parents' Magazine Press.

Charosh, M. (1971). *The ellipse.* New York: Crowell.

Goor, R., and Goor, N. (1981). *Shadows, here, there, and everywhere.* New York: Crowell.

Grifalconi, A. (1986). *The village of round and square houses.* Boston: Little, Brown.

Hoban, T. (1987). *Spots, speckles, and stripes.* New York: Greenwillow.

Hoban, T. (1986). *Shapes, shapes, shapes.* New York: Greenwillow.

Oakley, G. (1979). *Magical changes.* New York: Macmillan.

Shaw, C. (1974). *It looked like spilt milk.* New York: Crowell.
Silverstein, S. (1976). *The missing piece.* New York: Harper and Row.
Ungerer, T. (1962). *Snail, where are you?* New York: Harper and Row.

## Activities

1.  Invite students to create their own dictionary of terms for some of the non-geometric shapes found in the suggested reference books or in shapes of their own creation. Ask students to decide on the selected categories and how the "words" will be defined.

2.  Ask students to take a "walking field trip" around the school. Invite them to locate as many examples of geometric as well as non-geometric shapes as possible. These examples can be recorded in a large class journal.

3.  Explain to students that the shape of an object determines its strength. For example, a raw egg can be squeezed with one hand and not break. (CAUTION: Do this as a demonstration for the class.) Have students speculate as to why the egg does not break when it is squeezed. Discuss other examples in nature that might illustrate this principle.

4.  Ask students to decide on the perfect shape for (a) humans, (b) dogs or cats, (c) houses, or (d) schools. Discuss whether the shape of an object has anything to do with its function, mobility, strength, or usefulness.

# About the Authors

ANITA MEYER MEINBACH has worked for the Dade County Public Schools, Miami, Florida, as a classroom teacher, curriculum writer, and teacher trainer, providing seminars and guidance in curriculum development. As an adjunct professor at the University of Miami, she has taught courses in language arts, reading, and children's literature. Dr. Meinbach is the author of several textbooks and numerous resource books in reading and language arts. A frequent presenter at various workshops and professional conferences, she speaks on a variety of topics dealing with children's literature, the interdisciplinary approach to learning, and curriculum development.

LIZ ROTHLEIN, full professor, is an Associate Dean in the School of Education at the University of Miami, Coral Gables, Florida. She is coauthor of more than 20 books about reading, language arts, environmental and multicultural issues, and of other popular resource books for using children's literature in elementary classrooms. She is the recipient of numerous teaching awards, including Professor of the year at the University of Miami, and is listed in Outstanding Elementary Teachers of America.

ANTHONY D. FREDERICKS is an Associate Professor of Education at York College, York, Pennsylvania where he teaches methods courses in reading and language arts. A former classroom teacher and reading specialist, he is a frequent presenter and storyteller at school assemblies, inservice workshops, and reading conferences throughout North America. He is the author or co-author of more than two dozen teacher resource books in a variety of curricular areas including the enormously popular *Frantic Frogs and Other Frankly Fractured Folktales for Readers Theatre*, the award-winning *Social Studies Through Children's Literature: An Integrated Approach*, and the best-selling series of books — *Involving Parents Through Children's Literature*.

# Index